D1029363

What Is
Wrong with
Jung

What Is Wrong with Jung

Don McGowan

Foreword by
Mario Bunge

Prometheus Books

59 John Glenn Drive
Buffalo, New York 14228-2197

BF
109
.J8
m35
1994

Published 1994 by Prometheus Books

What Is Wrong with Jung. Copyright © 1994 by Don McGowan. All rights reserved. No part of this publication may be reproduced, stored in a retrieval system, or transmitted in any form or by any means, electronic, mechanical, photocopying, recording, or otherwise, without prior written permission of the publisher, except in the case of brief quotations embodied in critical articles and reviews. Inquiries should be addressed to Prometheus Books, 59 John Glenn Drive, Buffalo, New York 14228-2197, 716-837-2475. FAX: 716-835-6901.

98 97 96 95 94   5 4 3 2 1

Library of Congress Cataloging-in-Publication Data

McGowan, Don.
    What is wrong with Jung / Don McGowan.
        p.   cm.
    Includes bibliographical references and index.
    ISBN 0-87975-859-7 (cloth)
    1. Jung, C. G. (Carl Gustav), 1875–1961. I. Title.
BF109.J8M35   1994
150.19′54′092—dc20   93-38952
                                                                                CIP

Printed in the United States of America on acid-free paper.

LONGWOOD UNIVERSITY LIBRARY
REDFORD AND RACE STREET
FARMVILLE, VA 23909

"It is only shallow people who do not judge by appearances."

—Oscar Wilde

Contents

Foreword

Carl Gustav Jung (1875–1961) is a unique figure in twentieth century culture. He is unique in having been credited with important ideas in psychology, anthropology, religious hermeneutics, the philosophy of religion, and even the occult. He was a postmodern *avant la lettre,* and is a cult figure in the counterculture movement in addition to being respected in some academic circles.

What are Jung's contributions worth? Are they original? Are they true? Have they shed any light on the so-called mysteries of the human mind? And how does Jung's work look in the light of today's science and humanistic studies? These are the basic questions addressed in this book. The questions concern the very nature and value of science, philosophy, myth, and religion.

The author of this book, Don McGowan, is a brilliant young scholar. Like Jung, McGowan rejects the fragmentation and isolation of the various aspects of human life and knowledge. He is interested in psychology and anthropology, as well as in philosophy, religion, mythology, and the various cults that have mushroomed in the second half of our century. But, unlike Jung, McGowan believes that beliefs should be examined and tried out before being adopted: he is a critical thinker.

However, unlike most critical thinkers, McGowan is not impatient with popular beliefs. On the contrary, he thinks they are worth being studied. In particular, he believes that pop psychology and esoterica deserve to be investigated and understood, if only because they are popular.

I happen to share McGowan's conviction and believe that cultural anthropologists, social psychologists, philosophers, and culture watchers have been remiss in studying some of the most popular and influential myths and rituals of our time. As a result, academics are better acquainted with the exotic beliefs and practices of remote tribes than with those held or practiced in our own society. Surely this ignorance cannot help us understand, much less tolerate or correct, the beliefs and the behavior of our acquaintances.

McGowan has a knack for explaining in plain words Jung's often obscure ideas. Moreover, he does it in elegant and concise English peppered with a dry, perhaps Scottish, humor. Consequently his reader is bound to be entertained at the same time that he is being instructed and challenged. I, for one, am grateful to McGowan for having summarized and elucidated a sizable portion of Jung's writings, as well as a large part of the huge body of commentaries on the writings. Last but not least, I am proud of having learned much of this from one of my erstwhile star students.

Mario Bunge
Frothingham Professor of Logic and Metaphysics
McGill University
Montreal, Québec, Canada

Preface

It has been said that some of the greatest cultural achievements in history have actually been failures; John Milton, in his attempt to "justify the ways of God to men," succeeded "only" in producing one of the greatest works in English literature. In that respect, I cannot deceive myself that this work has managed to topple Jung from the throne of relative immunity on which he sits. In fact, my aims are far less lofty than Milton's: he wanted to justify the ways of God; I want to lambaste Jung. If there are any points of similarity between Milton's work and mine (and even I could hardly be so pompous as to believe that there are), they would be the unfathomable nature of our primary sources. If "the Lord moves in mysterious ways," then Jung and God bear the comparison on that level.

Keeping that in the back of my mind, I have set out to do exactly what Milton also tried: to explain the machinations of an unfathomable mind. In the end, after all the research I have put into Jung, I must admit that I can make neither heads nor tails of him. How one man could live through such a scientific revolution and still insist that synchronicity, archetypes, and alchemy have any bearing on modern society is beyond me. If anything, I am even more baffled by those who came after him. I must admit that at one time I too believed in these concepts, but then I moved into the tenth grade and started to notice the occasional flaw in Jung's logic. He and his followers purport to be educated; what is their excuse?

Enough of that; this is a preface, and as such it is my only chance to explain the method behind my personal madness. Jungian psychology and its subsequent adaptations are too broad a topic to be covered even in a work of this length, and their vagaries are enough to drive a legion of investigators off the deep end. Something had to give. So I have opted to concentrate on Jungian theory, leaving aside most of its practical aspects as well as those schools that came after Jung. For a good idea of what it is to experience Jungian therapy in practice, perhaps the best place to look is Robertson Davies' *The Manticore,* which chronicles the journey of its protagonist through Jungian analysis. The post-Jungians run the gamut from purportedly scientific to totally mystical. Some of the more comprehensible schools are described in Andrew Samuels' *Jung and the Post-Jungians.* As for the more way-out branches, you are on your own; the best I can do is to list a few of them in my bibliography and leave others to do the legwork from there.

Regarding the abbreviations and referencing system, see the following list of abbreviations and the bibliographical sections at the end with their explanatory notes. For those who would criticize me for not listing any of Jung's German works, I would like to point out that I do read German, and did read some of the more important papers in the original (such as the synchronicity series). I did not refer to the German works for the benefit of those readers who do not have access to the German copies or who do not read German. Unlike some, I do not consider dropping untranslated quotations to be the hallmark of education. I merely consider them pompous.

Being a student of both scientific method and comparative religion, I have combined the two approaches in this investigation to provide what I hope will be a reasonably comprehensive whole. I do not claim to have read everything Jung wrote in assembling this critique, and anyone who feels able to criticize my results based on the contents of "The Love Problem of a Student" or some other paper not listed in the special section of the bibliography is welcome to try. After all, in spite of my bold claim to have enumerated "what is wrong with Jung," I fully realize that no study could ever entirely disprove Jung. In the end, no one can ever disprove a pseudoscience. Nonetheless, I have tried, and if I have failed, I can only hope that my failure is of the magnitude of Milton's rather than the depth of Jung's.

Acknowledgments

This also seems to be the point in the book where I give my thanks to everyone who deserves them. Of the multitudes to whom I am grateful, the most important of them would have to be Professor Mario Bunge of McGill University. He gave me more than just the opportunity to produce this book; he gave me the skills and the desire to do so. If I could be half as clear a thinker as he, I would consider myself fortunate beyond measure. For those readers who are not familiar with Bunge's work, I would urge them to look him up posthaste.

There are also some people to whom I owe thanks for their nonacademic roles in the production of this book. First and foremost, I would like to thank Dougald Lamont, for sitting up with me until 3:00 A.M. reading the final version of this to make sure it made sense even to a "Jung-lover." And, for various reasons too numerous to list, I would like to thank Fred Kowalski, Rob Winters, Alex Usher, Fiona Doetsch, Neil Raymond, Frances Cable, Phil Richards, Tony Camacho, Bobby Kim, and everyone else who I forgot to list here.

Any errors in this manuscript are mine. Any credit for its clarity should go to the editorial staff at Prometheus, who took my often tortured prose and made it flow.

And, finally, I would be remiss in forgetting to thank my parents, Bob and Barbara McGowan, and my siblings, Rob and Sally.

Enough of this. We have Jung to bash.

List of Abbreviations

ABBREVIATION	FULL TITLE
"Complications"	"The Complications of American Psychology" (*CW* 10:946–80)
"Concerning the Archetypes"	"Concerning the Archetypes with Special Reference to the Anima Concept" (*CW* 9[1]:111–47)
"Confrontation"	"Confrontation with the Unconscious" (*MDR*, p. 170)
"Constitution and Heredity"	"The Significance of Constitution and Heredity in Psychology" (*CW* 8:220–31)
CW	*The Collected Works of C. G. Jung: Bollingen Series XX* (Jung, 1953–1971)
Kama Sutra	*The Kama Sutra of Vatsyayana: The Classic Treatise on Love and Social Conduct*, trans. R. Burton (1964)
MDR	*Memories, Dreams, Reflections* (Jung, 1963, 1989)
Qur'an	*The Holy Qur'an, with English Translation and Commentary*, vol. 3, ed. H. M. T. Ahmad (1949, 1988)
"Rumor"	"A Contribution to the Psychology of Rumor" (Jung, 1917)
"Synchronicity"	"Synchronicity: An Acausal Connecting Principle" (*CW* 8:816–18)
"The Syzygy"	"The Syzygy: Anima and Animus" (*CW* 9[ii]:20–42)
"Transformation of the Libido"	"A Transformation of the Libido: A Possible Source of Primitive Human Discoveries" (Jung, 1916)
Unconscious	*Psychology of the Unconscious* (Jung, 1916, 1951)

A Note on the Referencing System

Works by Jung compiled in the Bollingen *Collected Works* (*CW*) are cited as follows: title of paper, *CW*, volume number, and page numbers (see section 2 of the Jung Bibliography). Those works not included in *Collected Works* (see section 3 of the Jung Bibliography) are referenced by paper title and page numbers only. All other works are cited by author name and page numbers (see section 1 of the Jung Bibliography).

1

An Overview of Jungian Theory

Humanity is and always has been troubled by the unknown and the unknowable, especially the unknowable in itself. Through the millennia of civilization, people have tried to explain the workings of the world in terms of myths and legends. In the early years of the twentieth century, a Swiss psychoanalyst practicing the pioneering methods of Sigmund Freud noticed a relationship between these two factors, and decided that there must be some connection. This man, Carl Gustav Jung, looked at these myths and legends and saw in them explanations not simply for the workings of the world, but for humanity itself. Furthermore, he saw their contents reflected not only in other myths, but in the dreams and fantasies of his patients. More importantly, he saw them reflected in himself. From Pharaonic Egypt to Vedic India, from Gnostic Alexandria to modern Zurich, and at all other points in between, Jung found certain recurring structures and elements in the mind. Certainly, Zurich in the 1920s and 1930s hardly spoke the discourse of myth and legend. Or did it?

In fact, Jung came to realize that, the more people rationally behave in their daily lives, the more irrationally they think during their dreams and fantasies. The creature he describes as "modern man" in an essay entitled "The Spiritual Problem of Modern Man" is the rationally acting individual Jung saw everywhere around him. In Jung's eyes, such a person stands "at the very edge of the world, the abyss of the future before him, above the heavens, and below him the whole of mankind with a history that disappears in primeval mists" (227). The future is unknown, the past is shrouded in misty legend, which the modern person casts off with every step forward. However, Jung realized, people cannot cast off the misty legends quite as easily as they might like. They can ignore them, but this is not the same. Jung had learned something that has today become common knowledge—that ignoring a problem does not make it go away.

"The role of the unconscious is to act compensatorily to the conscious contents of the moment," Jung said in "The Role of the Unconscious" (*CW* 10.21). For Jung, this meant that when the conscious is acting in accordance with what has come to be called rationality, it is compensated by an irrational unconscious. However, the rational attitude is not natural for the mind. Therefore, when the mind is forced for too long to act rationally, it eventually gives way, and the unconscious contents push their way back to consciousness. These unconscious contents are of two sorts. Most directly accessible are those in the personal unconscious, which consist of painful thoughts, unpleasant memories, and undesirable personality traits of which a person would rather not be reminded. Unlike the Freudians from whose ranks he broke very early in his career, Jung was only marginally interested in the contents of the personal unconscious. He saw the problems of the personal unconscious as merely a distraction from the true problem endemic to all of humanity, not merely those who set foot in his office. He was willing to agree with Freud that the "overwhelming majority" of repressed personal material pertains to sexuality (ibid., 5). However, he did not believe that this sexually oriented material was all there was to examine. The unconscious contains not only repressed personal materials, but also "all of the psychic material that does not reach the threshold of consciousness" ("The Conception of the Unconscious," 446). This second type of unconscious content points to the most important distinction between Jung and Freud, namely Jung's concept of the collective unconscious.

The collective unconscious contains all the myths and legends of humanity, the inherited and omnipresent part of mental function (ibid., 452). "The archaic symbols so often found in phantasies and dreams are collective symbols," as are "primary propensities of forms of thought and feeling" and "everything about which men are universally agreed, or which is universally understood, said, or done" (ibid., 455). So a dream of a fish jumping from the water to the land is not a dream of a fish jumping from the water to the land, but a symbol for a message from the collective unconscious attempting to come to consciousness. The contents of the personality are collective; only the bounds of the persona are individual (ibid., 457). These collective contents are not only expressed in individual dreams and fantasies, but also through works of art and literature. In fact, all creativity comes from expressing symbols of the collective unconscious, which is symbolic activity of any sort. Good art, which Jung calls unrepeatable and amoral but simply image-laden, forces a return to "that level of existence at which it is man who lives and not the individual" ("Psychology and Literature," 198).

At a deeper level, the collective unconscious is bounded by race, descent, and family ("The Conception of the Unconscious," 452). This is shown by the fact that the most powerful works of art are also expressions of the attitude of the people from which the author descends. "Could we conceive of anyone but a German writing *Faust* or *Also sprach Zarathustra?*" ("Psychology and Literature," 197). However, although the symbols expressed are those of one particular race, "every great work of art is objective and impersonal, but none the less profoundly moves us each and all" (ibid., 199). Jung is not saying that the symbolic expressions of one race are incomprehensible to others, but rather that some races express some symbols as opposed to others, and that this tendency is innate. Repeatedly, he abjures people not to turn to Eastern religions such as Buddhism, in spite of their more developed spiritualism, because the patterns of thought that they require are not natural to the Western mind.

All of the above structures are ingrained in the same collective unconscious. However, these are not the only items contained therein. The entire structure of the self is also common to every person, although slightly differentiated for men and women. According to Jung, every personality is comprised of four elements: the ego, the shadow, the syzygy, and the self. The ego is "the complex factor to which all conscious contents are related . . . [that] forms, as it were, the centre of the field of consciousness. . . . The ego is the subject of all personal acts of consciousness" ("The Ego," *CW* 9[ii]:1). The shadow is the repository for all of those compensatory elements in the unconscious. When people seem to act contrary to their natures, the acting element is the shadow. For example, when a normally altruistic person behaves in a greedy manner, this is not the person's action, but the actions of that person's shadow. The syzygy is actually not one element, but two, differentiated by gender. Men, as a part of their psychological makeup, have an anima, a feminine component that compensates for their masculinity; women have an animus, a masculine element opposed to their femininity. When a woman acts in a male manner, this is the mark of the animus, and vice versa. Finally, the self is the wellspring from which all other personality elements emerge, as well as the repository for the collective unconscious. Psychological difficulty comes when people identify themselves too much with their ego and not enough with the rest of their personality components. Psychological wholeness comes when people become able to recognize the elements of the collective unconscious (the archetypes), as well as the syzygy and the shadow, and how these components affect them in their daily lives.

Before detailing the second half of Jung's personality theories, it is important to know why he felt so sure that everyone has these component elements. He asserted that these traits, and many more, arise from the collective unconscious, an area distinct from the personal unconscious where repressions lie. This collective unconscious is inhabited by elements Jung called archetypes, which are primal forms not unlike Platonic Universals. Archetypes such as The Hero, The Wise Old Man, The Witch, and many more populate people's personalities and dreams. Thus, the syzygy and shadow both arise from the collective unconscious and are formulated from the archetypes that are found as components of the self.

Every person has these archetypes in the collective unconscious, yet people are not all of the same general bent. Jung explains this dichotomy by postulating two basic types of personality traits, which interact to form a person's general world view. The most basic differentiation of personality is between introverted and extraverted people. Jung does not use introversion in the same way as Freud; for him, introverts see objects in terms of themselves, while extraverts see themselves in terms of objects. People are one or the other of these types, which are then modified by either thinking, feeling, sensation, or intuition. These four facets are arranged in two dichotomous pairs—thinking is contrary to feeling, and sensation is opposed to intuition. Because we will be devoting an entire chapter to an in-depth discussion of Jungian personality typology, no more need be mentioned of it here.

Having discussed Jung's three most important theoretical constructs, the collective unconscious with its archetypes, archetypes of the self, and personality typology, the most obvious question to ask would be how Jung discovered these phenomena. At first, patients served as his primary source. Jung never actually met the woman who is perhaps the most obvious example of someone whose dreams and fantasies he amplified, Miss Miller who was the inspiration for *Unconscious*. However, the method of amplification Jung used in *Unconscious*, elucidating Miss Miller's symbols by appeal to religious symbolism, points to the next step his general method would take—a movement into examining religious symbolism itself. Finally, he moved his investigation toward an often-overlooked aspect of Western thought—alchemy. In all of these pursuits he found common symbolism, which he believed to be related. However, rather than attributing the common occurrence of symbols to their pointing toward a higher power, such as God, Jung believed them to have their roots in something else common to all people—their humanity. For Jung, "God" is just a synonym for "unconscious" ("Late Thoughts," 327). Religion is simply a mass representation of a collective unconscious. Dreams and gods all spring from the same source.

Here, we can stop our introduction to Jung. Since at this point all we intend to do is to provide a sufficient overview of exactly what Jung believed for those who have only encountered Jung's theories in other sources, which very often do not provide a comprehensive treatment of his ideas. The rest of this book will consist of criticisms of the theory sketched in outline here. Those elements which seem to have been treated lightly will be further illumined later by the harsh light of criticism.

2

Religion in the Jungian Context

The most obvious place to start into Jungian criticism is in his interpretation of religions. Jung was definitely aware of the vital role religion plays in his allegations of universalism of human thought. If it can be convincingly argued that every world religion eventually reduces to certain common elements, it is not such a leap of logic, then, to say that these religions all descend from a common source; and if we wish to situate that common source in an atheistic manner, the only place left to situate it is in the human mind. This is not such an original approach as it might seem—ignoring mysticism, which is by nature non-scholarly, one major branch of religious scholarship is the phenomenology of religions. Mircea Eliade, one of its most prominent practitioners, sounds very much like Jung in many of his claims. Certainly, upon entering into an examination of Jung's religious scholarship, we step away from the comfortable grounds of science and into those fields that call themselves "the arts," where the rules all seem to change. No doubt some will bring us under fire for applying the methods of science and exact discourse where they allegedly do not belong. However, if university faculties of Religious Studies are allowed to situate their field among the "human sciences" then we can demand they be subject to the same sorts of justification as the traditional sciences. With these points in mind, let us delve into Jung's work with no further ado.

Repeatedly, Jung distinguishes between the West and the East based on what he perceives as their relative spheres of understanding, attributing intellect to the West and spirit to the East. In his eyes, the spiritual problem of the West today is its fascination with the psychic life, traditionally the domain of Eastern thought ("The Spiritual Problem of Modern Man," 251). But what exactly does he mean by "the East"? Again and again, we see these words refer to two distinct geographical and cultural entities—India and China. However, both of these regions developed as disparate units, linked only by one branch of Buddhism. Repeatedly, Jung justifies a European practice through reference to Indian writings. In this light, it will bear fruit to investigate exactly what differences exist between Jung's concept of Indian religion and the actual religion as practiced both in the past and today.

If we can make categorical assertions about Jung's views, we can say that he believed in the permanence of the self. Giving it the status of an archetype, he saw it as the underpinning for everything else in a person's life. Psychological healing, in Jung's eyes, comes from truly realizing that the archetypes are emanations of the self, rather than continuing to see them as independent projections. They are complex and often unfathomable, being unconscious, yet are quite unambiguously a part of the person who cannot fathom them. The archetypes are not the contents of a massive joint bank account into which everyone dips; an archetype has an individual quality. We should not be too quick to make any assertions about Indian religions, and especially Buddhism, but it is safe to say that the vast majority of Indian religions do not believe in a permanence of self. That is, liberation leads not to paradise but to nothing at all. Nirvana is not heaven; it is not anywhere or anything. The goal of the self is to obliterate itself. This is a hard concept for the Western mind to fathom, as it is educated from an early age in the discourse of the monotheistic faiths. For that reason, we will analyze it in some depth before we apply its ramifications to Jung's thought.

One of the standard jokes leveled at the so-called "New Age" movement is that nearly everyone at some point in time has to come out and admit that, in a past life, she was Cleopatra or he was Mark Antony. While the people who assert this may truly believe it, it is inconsistent with reincarnation as seen in both Hindu and Buddhist contexts. The Western-educated mind, accustomed as it is to dealing with the concept of transmigration of souls, has more than a bit of difficulty with the (admittedly quite oversimplified) idea that there actually is no underlying soul, a belief that both Hinduism and Buddhism share. This is about as much as we can categorically state about the Hindu and Buddhist belief; for those who call Christianity hopelessly fragmented, all that can be said is that they have never looked too closely at Hinduism or Buddhism, neither of which is a unified doctrine.

Fortunately, Jung himself saves us quite a lot of work in considering all of the different sects—he completely ignores the *nirguna,* or atheistic strand of Hinduism and, as far as Buddhism goes, he leans quite strongly toward the *Mahayana* version. For that reason, we shall look primarily at those aspects of Eastern religion to which Jung refers, considering the others only inasmuch as they do not support Jung's ideas either.

It is interesting to note that, in bibliographies to works on the theories of Hinduism, Jung is often conspicuous by his absence (e.g., O'Flaherty 1973); when he does gain admittance, he does so only as the instigator of one of several theories (e.g., O'Flaherty 1980). That is, serious scholars of Hinduism do not accept Jung's theories as entirely correct. While they do see him as having something to say about the nature of religion, they do not see him as making the definitive statement. This is important to consider in the context of our investigation, because Jung definitely saw himself as making the definitive statement. He did not propose that he had discovered an idea about Hinduism, but that he had discovered *the* idea underlying Hinduism. That kind of assertion requires quite a bit of supporting evidence, as well as a very thorough grasp of the concepts that Hinduism can be said to hold. And since speaking of "Hinduism" is somewhat of a misnomer (the term being an invention of the British to cover the entirety of Indian traditions, rather than self-generated by the believers), for Jung to say that he has grasped its essence is for him to admit that he has not even begun to understand. He is saying that his theories apply to all strands of what we have come to classify as Hinduism. Not only do they not do so, but for Jung to have truly understood the different strands of belief under the "Hindu" umbrella, he could at least be expected to know that Hinduism, to which he refers as "it," should actually be considered "them." Above and beyond the fact that Jung does not consider the nirguna tradition, as we have already said, it is significant to note that in the papers we have read, Jung seems to avoid *Vaisnava* or *Devi* beliefs, concentrating instead on the *Saiva.* That is, those systems that treat the god Visnu or any goddess as the supreme being, as well as or those in which the supreme being is not actually a being but a principle, go almost unnoticed in Jung's works. This glaring oversight prevents Jung's assertions from being categorical for all of Hinduism. However, the fact that Jung concentrates solely on Siva in his various incarnations and aspects does not by any means entail that his speculations in this regard are any more accurate. A couple of examples should bear this out well.

In "Aspects of the Libido," Jung makes repeated references to India and Hindu beliefs, which in the end all reduce to Saivism or, more precisely, to Saivism in its limited creative aspect. For example, he mentions the mythical tradition of Rudra (Siva in his destructive nature) and his thousand eyes, but relates them through the sun to Mithra and turns the story around to invoke Rudra as the creator-god ("Aspects of the Libido," 71). Certainly, Siva is sometimes referred to in his tradition as a creator, especially in his marriage with Parvati and his role as dispenser of boons to the pious ascetic. However, not only does Jung's one-sided interpretation ignore the destructive aspects of Siva, it ignores variants of the same myth where Rudra's thousand eyes are actually a thousand vaginas, the result of a punishment for admiring the *apsaras,* celestial water nymphs, at the expense of his kingdom.

This myth leads well into a second criticism of Jung's theories when applied to Indian religion, namely that Indian religion is packed full of blatantly sexual symbolism or even sexual representation. One of the most common forms of worship of Siva is of the *lingam,* a representation of the erect penis. This worship is hardly surrounded by symbolism; a long stone, often shaped to resemble a penis, is placed in a basin called the *yoni* ("vagina"). Milk is poured over the lingam, collected in the yoni, and then drunk for its creative power. No need to invoke arcane mythological and linguistic parallels to see the sexual symbolism here—the priests and the rituals come right out and glorify it. Moreover, desire, or *kama,* is considered one of the four acceptable goals for life, alongside duty, power, and liberation. A *Kama Sutra,* or guide to the pursuit of kama, has been written and preserved for at least sixteen centuries (*Kama Sutra,* 14), and details such subtle points of sexual enjoyment as what size penis will best satisfy a certain size of vagina and whether or not differing levels of sexual intensity aid or hinder enjoyment for both partners (ibid., 89–95). Certainly, such open and blatant sexual references in the Indian religious tradition do not by any means preclude the use of symbolism elsewhere. For example, Indian cinema is full of symbolism; in every film a hero chases a heroine around a tree, catches her, and then just when we might expect a kiss, they start to dance around in circles. This is a semiotic whereby the audience knows to assume that the actors are making love, sparing the director any trouble with the censors by showing it on the screen. However, some representatives of the Indian film industry have started to call for this taboo to be removed. G. D. Khosla, former chief justice and chairman of the Enquiry Committee on Film Censorship, has said, "In a country where the Lingam and the Yoni . . . are publicly worshipped and where a book on Kama Sutra has been written, what will happen if a couple is shown kissing as a mark of love and affection? Surely the Ganges will not catch on fire!" (Ramachandran, 540). Certainly, we will not deny that Indian traditions allow sexuality to be expressed in some areas (e.g., lingam worship) while not in others (e.g., cinema). However, this discrepancy indicates that the use of symbolism may have more to do with the milieu than with the inhibition. To put it another way, Jung's example of "a man the size of a thumb" being a symbol for the phallic libido ("Aspects of the Libido," 72) is more likely to reflect a metaphor, in the same way that Zeus is called "the Cloud-Gatherer" in *The Iliad,* than a disguising of phallic symbolism.

In spite of this rather obvious argument against it, later religious theorists such as Mircea Eliade have continued in this one-sided analysis of mythology. For example, Eliade calls the desire for orgiastic religion a desire for transmuting the religious condition of the believer, an interpretation that makes sense "if we keep in mind the fact that rural populations are in general only moderately interested in sex" (Eliade 1976, 91). This statement is justified by neither the context from which it is derived nor the rest of Eliade's work, but reflects an underlying assumption that must be made in order for this particular application of the symbolic hypothesis to make sense. The orgiastic religion is the primary fact, which is subjected to Eliade's interpretation to derive a conclusion. Without this interpretation, we could attribute orgiastic religion to any number of causes. For example, orgies might reflect an existing practice canonized to give them a sense of respectability, an allegation that has been made in the past of Tantrism. We should not mean to present our new interpretation as taking the place of Eliade's—we have just as little reason to believe it as Eliade does his. However, we can use it as a tool to show that one interpretation of a myth has as little validity as another, without corroborating evidence to support the one over the other. O'Flaherty tells how some people have described Eliade's method (or nonmethod) as that "he reads an enormous amount, remembers it all, and is very, very bright" (O'Flaherty 1980, 11). That is, he overwhelms us with evidence from which he then induces a conclusion and deems it universal. The same sentiment can be applied to Jung.

Jung's first and formative ideas about Hinduism come from Karl Abraham's *Dreams and Myths.* Abraham's theories are based upon Freud's in that they both see dreams, myths, and religion as wish-fulfilling (Abraham, 71), but they presage Jung's in their uses of mythology and

religion. Abraham uses the Prometheus myth as a basis for the assertion
that the process of rubbing two objects together to produce fire was
not discovered accidentally but rather was a result of displaced masturbation. In *Unconscious,* Jung adopted this stance as well. The argument
depends upon the myth of Prometheus, whose name Abraham declines
from "Pramantha," or "forth-rubber." From this other name, Abraham
extracts the idea that Pramantha brought forth people by rubbing, and
that rubbing to create fire is ritual reenactment of this primal creative
act (ibid., 31). *Matha,* according to Abraham, means male genitals, and
mantha is a Freudian slip contracting *matha* and *math,* which means
"to take or rob" (ibid., 45). Thus, Pramantha in both name and myth
reflects the fact that "all Indogermanic peoples produced fire by rubbing"
(ibid., 28), and that men can produce fire (i.e., semen—Sanskrit *agni*)
by rubbing as well. However, there are a few problems with this approach.
If Abraham wants to appeal to linguistic proofs, it would be nice if
he could at least give us the language or languages from which he draws
his *matha* and *math.* Some contention could be made about his deriving
"Prometheus" from "Pramantha," as well as his categorical statement
that all European myths derive from Vedic ones (ibid., 27), especially
in light of the fact that the Aryans migrated from Europe. Also, it
does seem a little odd that the Greeks "mistook the true meaning of
the Prometheus sage" and even "the meaning of the name Prometheus"
in assimilating the Pramantha myth (ibid., 33).

Unfortunately, Abraham does not cite his sources, and *Dreams
and Myths* is published without a bibliography, which probably means
Abraham did not include one. For that reason, we cannot even categorically assert the existence of the Pramantha myth. However, whether
or not it exists is irrelevant. The fact remains that, whether or not the
Pramantha myth exists, we have no reason to assume that the Prometheus
myth derives from it except Abraham's theory that all European myths
derive from Vedic ones. For all we know, the converse may be true:
Pramantha may well derive from Prometheus, and Abraham's theory,
unsupported up to now, would be falsified by a discovery of this type.
Hypotheses about the descent of myths and legends are exactly that—
hypotheses—and any scholar who mistakes them for facts quickly
becomes quite obviously wrong. However, Jung took Abraham's idea
in its entirety and supported a major work (*Unconscious*) with it. In
time, Jung took the ideas from *Unconscious* and used them as the basis
for the rest of his life's researches into the nature of the collective
unconscious.

We cannot here claim to have knocked out the entire foundation of Jung's thought because we have questioned the validity of Abraham's claims. That would be too simplistic, and would not acknowledge the incredibly vast corpus of work to which Jung would refer in later writings. Nonetheless, we can make some more specific statements deriving from our critique of Abraham. It is significant to note that, unlike Abraham, Jung is quite good about documenting his sources. He concludes both the foreword and the conclusion to *Aion* with the statement that, as best as he was able, he provided documentation of his sources to aid in the verification of his conclusions. This does not make these conclusions any more correct than Abraham's, but it does spare us the problem we had when wondering exactly who Pramantha was. But most importantly, *Dreams and Myths* does summarize nicely the problem of judging an idea in light of a preconceived theory. Deriving Prometheus from Pramantha is justified only by Abraham's assumption; when the assumption is removed, so is the derivation.

Enough of Hinduism; Jung refers to it extensively, but it by no means exhausts his interest in the subcontinent. Although Jung hardly deals at all with Jainism, an offshoot of Hinduism that has been more or less reassimilated, and *Bön,* a pre-Buddhist religion in Tibet, he does spend quite a bit of time looking into Buddhism. In chapter eight, we will discuss Jung's interpretation of the *Bardo Thödol,* and how it differs from the Buddhist's. When examining this book, it will be worth remembering that Jung, in calling the *Bardo Thödol* visions emanations of the psyche, makes the implicit statement that the psyche exists to produce these visions. The Buddhist, and the *Bardo Thödol,* treat these visions as independent of the viewer (inasmuch as anything is independent of everything else). That is, Jung considers the visions to be collective in that they are universal to human experience, but individual in that they do not reflect an objective reality, external reality. According to Jung the visions are the expression of an internal mechanism—the psyche. As for his conception of the after-death realm, this is harder to determine. In his doctoral thesis, Jung showed a predilection toward the paranormal, but even there he does not seem to believe that the incarnations that his subject claimed to have lived were actual people. Rather, he seems even to have seen the entire idea of life after death as having purely psychological content ("The Psychology and Pathology of So-Called Occult Phenomena," pp. 1–12, 23, 37–38). In any case, Jung saw belief in reincarnation and after-death experiences such as are described in the *Bardo Thödol* as purely psychological and personal.

The Buddhist sees the visions as personal in that perceiving them shows that the viewer still perceives a distinction between self and other, but collective in that they are actually a part of the viewer and all other beings.

This concept is very hard to describe, so alien is it to the Western development of thought, so we must look at it in more depth before we can see its ramifications for Jung. As far as a Buddhist is concerned, there is no distinction between self and other, but we perceive a difference because of our desire to maintain a sense of self. Once that desire is gone, the perception of difference goes along with it. In this light, the difference between the *Bardo Thödol* visions and their viewer is not real, but perceived; the visions are a part of the viewer not as products of the viewer's psyche but as everything in the world is a part of the viewer and the viewer is a part of everything. This viewpoint goes a long way toward explaining the Buddhist predilection toward nonviolence and respect of others. It also explains why the deceased "spirit" in its travels through the Bardo worlds should recognize the visions as part of the self, (and not falsely believe that the visions represent external reality). Recognizing the true nature of the visions removes the last self/other distinction before reaching nirvana.

In light of our understanding of the Buddhist viewpoint, we can now see why Jung's interpretation of the *Bardo Thödol* is so contrary to the Buddhist's. For Jung to call the *Bardo Thödol* visions simply epiphenomena of the psyche reaffirms the distinction between self and other in that while the visions are collective to the human species, Jung assigns them personal characteristics and individual meaning. As far as the Buddhist is concerned, these visions may appear different from person to person, but they are not personal. This distinction appears to be lost on Jung.

Just as Hinduism has different strands, so too does Buddhism. In its transmission from India to China, the context of Buddhism changed as it interacted with existing Chinese philosophies and beliefs. One of these changes diminished the role of *anatta,* changing it from a doctrine of the lack of self into a doctrine denying any sense of self-interest. This is reflected somewhat in Tibetan Buddhism, but really comes into its own once we reach China, Korea, and Japan, and their peculiar schools of Buddhism. In particular, the Chinese school of *Ch'an* represents a character more in common with modern schools of philosophy than Indian Buddhism. Better known under its Japanese name of *Zen,* this school often strikes Westerners as more concerned with linguistic paradox than with spiritual enlightenment. Certainly, the concept of the *koan,* or parable, depends heavily on linguistics for its effect. However, its intent is to bring the *bodhisattva* to instant enlightment, or *satori.* One major Zen scholar says that satori makes a person "consciously un-conscious" (Suzuki, 46). Terminology like this shows well how a con-nection between psychoanalysis and Zen could be drawn and maintained. However, Jung evidently had very little experience with the concepts of Zen, although, on the surface, it seems that Zen provides much support for his theories.

Jung, in all of his writings, only once dealt with Zen in anything more than a passing manner. In his twenty-paragraph introduction to D. T. Suzuki's *Introduction to Zen Buddhism,* Jung takes an approach that is clearly identical to his treatment of every non-Western religious tradition. Rather than interpreting Zen on its own terms, Jung pillages Zen for experiences analogous to those of other mystics, then explains them using the discourse he himself invented. For Jung, "the occurrence of satori is interpreted and formulated as a *break-through,* by a con-sciousness limited to the ego-form, into the non-ego-like self" (*CW* 11.883). Interpreted and formulated by whom?

Suzuki himself compares koans to archetypes (Suzuki, 44), but only inasmuch as both are said to be innate within us and the Zen master merely points them out. The obvious assumption to make from Suzuki's statement is that the koan and the archetype both lead to enlightenment. So far, he has not contradicted Jung. However, to assume that he and Jung are in agreement is to assume that he means the same thing by "enlightenment" as does Jung.

here are spiritual monuments . . . [that] are positive examples of our [individuation] process. Above all I would mention the *koans* of Zen Buddhism, these sublime paradoxes that light up as with a flash of lightning, the inscrutable relations between ego and self. ("On the Nature of the Psyche," *CW* 8.431)

For Jung, the enlightenment found through the koan points to the re-lation between the ego and the self. This may well not be the same claim as Suzuki makes when he attributes to satori the ability to make a person "consciously unconscious" (Suzuki, 46).

However, let us suppose that Jung's ideas are actually in accordance with Suzuki's. After all, we would be remiss in not noting here that Suzuki was a member of Jung's Eranos circle and that, although he thought the ideas of Jung and his followers primitive next to Zen, he did consider Jung at least beginning the process toward enlightenment. The question still remains whether or not Jung is in accordance with all Zen Buddhists. In the matter of a living tradition, be it religious or otherwise, the testimony of one expert should not be enough to make unqualified positive statements. Jung may well understand Suzuki's theory of satori. This does not mean he understands satori. Others who follow the Zen path may well look at satori through an entirely different light. For example, some who try to live by the strictures of a Zen master may well see satori as the experience that totally breaks down the barriers of the self. For such people, becoming "consciously un-conscious" would not "break down the barriers between ego and self" but break down the barriers between self and other. Jung, in his de-pendence upon Suzuki, ignores this possibility, choosing instead to take the moral high ground with his assertion that "the only movement inside our civilisation which has, or should have, some understanding of these [satori-like] endeavors is psychotherapy" ("Foreword" to Suzuki's *Introduction to Zen Buddhism, CW* 11.903).

So this is how Jung treats Zen when he deigns to look into it at all. The brief discussion just described is Jung's sole work investigating the phenomenon of Zen, yet he feels comfortable enough with it to make such positive statements upon its nature as the following:

> Our [psychological] paradox, however, offers the possibility of an *intuitive* and *emotional* experience [as opposed to an intellectual one], because the unity of the self, unknowable and incomprehensible, ir-radiates even the sphere of our discriminating, and hence divided, consciousness, and, like all unconscious contents, does so with very powerful effects. This inner unity, or experience of unity, is expressed most forcibly by the mystics in the idea of the *unio mystica,* and above all in the philosophies and religions of India, in Chinese Taoism, and in the Zen Buddhism of Japan. ("Psychology of the Transference," *CW* 16.532)

This is somewhat puzzling. After all, we can hardly say that he was not familiar with the thought of the Orient—repeatedly he invokes Taoism and the *I Ching* to support his theories (besides his commentary on the latter work, see "The Structure and Dynamics of the Self" for relationships between quaternities and the hexagrams of divination). And he must have felt comfortable with Zen, because he is willing to drop it in such overarching statements as mentioned above. However, because he seems to categorically avoid discussing Zen in any depth, we can only speculate as to why he would almost completely ignore one of the most prevalent philosophies in his "spiritual East."

Perhaps the fact that he called it "the Spiritual East" explains why Jung would steer so clear of Zen. If we can say one thing about Jung's methods of proof, we can reiterate our criticism of Eliade, that he is prone to giving almost a laundry list of examples to support his point, but never any counterexamples. Zen is a lot of things, but it is definitely not spiritual. In that respect, it parallels *Hinayana* Buddhism, or Indian Buddhism, which shuns metaphysical reflection entirely. It is interesting to note that Jung avoids discussing Hinayana as well. Now we may know why. Hinayana is fond of a particular proverb, telling of a man wounded by a poisoned arrow. The man's friends and neighbors all gather around to remove the arrow and treat the poison, but he will not allow them to do this until he has speculated about the caste of the archer, the particular material of which the arrow was made, from what plants the poison was derived, and the possible reason why the archer would want to shoot him. During this time, the man dies (H. Smith: Huston, 106). The Buddha would always conclude with the point of this proverb, namely that metaphysical reflection at the very least impedes enlightenment. Action, not reflection, is the way of the Buddha; it is the way of Hinayana and Zen as well. We do not meditate to expand the spirit, but to empty the mind, and while negative in effect, to empty is to act, not to reflect. This runs directly contrary to Jung's repeated assertion that the East is primarily concerned with the spirit and things metaphysical, at the expense of the intellect. Zen could not care less about the spirit, and for that reason Jung would never invoke it.

Other psychoanalysts have treated Zen as a philosophy comparable in approach to psychoanalysis. Erich Fromm, for example, sees Zen as quite compatible with the psychoanalytic procedure. As far as Fromm is concerned, the aims of Zen are the same as those of psychoanalysis: to liberate energy, to see true human nature, and to stop people from going insane or being crippled by their mental limitations (Fromm 1960, 122). To Fromm, the psychoanalyst is the secular equivalent of the Zen master, who cannot enlighten someone but can show the path to enlightenment (ibid, 113). The psychoanalyst does not cure someone, this view would say, but instead leads the patient down the road to an eventual self-induced cure. Perhaps this shows the modern appeal of

Zen to psychoanalysts—that it is a parallel system of thought where even the best master cannot lead supplicants to enlightenment without some help from the supplicants themselves. That is, both Zen and psychoanalysis blame the seeker of knowledge in the event knowledge is not attained, rather than blaming the person who claimed to be able to enlighten, effectively removing the burden of proof from the master or the psychoanalyst.

However, to say that psychoanalysis would be interested in Zen simply because of the shared beliefs about the roles of the recepient and practicioner does not do credit to the depth of the relationship. In fact, many concepts of Zen find a mirror in psychoanalytic theories. For example, as far as both techniques are concerned, the ego comes to be through an affirmation of the self; when the distinction between self and other is gone, so too go the current boundaries of the ego (DeMartino, 143). However, this brings us back to the difficulties we found between Jung and the Tibetan strand of Buddhism. Both De-Martino and Fromm seem to miss the point that, while both psycho-analysis and Zen advocate the destruction of the boundary between self and other, they do so for different reasons. As far as the psychoanalyst is concerned, removal of this distinction will help patients live more comfortable lives and aid them in their interactions with other people, leading to a sort of "Golden Rule" approach to life. But to the Zen master, interactions with other people are irrelevant—the quest is for ultimate knowledge, not a more comfortable social life. In response to Fromm's assertion that the aims of psychoanalysis and Zen are the same, we must reply that they are the same only in those general terms by which he enunciates them (Fromm 1960, 122). That is, the Zen master and the psychoanalyst may both intend to show their followers the true nature of humanity, but that true nature is categorically different from one ideology to the other.

Although Jung did not want to consider Zen in his analysis of "Eastern thought," he could not afford to leave China untouched. If he had completely ignored a society that had developed not only a high degree of technology (e.g., gunpowder) but also highly refined philosophies, he would have been accused of ignoring almost a quarter of the world's population. This would have made any claims to uni-versality for his theories appear ludicrous. Fortunately for him, China did provide two different systems for him to invoke in support of his ideas. The more arcane of these, coming to the fore in such works as *The Secret of the Golden Flower*, deals with ideas Jung considered

Chinese forms of alchemy; we will deal with them when we deal with alchemy in general. However, one very mainstream strand of Chinese thought did lend itself well to Jung's metaphysical reflections, and crops up again and again throughout his works. This system, Taoism, came to play a very large role in Jungian thought and analysis and for that reason it bears looking into here.

In a nutshell, Jung saw Taoism as an Oriental counterpart to Heraclitus's *enantiodroma,* "the reversal into the opposite" ("Psychotherapists or the Clergy," 275). Enantiodroma was one of Jung's favorite occidental ideas, and finding it supported by Taoism must have reinforced his belief in it. Like any capsule definition, calling Taoism simply an Eastern form of this Greek idea oversimplifies the intricacies of Taoist thought, yet it may go a long way toward explaining why Jung was so fascinated with them. However, in the past we have seen Jung get rather excited about ideas without truly understanding them. In his considerations of Taoism, Jung continues this fine tradition. In fact, Taoism is more concerned with maintaining balance, or homeostasis. The *Tao Te Ching,* promoted under the auspices of one Lao Tzu (who more probably edited than wrote the work), was concerned with the whole of the unfathomable universe rather than the place of humanity in that universe. Basically a sort of nature mysticism, Taoism becomes significant to Jung through its development of the theory of *yin* and *yang,* two opposing principles around which the universe is organized. So far, we see here nothing new—any reasonably developed monotheism posits a similar set of opposites. However, Taoism puts a bit of a twist to the bipolar idea by assigning each of the poles a set of values specifically devoid of any idea of divinity. Yang comprises ideas such as goodness, activity, positivity, light, and summer; yin such elements as evil, passivity, negativity, darkness, and winter (H. Smith 211). Again, we have here a slightly different set of opposites in that no gods are associated with either one. If this were all that Taoism offered, Jung would probably not have been very interested in it. But we have left out the most important differentiating criterion between the yang and yin, that of gender. Not only does yang consist of all the attributes we listed above, but it is also masculine, whereas yin is feminine.

Here we find enshrined in a Chinese philosophy an idea that Jung would espouse over twenty-four centuries later, that the two genders exist in a state of balance, and only fall out of balance due to effort expended by people to alter that state (ibid., 211). We see this most clearly in Jung's concept of the syzygy, the animus and the anima inside

of everyone, which we will further investigate in the sixth chapter. Jung's animus reflects very precisely the attributes given to the principle of yang, and his anima those of the yin. For example, Jung equates the animus with the paternal Logos, and the anima with the maternal Eros ("The Syzygy" *CW* 9[ii]:29). Taoists conceived each principle as containing some part of its opposite. When we look at the diagram on this page, the most famous Taoist symbol, we see that the white "tadpole" (yang) contains a black "eye," and the black "tadpole" (yin) contains a white "eye." This is meant to show that, even immersed in the very heart of the yang, we will find an element of yin (the black "eye"), and vice versa. The syzygy reflects this in that every man is said to encompass a feminine element, and every woman an element of the masculine. In Jung's syzygy, the masculine and feminine elements balance and complement each other, just as they do in the Taoist system.

If this relationship between the yin and the yang represented the sum total of Taoist philosophy, then we would be able to say that Jung based many of his ideas upon this system and, if Huston Smith is correct in saying that Zen is Indian Buddhism filtered through Taoism (H. Smith, 212), we could here find an explanation for why Jung ignores Zen. In his neverending quest into the past to find a "golden age" for every theory, before its becoming tainted by interaction, Jung may well have seen Taoism as the "pure" form of Zen, and therefore found it a more appropriate subject for inquiry. However, Taoism is not as simple as Jung's consideration of it would make it seem, or at least it does not correspond so well with his theories as he might like. One important difference between Jungian theory and Taoism is exemplified by the Taoist metaphor of the river. Like the river, the Taoist says, people should seek their own personal levels, never aspiring to something higher. Like Jung, Taoists hearken back to a golden age, when people were happy and well-adjusted, but the reasons they give differ quite substantially from Jung's. In the Taoist golden age, people had no curiosity, no ambition, no sense of personal property. The true Taoist, living in the true Taoist land of this golden age, could go an entire lifetime never visiting the neighboring land, even though that land might be just over the next hill (ibid., 210). While Jung would agree that people should try to live well-adjusted lives, he sees this as being a result of constant interaction with the archetypes and realizing them for what they are. That entails a certain sense of curiosity, a desire to find out the underlying causes for things, a drive to cross the hill and visit the neighbors to find out that they are actually us. The Taoist would not share this concern.

More damaging to Jung than the metaphor of the river in consideration of Taoist principles are the tenets of Chuang Tzu, a Taoist sage who lived sometime around the turn of the third century B.C. Not only did Chuang Tzu recommend a calm acceptance of things as they are, but he also believed people should respond to their environment spontaneously, instantly, and unthinkingly. That is, he did not recommend any reflection on life and its underlying meaning. How different this is from Jung's constant inquiry into the unconscious causes for events. But perhaps even more damning to Jung's ideas is Chuang Tzu's injunction that no knowledge can be universally extended. Huston Smith relates a discussion between Chuang Tzu and Hui Tzu, a Confucian. In this anecdote Chuang Tzu, looking over a bridge at some fish swimming in the river below, is moved to comment about the pleasure the fish enjoy, to which Hui Tzu, thinking he had caught the Taoist in a quandary, asked how Chuang Tzu could know what gives pleasure to a fish. Chuang Tzu replied by asking how Hui Tzu, he not being Chuang Tzu, could know whether or not Chuang Tzu knew what gives pleasure to a fish (ibid., 214). Certainly, no Taoist would claim that Chuang Tzu was implying that he knew what gives a fish pleasure. However, whether or not Chuang knew what pleases the fish, Hui did not know whether or not Chuang knew. Hui had his experience, Chuang his; for all Hui knew, Chuang may well have known that fish actually enjoy swimming. Again, we see the contrast with Jung's views, where the experience of one person, such as Miss Miller in *Unconscious,* is extended to be representative of all of humanity. Chuang Tzu would call this view ludicrous—how could Jung have any knowledge of Miss Miller's personal experience, let alone say that he has knowledge of our experience as well, and that the lot are the same?

Finally, Chinese philosophy in general still has one blow left to administer to Jung's neat, precise interpretation of it. Repeatedly, in his discussions of quaternities, Jung appeals to the traditional elements of earth, air, fire, and water to show one popular application of four disparate things combining to make one totality, in this case everything in the world. Here again, China has something to add that Jung would rather not consider, and unlike the two discrepancies discussed above, we cannot allow Jung the liberty of claiming never to have encountered it. In many major Chinese schools, the four traditional elements gained a fifth—wood. This destroys any assertions of universality Jung could make for the quaternity of the elements. We will explore quaternities as part and parcel of our later discussion of alchemy; for now, it is enough to point out that, if any belief about the world should be universal, we could expect that belief to be the actual components of the world itself. However, the *Book of History,* Mo Tzu, Hsün Tzu, Tsu Chuan, and Kuo-yü all advocated a system of elements with one more element than did the Greeks. This time, Jung cannot plead ignorance. In his discussion of the mandala, he discusses a Chinese figure that he himself indicates deals with earth, water, air, fire, and wood ("Concerning Mandala Symbolism," *CW* 9[i]:640–43, fig. 2). During this discussion, he makes no attempt to explain the presence of wood.

Now we will leave the religions of the East for what may be more familiar Western ground. But before we go, we have here a good opportunity to stop and make one very important point. Throughout our comparison between Jung's theories and the various religions we have considered, we have made a distinct attempt to avoid the claim that, through our investigations, we have disproved Jung's theories by use of these religions. After all, if one religion could prove or disprove anything, then we would not see the plethora of religions with which we are presented today. However, this is not to say that we have gone to all this work for nothing. Quite the contrary; we have so far covered enough ground that we can make some very substantial claims. First and foremost, this analysis of Eastern systems of belief has shown us that, far from bearing out Jung's statement that the East is primarily concerned with spirit, leaving intellect to the West, the systems of belief in Asia show no more predilection toward the spiritual than do those of Europe and North America. Those examples that support Jung's statement, such as Tibetan Buddhism and Taoism, are hardly representative of the totality of Asian religion; and even these supports have been shown to uphold his ideas only when first removed from their original contexts. Those examples that do not support Jung's statement, such as Indian Buddhism and Zen, may as well not exist for all the discussion Jung gives to them and their tenets.

To say this of someone who is bold enough to start a paper with the subheading "The Difference Between Eastern and Western Types of Thinking" ("Psychological Commentary" to *The Tibetan Book of the Great Liberation, CW* 759–830) is to cut a substantial support from under his theories. He says that the East sees "mind" as having metaphysical connotations, while the West does not (ibid., 759) However, we have seen Hinayana Buddhism reject metaphysics unequivocally. To Jung, the East sees the psyche as the "main and unique condition of existence," liberation from which must come from within; the West posits the world at large as dominated by objects, one of which can liberate the individual from suffering (ibid., 770). However, Taoism has no concept of liberation in any way with which Jung can associate his theories, and we will see that the Levantine Gnostics saw liberation as coming from within. Jung attributes the difference between Eastern and Western types of thinking to typically introverted (Eastern) and extraverted (Western) viewpoints (ibid., 779). Not having discussed intro- and extraversion, we are not in a position to comment on this statement as yet. However, when we do look into Jungian personality theory, we will find this to be possibly the one statement that, while not totally true, at least leads us to something that approximates truth. That is, while we do not want to call Eastern thought introverted, we will find ourselves able to call "introverted" that way of looking at the world that Jung calls "Eastern."

At this point, it is worth noting that our contradicting Jung's statements about Eastern religion does not make these statements scientific. While it is characteristic of scientific statements that they are falsifiable, no one would assert that, because something can be falsified, it is therefore scientific. If that were the case, the statement that Elvis Presley and Marilyn Monroe were the same person would be scientific, because it can be proven false. So while Jung's wild statements can lead us to something that approximates accuracy, this does not make him a scientist.

Having embarked on that brief diversion, we should now continue our analysis of Jung and religion, moving from the Far to the Near East. Having shown that Jung did not have a real grasp on the basic structures of Eastern religion does strike a rather serious blow at his early work, or at least his own ideas based upon those that he claimed to find in the East, but it leaves his later work relatively unscathed. In later years, Jung left Eastern religion behind for a return to the West. However, the ideas and images of Christianity have been analyzed for almost 2000 years; any input Jung could have, no matter how much weight his name may have carried, would not elevate his theories beyond the one-of-many stage to which we saw him relegated in the Hindu context. This is not to say that Jung shied away from Christianity entirely.

In fact, he did refer quite frequently to Christian symbolism, especially the Mass, throughout his writings. However, when he turned his attention to the vagaries of Western religion (that is, the non-monotheistic strands), Jung found himself in a situation similar to Freud's when he first started to investigate dreams. Before him lay a huge body of undigested facts, which he had free rein to interpret in any way he pleased. Any theory that made sense out of what had been previously unintelligible material was better to Jung and his contemporaries than admitting the material to be inscrutable. This idea applies in particular to alchemy, with which we will deal in a separate investigation, but it also assists any inquiry into Jung's treatment of other Western strands of belief as well. When looking at Eastern religion, Jung was able to rely upon the relative lack of knowledge and theories about his subjects to promote his own, and selected his supporting evidence accordingly. We will find that he carried out the same procedure in investigating the lesser-known Western beliefs.

This idea, that Jung only invokes the unexplored strands of Western religion in his proofs, is borne out by what may be his greatest omission. For someone who places so much stock in referring back to myths and legends, it seems more than a bit odd that Jung very rarely hearkens to the tales of the Greeks. He could definitely read Greek—the untranslated quotations and footnotes throughout the *Collected Works* more than attest to that. Moreover, at the time Jung went to school, a "classical" education was the only one offered, and that involved liberal doses of Homer. So why does he almost completely avoid both the *Iliad* and the *Odyssey*? The only reason that seems logical is the one presented above, that he wants to avoid using those materials where theories conflicting with his have been presented to explain (or explain away) the subject matter, or where the subject matter itself conflicts. In chapter eight, we will discuss the dichotomy between the primary fact and the interpretation; for now it will suffice to say that Jung avoided those sources that had already been shrouded with several interpretations. Perhaps he did this because his theory might not stand up to competition with another? We will not try to climb inside Jung's thought processes here; suffice it to say that his staying away from previously analyzed sources conveniently circumvented this difficulty for him.

However, we cannot let Jung off so easily. The fact that Jung presented his ideas as being universal means we can expect them to hold both in areas he considered when deriving them and areas he either did not consider or had never even heard of. If evidence from Greek mythology and belief provides us points we can use here against him, the fact that he himself occasionally invoked the Greek sources as proof or referred to the Olympians (e.g., "The Idea of Redemption in Alchemy," 233) becomes irrelevant. Instances such as this allow us to presume Jung had a certain level of familiarity with the Greek tradition. Accordingly, if we can find differing explanations from Jung's, we can at least see how he stands up against them. In the Greek context, we can draw such evidence from many different angles; here, we shall explore one only.

The particular route by which we shall approach Greek myth, following a path laid down by Pausanias and described by Paul Veyne, asks one simple question: did the Greeks actually believe in their myths? The ramifications of this statement for Jung should be instantly apparent—if the Greeks can be shown not to have believed in their myths, then the same assertion can be at least postulated about peoples and myths from other traditions as well. If that is true, and most people, or even one person, do not truly believe in the myths that their cultural and religious traditions put forth, then Jung's universality in invoking mythology as proof loses a lot of its credibility. Asserting the universal nature of a symbol by means of a myth not even believed by the people to whom it is current seems more than a bit ludicrous.

Veyne credits Greeks with a belief in their myths comparable to a child's belief in Santa Claus. The child, looking around, can very easily determine that in no way could any adult fit down any but the largest of chimneys and that children living in apartments without fireplaces get presents as well, yet he or she continues to believe in Santa because of the results. Three hundred sixty-four days a year, there is no Santa Claus, but what about Christmas morning? How can we tell a child tearing apart a parcel marked "From Santa" that Santa is just a myth? At this point, the argument that would persuade the child on any other day holds absolutely no weight. Santa must exist, because the toy exists, and it says right on it that Santa brought it. Certainly the next week, when well-meaning adults ask, "What did Santa bring?" the child becomes quite embarrassed; now we are back in the normal world, where reality reigns and there is no such thing as Santa Claus. Adults submit themselves to the same effect when watching a film—before sitting down to watch, the characters do not exist and afterwards they do not exist. But while the pictures are moving, then those characters are as alive as anyone else—they have wants, cares, needs, fears, and the rest of the spectrum of human emotion. It is a very bad movie that reminds the audience they are watching a movie, unless the intent is self-reflexive, which mocks the whole idea of suspending disbelief to begin with and in any case is very hard to pull off. Stephen King calls this effect the "mental clean-and-jerk," where the audience has to lift and suspend the weight of disbelief for a while. One "barometer" for the merit of a film "tests" the pressure that this weight places upon us. Once disbelief has been suspended, the moviegoer is in another world whose characters seem as real as friends and neighbors. Veyne proposes that the Greeks saw their myths in a similar vein, that most of the time they were just fictions, but occasionally they took on a special significance and became real. And the evidence he brings forth is very convincing. For example, he cites Aristotle's "Poetics" 9.8 to show that the Athenian public was aware of the existence of a double, mythical world in which tragedies took place rather than that they existed in the real one (Veyne, 45).

This concept, which Veyne calls "modality of belief," again brings us dangerously close to the problem of relativism. If we say that people can watch a film, do the "mental clean-and-jerk," and not engage in logical fallacy, then do we also have to say that Jung can call some concepts archetypally inspired while attributing the rest to daily life? In a nutshell, no, we do not. If two people, John and Jane, go to the cinema, and John watches a murder mystery while Jane watches a science-fiction fantasy, they go in with certain differing expectations. John can reasonably expect that no one will appear on his screen with more than the usual number of heads and other appendages, but Jane cannot. The difference is in the cognizance, and the context—by its very nature, a science-fiction film is not meant to represent a possible scenario, but a murder mystery just might. If a murder mystery appeals to such constructs as interplanetary travel or beings from another planet to reconcile its plot, it is no longer a murder mystery but a science-fiction fantasy involving a murder as part of its plot. The 1983 film *The Keep* failed miserably for exactly these reasons; reconciling the stereotypical "Nazi movie" plot by appeal to supernatural beings breaks the genre that the film chose for itself. The *deus ex machina* is no longer an adequate resolution to drama. Heroes in the *Iliad* as often as not find themselves fighting gods and goddesses, and the Greeks could accept this, but when a medieval text claims that God and all his angels were fighting for one side in a battle, we do not take this literally. However, if both Sophocles and Shakespeare write a tragedy, and neither appeals to the gods, they are still not perceived as equivalent. Certainly, Shakespeare's audience did not believe that the episodes detailed in *Hamlet* actually occurred, but they could have, and this would have required no "mental clean-and-jerk"—the play may not have been believed but it was believable because its setting was considered plausible. The alternate world Veyne cites as the location for Greek tragedies (ibid.) was considered categorically different from the actual world in which the Greeks lived. As such, they had no difficulty postulating interaction between people and gods in this realm. Shakespeare's world is the world of the murder mystery, Sophocles' the world of science fiction; neither is the actual world of real life. Categorically different things can happen in each realm, and they do.

In this case, we escape the problem of relativism—people allow themselves certain liberties when dealing with drama and literature, which would stretch the fabric of truth were the stories actually real. However, these differences only exist because the audience allows them to. In this respect, modern advertising techniques have been very helpful. Through advertisements, the public becomes aware of which modality of belief it must adopt when stepping through the door of the theater, whether it should expect aliens to be from another planet or simply another town, and as such advertisements give a warning of how heavy the weight of disbelief will be. If an audience goes into the theater expecting *Hamlet,* it might be disappointed to see the Dane come out wearing a three-piece suit, unless it knew in advance to expect a modern interpretation of the drama. This is not relativism, because it is calculated. Relativism assumes that religious belief and ordinary belief are not epistemologically distinguished in the mind of the believer (Sperber, 165). Here, we would like to contend that they are.

This also gets us nicely around a possible contention that could be raised by Eliade, his concept of ritual time and space. Throughout Eliade's work, he proposes the idea that rituals such as creation festivals are actually attempts to partake in the primal creation act. Jung's frequent reference to the Pueblo Indians of Arizona makes the same claim— that they had to help the sun rise every morning, or else it would stop rising ("Travels," 252). It is this sort of statement that causes Jung to see a parallel between the mythical thinking of ancients, children, "lower races," and dreams ("Concerning the Two Kinds of Thinking," 14). Just as the child has not yet learned the dichotomy between Santa Claus the concept and Santa Claus the bringer of presents on Christmas morning, so too do the Pueblos need to learn the difference between the sun as a god and the sun as the thing in the sky, or so Jung would say. Veyne gets us out of this difficulty with his concept of the modalities of belief—"Men do not find the truth; they create it, as they create their history" (Veyne, xii). A tribe of Ethiopians, the Dorzé, see the leopard as a Christian animal, and they believe that it observes the fasts of the Coptic Church every Wednesday and Friday, but they do not abandon their livestock on those two days. Tradition says that leopards are Christian, but experience teaches that they eat when they can (ibid., xi). By the same token, tradition tells children that Santa brings presents, but years of staying up all night on Christmas Eve teaches them experientially that Santa looks remarkably like someone with whom they live; or tradition tells the Pueblos that they must raise the sun every morning, but if they were forced to abandon their ritual, they would still find the disk in the air. The differing beliefs are in differing modalities, and can therefore be simultaneously sustained, just as the Greeks could believe in divine intervention in their plays but not in their homes.

As nice as the idea of modality of belief sounds in descriptive terms, we are no better than Jung if we cannot explain how this concept is formed in the human brain. While we have set ourselves epistemological limits based upon which theories of knowledge have been scientifically supported, and thus cannot give a full explanation for this phenomenon, we can propose something and do so using acceptably scientific terminology. B. F. Skinner, in a paper detailing a type of "superstitious" behavior he had conditioned into a group of pigeons, told how, when presented with continual reinforcement at regular intervals with no regard for the pigeon's behavior, each pigeon conditioned itself to some randomly occurring behavior (Skinner 1959c, 405). More interesting to see was the fact that each pigeon had developed a different conditioned response, such as circular movement, patterned pecking, and the like. After a second investigation into the same phenomenon, Skinner reported that "pending an investigation of . . . parameters, it may at least be said that incidental stimuli adventitiously related to reinforcement may acquire marked discriminative functions" (Skinner and Morse, 412). That is, when presented with an incidental stimulus (i.e., a stimulus uncorrelated to the the reward), the pigeons performed their conditioned response in its presence, even when no other stimulus was provided to announce the imminent reward.

We can transfer this analogy to the human context quite easily. When on a streak, baseball players develop some very bizarre habits, such as not shaving or changing their socks. Hockey goaltenders often kiss or in some other way consecrate their goal posts before every game. If we were to ask either type of athlete whether or not these rituals actually help them play, they would answer in the negative. However, keep them from their ritual, and performance often suffers—not always, but often enough that we can posit some form of diminished capacity correlated with non-performance of the ritual. Here Jung, Eliade, and their followers would invoke a human need for ritual to explain the decreased performance. However, any profession that depends on reacting to unpredictable situations will show a higher frequency of rituals (Persinger, 119). The analogy with Skinner's experiments explains the phenomenon as well, and with less excess baggage.

If we marry Skinner's results to Leon Festinger's concept of cognitive dissonance, we have the makings of a theory of religion to contest Jung's. When the ritual is performed and a good result ensues, the ritual was correctly performed; if a good result does not ensue from the ritual, it is the fault of the actors, not the act, and if a good result ensues without the ritual, the actors consider themselves lucky. Using the creation myth example, if the ritual is performed, then the fields will be fertile, and if the fields are not fertile, it is not that the ritual is useless but that it was not properly performed. If the ritual is not properly performed but the fields become fertile anyway, the people see themselves as fortunate, but this does not mean they abandon the ritual forever. The Judeo-Christian tradition captures this in its histories of the nation of Israel—when they worshipped God they prospered, but when they came upon hard times, it was not God's fault but theirs, and when the people were faithful but still suffering, they were suffering for the sins of their parents or their neighbors. God can do no wrong, but people can, therefore the people must have been doing wrong if bad things happened to them. Tradition has taught them to venerate God and they will prosper, and "the Lord may well provide," but he provides much better if we farm the land he has given us.

Are people born with an innate sense of this difference between tradition and experience? Through the combination of Veyne's, Skinner's, and Festinger's ideas, we can advance a hesitating answer to this question. The stimulus-response patterns of tradition are established through experience, but once these patterns are established they then form the basis for our subjective interpretations of experience. Certainly, we have not experienced beings from other planets, but the social convention of the cinema allows us to do just that, and while on one level these beings are real, on another they are not. So long as we maintain the socially determined metaphor, so long as we "clean-and-jerk," then the aliens are real. Once the weight falls, or if we have not been warned to lift it, then we do not separate the modalities of belief. Tradition tells us that a murder mystery does not contain aliens, but our experience of the figures on the screen may indicate otherwise. At this point, we either reinterpret the film as a science-fiction fantasy or drop the weight of disbelief and walk out. But once outside the theater, even if we have been watching a science-fiction fantasy, we do not expect aliens to swoop down from the sky. When Jung reinterpreted the phenomenon of the UFO, he did so assuming that they were psychological, because our version of reality does not allow for beings from another planet. In the theater, however, aliens can and often do exist, but only if we have been prepared in advance to receive them. People who see UFOs in the skies at night may just have lifted the weight so effortlessly that they have not realized the time has come to put it back down.

Veyne's idea of there being different modalities of belief led us on that rather extended tangent, and it will lead us back to our main point as well. Just as modern citizens can sometimes believe in aliens and sometimes not, the Greek citizens could believe that Achilles' mother was a goddess but also that they will never meet anyone whose mother is a goddess. In short, the evidence in Veyne's book is enough to call into question the constancy and extent of the Greeks' belief in their myths. At the same time, Veyne's limitations, such as acceptance of psychoanalysis, do not curtail us, because we have been able to combine his theory of modality of belief, which does not depend on psychoanalysis for its truth claim, leaning instead on other theories to produce empirically testable hypotheses, such as one that people are more likely to believe in aliens while watching a science-fiction film than while writing a chemistry final. Certainly, Jung could say that special beliefs such as that of Santa Claus reflect the activation of an archetype. However, it takes less effort to say that the child on Chrismas morning and the adult in the theater believe at their particular moments because they want to believe—because they have made the "clean-and-jerk"—and that they stop believing afterward because they no longer want to. But considering that Jung does not often use Greek mythology in his proofs, we could be forgiven for stopping here and considering that Veyne's hypothesis, while interesting, has no ramifications for Jung. That will not do. While the scope of Veyne's investigation may be limited to Greece, its implications stretch far beyond the Adriatic, in more contexts than the one we have just explored. In general, it is safe to say that religions are only truly believed by a fraction of those people who consider themselves practitioners of the religion. Upon the death of Muhammad, many of the Bedouin tribes considered themselves free from Islam because of the nature of their understanding of the religion. It took the succeeding caliphs quite a long time and not a little bloodshed to convince the Bedouin that their allegiance was with God, not Muhammad, and that God is eternal. They were overpowered by the presence of Muhammad, but once Muhammad was gone, so too was his influence over them, and they became like the child once Christmas Day has passed. They did not believe in the religion of Islam but in the cult of its the Prophet's personality, which was categorically different.

In a more modern case, North America is full of "Christians" who have not seen the inside of a church in years, but who generally think that God is a good thing and that Jesus had some interesting ideas. When questioned, these people will often call themselves Christian simply because their parents took them to church when they were young. Often, children will say, "My mother is a Catholic and my father is a Lutheran; what does that make me?" as if religious denomination were an ethnic group or a can of paint. Though faith may show itself through works, works can exist in the absence of faith; by the strict definition of its terms, these people are not Christian. For example, the Anglican Church sets down a very strict set of terms and beliefs that the true believer will hold, listed in its *Book of Common Prayer* (pp. 695-714), and while these are acts of faith, they are categorically different from works. Other denominations have loosened, tightened, or altered this set as they have desired, but none has abolished it altogether. Very many so-called "believers" would recognize none of these articles of faith but consider themselves Christians nonetheless. Put them in a church, under the influence of an effective speaker, and this belief will come to the fore; but once the speaker is gone, so are the effects, and the believer has returned to "normal" life where religion is comfortable, and Santa Claus is not real.

It would be a mistake to say that, because this sort of modal belief has shown up in the above cases, it is universal. However, the fact that it exists allows us to say that its opposite is not universal either. If there exist people who do not believe those tenets they claim to believe, such people cannot be said to entertain any religious belief at all. Jung and the post-Jungians circumvent this problem through the archetypes and the concept of the "secular myth." However, chroniclers of such "secular myths" end up collecting the type of stories found in such books as *The Vanishing Hitchhiker.* Urban legends such as these are epistemologically different from religious beliefs. As for those religious festivals that have adopted a secular context, such as Christmas, their persistence can be explained away through our Veyne-Skinner-Festinger hypothesis. Little Jane may not understand the Christmas story, but she does know Santa, and she knows what he brings. That is, because of examples such as the crypto-Christian described above, we cannot say that total belief in mythological systems is universal to the human species. And this leads us back to our main topic for this chapter from what may seem like a very long diversion. It is quite probable that Jung, while not having access to Veyne's book, did have access to Pausanias and the other authors from whom Veyne derives his conclusions. And it is significant to note that Jung very rarely invokes Greek pagan examples to support his hypotheses. Of course, these two facts do not prove that Jung conspicuously avoided the Greek mythos because it could lead to works directly contradicting his hypothesis. To conclusively support such an assertion would require far more proof than that to which we currently have access, such as a complete bibliography of every book Jung ever read and a total diary of every thought he ever entertained. However, we can make some limited statements from this discovery, and we can use works such as Veyne's if not to contradict Jung's assertions for the universality of his theories then at least to undercut them.

Even the briefest analysis of Jung's work will show that he by no means kept away from the Western world when formulating his theories. However, if our hypothesis that Jung deliberately chose little-explored religious systems to support his ideas is to hold here, we would have to see him invoke the lesser-known religions of the West. This would seem to be impossible—in the Western world, only three traditions have flourished, Islam, Judaism, and Christianity, and none of these is obscure. In any case, we will soon see that Jung's approach to Christianity is at best questionable, his interpretation of Judaism was solely Qabalistic, and his approach to Islam was almost no approach at all. In this light, we would expect Jung to hearken back to the past, to the time before these major faiths. However, we have also seen that he left the Greco-Roman pantheon almost untouched. So this leaves us to look in the darker corners of Western religion. This search will prove rewarding, for Jung did not ignore Western systems of belief altogether, but he did manage to find some sufficiently untouched by previous interpretation that he felt free to offer one. In particular, we shall look into two of these—Mithraism and Gnosticism.

Mithraism has been called the greatest enemy of the early Christian Church. For that reason, the dearth of evidence available today to study the religion of Mithra is somewhat surprising, even if we consider that perhaps the Christians burned all the Mithraist documents. Franz Cumont, for years the eminent scholar of Mithraism, described the problems in exploring his field of study in this way:

> Our predicament is somewhat similar to that in which we should find ourselves if we were called upon to write a history of the Church of the Middle Ages with no other sources at our command than the Hebrew Bible and the sculptured *débris* of Roman and Gothic Portals. (Cumont, vii)

This, of course, is exactly the environment that would fascinate Jung, and Cumont's explanation of the existing evidence coincided well with Jung's own ideas about religion in general. From the evidence we have available today, Mithraism seems to have centered around a ritual called the *tauroctony,* or the ritual killing of a bull. The "Holy of Holies" of a Mithraic temple, or *mithraeum,* invariably contained a statue or an engraving of the tauroctony, where Mithra would kill a bull by stabbing a knife into its flank. Present in every representation were Mithra, the bull, a dog, a snake, a raven, a lion, a cup, and a scorpion in reasonably stereotyped forms (Ulansey, 11). Tracing the descent of the god Mithra, Cumont follows him back through Persia to the Vedic Mitra (Cumont, 2), the god of light and protector of truth. The Roman imperial army adopted this god from Asia Minor and spread his worship throughout the Empire (ibid., 40).

With the onset of Christianity, the similarities between the two faiths were so instantly apparent that the Christian heresiologists would later talk of a "Satanic travesty" (ibid., 193)—to invoke just one example, both Christian and Mithraic rituals use bread and a cup of water in ceremonies (Justin, quoted in Gwatkin, 55). However, the two faiths only came into direct conflict in the Rhône Valley, North Africa, and Rome itself; Christianity developed in places of Israelite settlement, while Mithraism followed the slave trade and armed conquest. Jung saw this simultaneous development as a perfect example of synchronicity, where two very similar ideas occur together with no causal connection to link them, and thus became intrigued by Mithraism. He went on to invoke it liberally throughout *Unconscious,* going so far as to equate Mithra with Christ. By transition, this makes Mithra a symbol representing the archetype of the self, because Jung sees Christ as a symbol of the self. This relation is reflected in Jung's choice of title for his most comprehensive study of the self; Aion is another name for Mithra. Undoubtedly the coincidental appearance of Christianity and Mithraism played a very heavy role in Jung's conception of synchronicity.

Certainly, Mithra and Christ share some characteristics. Nonetheless, they do differ in many ways, as even Cumont admitted (Cumont, 195–98). Cumont saw these differences as exemplifying the inherent superiority of Christianity; even without the polemic, they suffice to show that while Mithraism and Christianity "embodied two responses to the same set of cultural forces" (Ulansey, 4), they did not represent exactly the same process. For that reason, alternative hypotheses about Mithraism become very important. Throughout Jung's life, no one questioned Cumont's hypothesis. However, that is not to say that other ideas about Mithra were never proposed. As far back as 1869, K. B. Stark had proposed the idea that the iconography of the tauroctony did not actually refer to a sacrifice, but in fact symbolized a sort of star map of important constellations (ibid., 15). This idea lay dormant for over a hundred years, but caught fire in the early 1970s. The different versions of the astrological hypothesis are cataloged and discussed in David Ulansey's *The Origins of the Mithraic Mysteries,* and while no particular version has convinced everyone, it is safe to say that the astrological hypothesis has at least assumed the status of viable alternative to Cumont's idea. In fact, the astrological hypothesis at least goes part of the way to explaining the series of initiations, secrecy of doctrine, cavelike temples, and iconography of the tauroctony, all taking on different forms from the Anatolian to the Roman incarnation of Mithraism (ibid., 8). We have no evidence that the Persian Mithra ever killed a bull, and while Cumont found a myth of a bull being killed in the Persian mythos, the slayer was Ahriman, the power of evil (Cumont, 35). Cumont took this myth and posited a variant where Mithra did the killing, but there is no evidence for this variant in the Persian sources (Ulansey, 9).

Ulansey is not the only person to put forth the idea that Mithraism, rather than actually being a parallel to Christianity, is actually a disguised form of astrology, and he himself admits this, citing several other works from which he drew his ideas. However, Ulansey seems to have missed one other source that attests to the astrological nature of the Mithraic religion. We cannot fault Ulansey for not being well-read in the works of Aleister Crowley, because they take on a singularly unfathomable tone at least five times a page. Nonetheless, Crowley did publish quite a substantial library, and although his works are written from a slightly different perspective than Ulansey's (for example, Crowley actually believes in the "power" of the Tarot), they do lend more than a bit of insight into astrology, the occult, and other little-studied phenomena. One particular passage is worth quoting here in full:

> 3. Early astronomers calculated that the Sun took 360 days to go round the Zodiac. This was a closely guarded secret of the learned; so they concealed it in the divine name Mithras, which adds up, according to the Greek Convention (**M** 40—**I** 10—**Th** 9—**R** 100—**A** 1—**S** 200) to 360. Better observation showed 365 days to be more accurate, so they decided to call it "Abraxas" (**A** 1—**B** 2—**R** 100—**A** 1—**X** 60—**A** 1—**S** 200). When the others found this out they put themselves right by altering the spelling of Mithras to Meithras, which adds (like Abraxas) to 365. (Crowley 1944, 27-28)

One drawback to Crowley (or any other occultist) is his absolute disregard for citing sources, if in fact he uses sources at all. Nonetheless, it is interesting to note that Crowley seems to have come up with an astrological meaning for the name Mithras that supports Ulansey rather than Cumont. Also of some import here is Crowley's method of proof. Although no sane person believes that numerology is support for scientific proof (and, fortunately, we are spared here the question of whether or not Crowley is correct in his reasoning), what should interest us is the fact that Crowley does use numerology in asserting an astrological origin for the name of Mithra. It should have interested Jung as well. We have seen Jung use far more tenuous numerological grounds in psychoanalysis than Crowley uses here (c.f. "The Psychology of Number Dreams," *CW* 4:95–128), so he could not discard Crowley's interpretation categorically. As well, we can expect that Jung would have at least heard of Crowley; they shared a mutual fascination with the occult, were contemporaries, and both received a substantial amount of press. When Crowley died, on December 1, 1947, he was "reviled by the English press as the wickedest man on earth, [and] scorned by many who should have known better" (Wasserman, 5). In short, if Jung was to consider himself an expert on the occult, or at least a scholar of it, he should at least have known other scholars who had written in the field. If not, he should have been expected either to yield to their opinion or to work toward falsifying it. Of these other writers, Crowley stood head and shoulders above the rest, if not for scholarship then at least for notoriety. Of course, to see Crowley's work support Jung's would not necessarily prove that Jung's was right any more than seeing the two conflict proves that Jung was wrong. Nonetheless, it is interesting to see that Crowley seems to support Ulansey, not Cumont, on this point; this is interesting because Cumont studied more than just Mithraism. In fact, for a long time Cumont was considered the eminent authority on ancient systems of astrology (Ulansey, 13). Cumont consummately dismissed the role of astrology in Mithraism, so Jung, who was also known to invoke astrological proofs (c.f. "The Sign of the Fishes"), dismissed astrology in this case as well; because it fit in with his interpretive hypothesis, Jung yielded in the face of greater authority. To be honest, he would have had to at least consider the ramifications of others as well.

Note that we are not concerned here with whether or not Ulansey's hypothesis is better than Cumont's. In spite of the limited support we have just seen Ulansey receive from Crowley, for our purposes it is enough to say that Ulansey's idea has been proposed, and at least rates the status of "serious alternative" rather than "flat earth." As Cumont himself admitted, we do not have enough evidence to be sure of any Mithraic hypothesis (Cumont, vii). Yet Jung, in *Unconscious,* seems very certain of Cumont's conclusions. In fairness to Jung, we must admit that the explosion of astrological theories did not take place until after his death, and even though Stark's paper had been written well before Jung was born, we cannot expect Jung to have read every work published on every topic he has ever discussed. And although we have said that Jung should have been familiar with Crowley, it is possible that he was not. Nonetheless, the widespread existence and success of the astrological hypothesis does give us grounds to question whether the conclusions drawn in *Unconscious* could be presented quite so categorically today. Ulansey's hypothesis actually explains more than Cumont's, so if Jung was writing today, we might expect him to consider it the more probable, or at least to consider it at all. At the very least, we can discount any conclusions Jung draws based on Cumont's ideas if they do not stand the test of Ulansey. When Charles Darwin wrote *The Origin of Species,* the conclusions of Lamarckian biology were weighed in the balance and found wanting. The same standard should apply to Mithraic research—guardedly, to be sure, because of the very limited evidence we can use on which to base our conclusions—but it should apply nonetheless. And if we discard Cumont's ideas in favor of Ulansey's, we can then at least reconsider Jung's ideas at the same time.

Before leaving this discussion, it is worth offering a bit of an apology for having treated Aleister Crowley as if he were a legitimate scholar. Certainly, his writings are utter tripe. However, Jung has different standards than we do, and Crowley does meet Jung's standards inasmuch as Crowley firmly held his beliefs to be true and, while that does not make them true beliefs, it does make them real and therefore worthwhile to investigate ("The Real and the Surreal," *CW* 8:747). Certainly, as far as scholarship goes, Crowley is about as much a scholar as Nostradamus or Meister Eckhart. However, Jung does accept both Eckhart's and Nostradamus' work, even going so far as to base theories upon them. Using Crowley against Jung in his consideration of Mithraism does not imply acceptance of Crowley's beliefs. However, it does point nicely to the fact that, whereas in other situations Jung rejects traditional scholarship in favor of mysticism, in this regard he has done the opposite. If he was correct in accepting traditional scholarship here, why would he not have been in other locations?

It is interesting to note that, as his career progressed, Jung completely abandoned Mithraism in favor of Gnosticism. Gnosticism, like Mithraism, was contemporary with Christianity, and, like Mithraism, was vigorously persecuted and suppressed once Rome became Christian. In *Aion,* Jung's work considering Christ as a symbol of the self-as-redeemer, it may not be insignificant to note the absence of any consideration of Mithra, where in *Unconscious* Mithra was constantly equated with Christ. It is tempting to draw from this omission something about Jung's academic standards—to believe that perhaps he had heard of the astrological hypothesis, realized it was more probable than Cumont's, and abandoned Mithraism because of this—but we should not do this. In any case, having weighed Jung's Mithraism in the balance and found it wanting, we can turn to his analysis of Gnosticism. But before we investigate Gnosticism proper, we must admit that the fact we are able to analyze it at all is a debt we owe to Jung, though perhaps not for the reasons he might wish. For nearly two thousand years, our entire knowledge of Gnosticism came from deciphering the polemics against it written by the Christian heresiographers. Then, in 1944, the Nag Hammadi Codex, twenty-two volumes of Gnostic writings, was found. Jung got a taste of one fragment, and his appetite was so whetted that he started avidly to collect as many fragments as he could find. Even today, these fragments are called the "Jung Codex." For this reason, we should be able to expect Jung to have a very thorough understanding of the contents of the Gnostic Scriptures, with all their points of similarity and difference. Although Gnosticism does not encompass quite so diverse a set of beliefs as Hinduism, this term by no means subsumes one definite, particular set of beliefs. Certainly, all strands of Gnosticism share some beliefs in common besides their being suppressed by the church fathers, otherwise they would not be grouped together. However, the strands differ on some major points, which once we have looked into the common beliefs will bear looking into as well.

Gnostic cosmogony posits one major difference from almost every other system of belief in that it ascribes the creation of the universe to an evil god with various names, one of which was Jehovah. The accounts vary, as do the evil god's reasons for creation, but this idea remains permanent. Gnostic soteriology also remains constant from strand to strand—people can attain salvation only by recognizing the spark of divinity inherent in themselves and transcending the world of the evil god to the good God and his wife, Wisdom (Sophia). This good god can only be described by a *via negativa*—we cannot make any positive statements about him because the entire world was created by a god who wants us to remain ignorant of the true God. Gnosticism also posits the concept of the *anima mundi,* or world soul, which closely parallels the concepts of atman and yin-yang. However, one major difference between the strands of Gnosticism arose with the age of Christ, when Gnosticism split into two divergent schools, one that saw Christ as a redeemer who could lead humanity to recognize the spark within, the other that saw Christ as a creation of the evil god who would distract humanity from recognizing the spark. (For an expansion of the ideas in this paragraph, see Rudolph 1977 and Singer 1987.)

In a pattern that is beginning to take on the characteristics of a broken record, this divergence in the schools seems to be where Jung picks up on Gnosticism. Perhaps the importance he ascribes to the Christ symbol would explain why Jung would consider the Christian schools of Gnosticism so exclusively. Singer posits that Gnosticism caught Jung's eye with its soteriology, the idea of redemption through self-recognition (Singer, 84). Singer further postulates that the "Anonymous Treatise on the Origin of the World" would have fascinated Jung (ibid., 79). The reason Gnostics saw the creator-god as evil, because he withheld knowledge from Adam, would find sympathy in Jung's view that people should aim for complete knowledge (ibid., 80). Gnosis seeks wholeness, not perfection; it abjures people to integrate with the shadow, not overcome it (ibid., 89).

That last statement may well be the reason why Jung concentrated so totally on the Christian Gnosticism. Completely beyond Singer's contention that the world of the Gnostic god is that of the archetype, the syzygy (ibid., 73), Jung saw Christ as a symbol of the self, as the psychological magnet for unconscious symbols of redemption ("Background to the Psychology of Christian Alchemical Symbolism," *CW* 9[ii]:283). "In the world of Christian ideas Christ undoubtedly represents the self" ("Christ, a Symbol of the Self," *CW* 9[ii]:115). However, the Christian religion cannot tolerate any form of evil in it— the doctrine of the *privatio boni,* that evil does not exist in itself but is simply the absence of good, repeatedly raises Jung's ire, because it does not allow for the opposite he sees so necessary for psychological health (e.g., ibid., 116). Christians aspire to be like Christ—to be perfect, as perfect as they see him as having been. However, Jung says, the Christ-image is not the same as the archetype of the self. The Christ-image is "as good as perfect;" the archetype is "completeness but is far from being perfect" (ibid., 123). Gnosticism, on the other hand, does not urge perfection, but rather integration of the opposing elements (Singer, 89). Do not try to be perfect, says the Christian Gnostic, because we have been created imperfectly by an evil god. Instead, transcend this evil god through the example Christ set for us.

Jung claims Gnosticism is important in considering the idea of the Redeemer because of the synchronicity between it and Christianity ("Gnostic Symbols of the Self," *CW* 9[ii]:287). That is, because the two religions arose at around the same time, they must be related, and Jung invokes Rhine's ESP experiments to support this statement. If Jung's interest in Gnosticism springs from this source, no wonder he would not consider the non-Christian strands. Ignoring the absurdity inherent in Rhine's proofs (and the refutation of them in Hines), we nonetheless have here an instance of Jung ignoring evidence that conflicts with his theories. As far as he is concerned, Christ is a symbol of the self. Therefore, those people who did not consider Christ to be that redeeming symbol but instead saw him as a creation of an evil god sent to lead people astray would also disagree with Jung's statements about Christ. For that reason, Jung would not want to consider these people when formulating his statements. After reading Jung, we could be forgiven for thinking that all Gnostics were Christians. This was hardly the case, but Jung would have us believe it was, because if he is forced to admit that intelligent, highly literate, myth-forming people, living in the time when he claims psychological ideas such as redemption were assimilated to the Christ-image, were able to formulate a cogent counterargument, he would then have to consider counterarguments to his own as well.

Perhaps not a counterargument to Jung's view but definitely different from it, the role of Jesus Christ in Islam is greatly scaled down from the one that Christ plays in the religion bearing his name. To the Muslim, Jesus was a prophet like any other, certainly very important and definitely blessed by God, but merely a prophet—no more, no less. However, we cannot accuse Jung of ignoring this aspect of Islam while simultaneously promoting others; we have in Islam an instance of a religion that Jung very nearly ignored. In fact, despite several tangential references in other papers, Jung only deals directly with Islam in one paper, "Concerning Rebirth," which pertains to the eighteenth *sura* (chapter) of the Qur'an. But even in this one paper, Jung shows that he did not really understand the structure of the Qur'an, nor did he truly have a grasp of the message of Islam.

The eighteenth sura of the Qur'an, "The Cave" (*Al-Kahf*), takes its name from the long parable that opens it. This story relates the account of "a few young men" (*Qur'an,* 18.13)* who condemned the religion of their society and, fearing persecution, went and hid in a cave. God hid these men under the cover of sleep and with the protection of their dog for "a number of years" (ibid., 18.11). Eventually they awakened and sent one of their number down to the town for food, with the injunction that he be careful not to let his presence be known:

> If they come to know of you
> they will stone you to death,
> or force you to go back to their creed;
> then you will never succeed.
>
> (ibid., 18.20)

Jung saw the parable as telling of rebirth, a subjective transformation by enlargement of the personality ("Concerning Rebirth," *CW* 9[i]:215). The cave he saw as a mystery in the same sense as the Eleusinian or Mithraic mysteries, a "secret cavity in which one is shut up in order to be incubated and renewed," and anyone who enters it will penetrate

---

*This is the standard method for footnoting the Qur'an. It takes the form chapter.verse, and is similar to the form used in numbering biblical verses. The various chapters of the Qur'an are traditionally referred to by number rather than by name.

into the unconscious and make contact with unconscious contents, causing an unconscious process of transformation (ibid., 240–41). He interprets the sleepers as gods because there are seven of them (ibid., 242).

> Some will say: "They were three,
> and their dog was the fourth;" and some
> ill also say: "They were five and their dog was the sixth,"
> guessing in the dark. And some will even say:
> "They were seven, and their dog the eighth."
> Say: "My Lord alone knows best their number;
> none but only a few know of them."
> So do not argue about it with them but lightly,
> and do not enquire about them from any one of them.
>
> (*Qur'an*, 18.22)

But by no means does this say that there were seven sleepers. On the contrary, it says that only God knows how many there were, and that people should not concern themselves with the number. So Jung's allusion between the seven sleepers and the seven planets, and all other sevens he invokes ("Concerning Rebirth," *CW* 9[i]:242) are based on a fallacy, namely that the passage numbers the sleepers at seven. It is for that reason we were so scrupulous when recounting the passage to quote the relevant section that says there were "a few" sleepers (*Qur'an*, 18.13). The Qur'an never says how many people slept, nor how long they stayed (ibid., 18.26), choosing instead to leave that information up to God. Jung considers the dog important, because it makes the seven sleepers into an "ogdoad," which is a double quaternity and therefore a totality ("The Components of the Coniunctio," *CW* 14:8), or the three sleepers into four, which forms a single quaternity ("Concerning Rebirth," *CW* 9[i]:242)

Following the parable of the cave come a set of edifying instructions such as an injunction to recite the Qur'an (*Qur'an*, 18.27). Jung sees these morals as coming for those who cannot be reborn through the mystery story of the cave and must be content with a set of moral laws. As well, the section contains a brief discussion of heaven and hell, which Jung ignores. So long as we remove the idea of the rebirth mystery, we can actually rest reasonably content with Jung's analysis here; to say that the rules are in place so that those who cannot understand the parable will not walk away thinking it was just a pretty story, does us no harm. However, this presumes that the chapter was actually written in the order in which it is presented, which no serious student of Islam would ever put forth so categorically. Even Muslims, who do believe the Qur'an to be the actual words of God, do not believe that these words are in God's own order. In fact, the words that are generally believed to be the first revelation received by Muhammad do not occur until chapter 96, "The Embryo" (*Al-Alaq*). Certainly, the edifying instructions found after the parable of the cave (*Qur'an,* 18.23–31) do seem related (witness the interjection of the cave story again at 18.25–26). However, we have no reason to assume any more relation between the cave story and the later story of Moses, which starts at 18.60, than we do to relate the cave story to "The Embryo." The best we can do is to point out that "The Cave" is a Meccan sura, so both the cave story and the Moses story occurred before the *hijra* to Medina.

Before we discuss the Moses story, it is worth pointing out that Jung skips the twenty-eight verses coming between the rules following the cave story and Moses. These verses tell a parable, present another list of instructions, again tell of the punishment of sinners, and tell some reasons for sending prophets. Seeing as Jung skipped over these, we could be forgiven for doing so as well. However, it is worthwhile to look into the parable of two men, one with gardens and one without. The man with the gardens exalted his land, so much that he said:

> "I cannot imagine that this will ever be ruined,
> Nor can I think that the Hour (of Doom) will come.
> And even if I am brought back to my Lord,
> I will surely find a better place there than this."
>
> (18.35–36)

That is, he put the land before God. At this, the other man rebuked him, with the message that all things come and all things go because of God. Because of their owner's pride, the gardens came to ruin, and the man who had once been so proud was reduced to wailing, "Would to God that I had not/ associated any one with my Lord" (ibid., 18.42). Again, we see the message being presented that God gives and he takes away for his own reasons, which may or may not make sense. This is hardly the sense Jung intends us to draw from the chapter and is worth keeping in mind as we look at the story of Moses starting from verse 60.

Jung splits the Moses story into two halves, verses 60 to 64 and 65 to 83. The first half tells of Moses and his servant Joshua making a journey to the confluence of two seas, then going past it and realizing that they had forgotten their fish. At this, Moses says, "But that is exactly what we were seeking" (ibid., 18.62), and they retrace their steps until they find a votary of God. At this point, the second half of the story begins. Jung calls Moses a man who seeks, and seeks knowledge of the self, which is the fish ("Concerning Rebirth," *CW* 9[i]:244). Under the influence of several commentators, Jung calls Moses' servant Joshua ben Nun, and ignoring the fact that the Arabic name would contain *ibn* rather than *ben,* the whole idea of telling us who was Joshua's father is nowhere justified by the rest of the passage. Undaunted by this, Jung goes on to draw the connection between Nun and the Egyptian Nun, the primal chaos, which is the father of the shadow. Joshua is therefore Moses' shadow (ibid.). Thus, Jung says, it was actually Moses himself who lost the knowledge that he seeks. Jung never draws a connection between Joshua ben Nun through the shadow to the fish and the self, thereby calling Joshua a symbol of the self; nor does he equate the lost fish with Christ, thereby having Moses lose his self, and this despite the fact that the latter idea has been proposed by at least one modern commentator (Ahmad, §2101). Instead, he says that the fish coming alive and leaping from the basket shows the animal ancestor separating itself from conscious humanity ("Concerning Rebirth," *CW* 9[i]:244). This disregards the actual text of the passage, which says that Joshua simply forgot the fish (*Qur'an,* 18.61). One puzzling element of the passage is the fact that Joshua ascribes his forgetting the fish to Satan (ibid., 18.63), but Jung does not make a point of this.

Instead, he follows Moses and Joshua as they retrace their steps and find "one of Our [i.e., God's] votaries/ whom We had blessed/ and given knowledge from Us" (ibid., 18.65). We make this distinction to show that giving the name Khidr to the man is not Qur'anic, but rather was added in a later commentary (see the article "Khizr" in Hughes —the different spelling merely reflects a different style of transliteration). Khidr's name brings us back to the problem of the interpretation and the primary source, the ramifications of which will be elucidated in chapter eight. Moses asks if he can join with Khidr, to learn knowledge of the right way. Khidr tells Moses that he is far beyond Moses' comprehension, and that Moses must not ask him anything until he speaks of it himself (ibid., 18.70). Moses agrees, and goes with Khidr. They come across a boat, in which Khidr makes a hole, and then a boy, who Khidr kills, and finally a city that will not be hospitable to them, where Khidr repairs a crumbling wall. At each stop Moses questions Khidr's motives until finally, after fixing the wall, Khidr sends him away, but not without telling Moses the reasons for his actions:

"That boat belonged to poor people
who used to toil on the sea.
I damaged it because there was a king after them
who used to seize every ship by force.
As for the boy, his parents were believers,
but we feared that he would harass them with defiance and disbelief.
We hoped their Lord would give them a substitute
better than him in virtue and goodness.
As for that wall, it belonged to two orphan boys
of the city, and their treasure was buried under it.
Their father was an upright man. So your Lord
willed that on reaching the age of maturity
they should dig out their treasure as a favor from their Lord.
So, I did not do that of my own accord."

(ibid., 18.79–82)

We are reminded here of one moral from the parable of the gardens. Again, we see that God reserves the right to act as he wills, without regard for telling mere mortals his reasoning. The Lord moves in mysterious ways. Jung believes "Khidr may well be a symbol of the self" ("Concerning Rebirth," *CW* 9[i]:247), but that he is equally a symbol for God, that he is a "human personification of Allah" ("Flying Saucers: A Modern Myth of Things Seen in the Skies," *CW* 10:622). This would also explain why Khidr has become a favorite person for Sufis such as Jung's safari leader, who told Jung he should always be on his guard in case he meets Khidr in any form—as a man, a blinding light, or even a blade of grass ("Concerning Rebirth," *CW* 9[i]:250). Certainly, the greatest heresy a Muslim can ever commit is to associate a partner with God, as we saw in the parable of the gardens, but that is not to say that they do not symbolize God. However, when they do symbolize God, they anthropomorphize, and even then only aspects of God. Some of the "99 Names of God" describe physical attributes (c.f. Nurbakhsh), but none is another name; we can have "God the Merciful" but not "God Smith." As well, Jung has never given us a solid reason to accept that Khidr is the fish ("Concerning Rebirth," *CW* 9[i]:246).

After the story of Khidr comes the story of Dhu'l-Qarnain. Jung agrees with most commentators in ascribing to this figure the identity of Alexander the Great, and promptly links him with Khidr by assigning both the role of two friends, equivalent to the Dioscuri (ibid., 252). However, Ahmed Ali sees Dhu'l-Qarnain as closer to Cyrus the Great, citing the travels to east and west, wisdom, and qualities of prophethood, and using Isaiah 42.1–3 and Ezra 1–2 in support of the idea that, of all foreign kings, God has anointed Cyrus (Ali, 259—note to 18.83 in the *Qur'an*). Whether or not Ali is correct in his assertion, it is worth remembering that the identity of Dhu'l-Qarnain is by no means settled. Jung equates Dhu'l-Qarnain with Moses, probably on the basis of the fact that Dhu'l-Qarnain is Arabic for "He of the Two Horns," which may have reminded Jung of Michelangelo's famous statue. The actual story of Dhu'l-Qarnain is highly allegorical and symbolic, and we do not have the same benefit of a preconceived interpretive hypothesis as Jung had in looking at it. Nonetheless, we can point out certain important elements and highlight discrepancies between Jung's analysis of them compared to other possibilities.

Jung explained the insertion of the Dhu'l-Qarnain story as Moses' having an experience of self, but not being able to tell the Jews directly because they were infidels ("Concerning Rebirth," *CW* 9[i]:252). However, the Qur'an makes it very clear that "for every people there is an apostle" (*Qur'an* 10.47). That is, at the time of Moses, Muhammad had not yet brought the revelation, so God was still sending prophets to every people and giving them the revelation, however incomplete, in that way. So Moses would not have been bound to use a story to tell people of his experience of the self, assuming that is what he had, because at this point the Jews were not yet infidels.

However, that point assumes that Moses is the one telling the story, which we have no reason to assume. We have already pointed out that each chapter of the Qur'an is composed of several fragments, but we have not pointed out any way to tell them apart. Without getting into the vagaries of Qur'anic scholarship, we can point out one method that is often used to differentiate the different sections. Throughout the Qur'an, the command, "Say!" crops up. Since the Qur'an is taken to represent God's exact words to Muhammad, as opposed to the Bible (whose words are simply inspired by God), the imperative is always taken to be an imperative from God to Muhammad. Without giving us any reason to abandon this tool here, Jung does exactly that, interpreting the command as Khidr inviting Moses to tell the story using Dhu'l-Qarnain to symbolize himself. According to Jung, this stops Moses from seeing the story as something personal, something happening to his ego-consciousness, and associating that ego with the self ("Concerning Rebirth," *CW* 9[i]:254). However, we have no reason to believe that this story is being told by Moses at all. In fact, the occurrence of the imperative gives us reason to believe that Muhammad, not Moses, is telling the story. Certainly, all Muslim interpretations have followed this general structural interpretation. This would also explain the eschatology beginning at 18.97. Muhammad brought the revelation; Moses just brought the law. If Moses is not telling the story of Dhu'l-Qarnain, this strikes a very serious blow at Jung's general hypothesis, making the story just another part of the Qur'an—important, definitely, but not psychologically interpretable.

Certainly, this is the most allegorical chapter of the Qur'an, as Ali himself testifies in a footnote to the chapter. For that reason, we must be very much on our guard that we do not fall into the trap of walking in with an interpretive hypothesis and promptly finding that which we seek. This would make us subject to the same sort of criticism as we have applied to Jung, and is why we have categorically avoided making any positive statements about the identity of any of the characters we have seen. However, we can make some limited claims about the content of the chapter in general, so long as we are careful to remember several caveats. Jung calls the entire chapter a rebirth mystery; this runs totally in the face of the fact that the chapter is composed of several disparate elements. Jung could be in some way supported if all the elements of the chapter had presented a fairly unified whole, but they do not, and "Concerning Rebirth" actually concerns only those elements that do support Jung's hypothesis. If anything at all can be said about the contents of the eighteenth chapter, it can be said that the chapter reserves for God the right to give or withhold knowledge or goods from people as he wishes. In the parable of the cave, God withheld knowledge of the number of sleepers and how long they slept. In the parable of the gardens, God took away the man's garden when he began to venerate it above God. In the story of Moses and Khidr, God denied Moses knowledge of Khidr's motives. In the story of Dhu'l-Qarnain, God gave a story of what would happen on the Day of Judgment and made the categorical assertion that he is One. Certainly, these can be perceived as rebirth mysteries—Jung did exactly that. However, that does not say that perceiving them that way is correct.

We have spent so much time looking into this one portion of the Qur'an because it gives us a very good insight into Jung's treatment of religious sources in general. Of the traditions Jung invokes, the only ones active today are Buddhism, Hinduism, Islam, Judaism, and Christianity. Christianity and its interpretations so pervade Jung's writings that they are pointless to try to summarize here—we would find ourselves hundreds of pages later only having scratched the surface. Jews would not have found too much to question about Jung's interpretations of their religion, because he left it relatively unscathed—he only looked into Jewish mysticism and astrology, about which even knowledgeable rabbis hotly debate. As for Hinduism and Buddhism, the odds of Jung finding a substantial body of practitioners of either of those while based in Zurich are slim to none. For this reason, Islam could have provided Jung with a very valuable source of verification for his ideas. While not a Muslim area, Europe definitely contained and contains many Muslims, and while Jung was based in Zurich, we know he did leave Switzerland occasionally. During any of those trips, he could have found some Islamic scholars and approached them and asked what they thought of "Concerning Rebirth." The fact that Jung never did so tells us something very important about his appeals to religion, and especially those external to his own upbringing. He was unconcerned with whether or not his interpretation would be acceptable to those who actually believed the religion currently under his slightly fuzzy microscope. In psychoanalysis in general, a patient who refuses to accept an interpretation is seen as impeding progress. "Anyone who insists on denying it [i.e., projections] becomes identical with it" ("The Self," *CW* 9[ii]:44). In light of this, we can see why Jung felt such impunity to be so wrong so often—because in his mind, he was actually right, and the believers of the religion could see it because to him they were identical with the error. The self is a God-image, Jung held ("The Syzygy," *CW* 9[ii].42), and since the believer's self is incomplete and unconscious, so too is the God-image. After help, meaning psychoanalysis, people learn to see how their religious works had actually already been leading them toward individuation, although they had not been aware of it.

Herein lies the whole crux of Jung's use of religion. Once religious believers undergo psychoanalysis, they see in their holy works what Jung sees in them as well, or they reconvert and individuate by these means. Believers who do not undergo psychoanalysis think Jung has misinterpreted the primary source material. Jung would say they do not agree with him because their archetypes of the self are unconscious. The believers would say they do not agree with Jung because his disbelief colors his writings, forcing him to reduce God to the human level. Certainly, Jung claimed a parallel such as that between Christ and the self is "not to be taken as anything more than a psychological one" ("Christ, a Symbol of the Self," *CW* 9[ii]:122), and that the archetypes are not metaphysical ("Religious and Psychological Problems of Alchemy," *CW* 12:15). However, his denial of Christ's divinity effectively puts him in the position where the believers can call him an unbeliever and therefore take him with a grain of salt.

This whole discussion of Jung's belief or disbelief coloring his works is, for our purposes, more or less irrelevant. What is important to note is that Jung will not allow for divergent views to his own, yet only experience of the psychoanalytic procedure or detailed study of the *Collected Works* could give someone the same views as Jung. That is, in order for Jung to consider someone to have correct views, that person must also have the correct viewpoint from which to be looking. It is as if Jung had been born with blue filters in his eyes, and would only accept a photograph as accurate if it had been taken through a blue filter. So he goes a step further, and convinces other people to put blue filters into their eyes. Now he and they see the world in the same way, and therefore he will listen to their opinions.

To continue the metaphor, certain religious traditions are better suited to receive the blue filter than others, these being traditions not so deeply explored through filters of other colors. Jung has capitalized on this, and scoured the religious traditions of the world for instances that he can invoke to support his views wherever necessary. Since he places such great stock in proofs from mythology, for us to spend so much time analyzing religions has paid off in spades. Certainly, we have not had time to look into every religious tradition ever invoked by Jung. Instead, we have concentrated on some major traditions. In this concentration we have found that Jung ignores major systems of belief, and even in those systems he does consider, he is very often off base. "Concerning Rebirth" was an especially important example of this, in that it gave us the opportunity to look at Jung's work in comparison to a well-established system of theology, honed over more than a thousand years of constant self-reflection. Jung therefore had a substantial body of literature against which he could have compared his theories to see if they aligned with the previous scholasticism. Yet he did not choose to undertake a thorough study of Islam; instead, he applied his own interpretive hypothesis, a method he followed in every analysis of every religion he ever undertook.

3

The General Archetypes

So far, we have covered quite a lot of ground in our investigation of Jung. However, one objection which could be leveled at our inquiry is that we have dealt solely with generalities. That is, while we have made many sweeping statements and allegations, we have not criticized Jung in any particular aspect as yet. While it is very important that we show how he misuses religion, we would not live up to our mandate if we did not analyze any specific ideas and concepts of Jungian theory. In that regard, probably Jung's most famous and most contentious particular concept is that of the archetype. The archetype is absolutely central to Jung's theories. His phenomenology of the self, his ideas about human behavior, his interpretations of alchemy; all of these and more hinge on our first accepting the archetypes. In fact, his first conception of the archetypes was as "the *a priori,* inborn forms of 'intuition' . . . which are the necessary *a priori* determinants of all psychic processes" ("Instinct and the Unconscious," *CW* 8:270). Ignoring all the problems we have had with accepting any a priori concepts, we nonetheless see that from the very beginning, Jung did posit the archetypes as being universal to all of humanity. For that reason alone, they bear looking into. After all, even though we will not allow ourselves to posit any sort of universal trait without experimental justification, Jung did not limit himself in the same way, and if he based so many of his central concepts on this one, he must have felt it so well supported as to be impregnable to all attacks. As such, we will attack and see what effects ensue.

Probably the best place to look into the archetypes is at the beginning, or at least their beginning to Jung. The first encounter he describes with a patient's reenacting the mythical came early in his career, in 1906, when he was making his rounds. We will let Jung tell the details himself:

> One day I came across him [in the corridor], blinking through the window up at the sun, and moving his head from side to side in a curious manner. He took me by the arm and said he wanted to show me something. He said I must look at the sun with eyes half shut, and then I could see the sun's phallus. If I moved my head from side to side the sun-phallus would move too, and that was the origin of the wind. ("The Structure of the Psyche," *CW* 8:317)

The significance of Jung's having had this experience in 1906 becomes clear as he continues the description, telling that he happened upon the same idea when he studied Albrecht Dieterich's inquiry into Mithraism in 1910: "And likewise the so-called tube, the origin of the ministering wind. For you will see hanging down from the disc of the sun something that looks like a tube" (quoting Dieterich, in "The Structure of the Psyche," *CW* 8:318). Since Jung did not encounter Dieterich's idea until 1910, while his patient had produced it in 1906, he saw something more than coincidence. Of course, during those four years, he had probably received reports of hundreds of other visions from hundreds of other patients, but this one stuck in his mind. If we consider this in light of his ideas on synchronicity, it quickly becomes clear that Jung's remembering this particular incident would be half the proof of its significance to him and in general. Despite the fact that he had not developed the concept of synchronicity at this point, Jung does see a relationship between the two events and looks for the idea to recur in other places, finding it in "certain medieval paintings [where] this tube is actually depicted as a sort of hose-pipe reaching down from heaven under the robe of Mary. In it the Holy Ghost flies down in the form of a dove to impregnate the Virgin" (ibid., 319). Remarking that the Holy Ghost (or Holy Spirit) was originally conceived of as "the wind that bloweth where it listeth," Jung also points out that "a Latin text" (he does not tell us which) reads "they say that the spirit descends through the disc of the sun" (ibid.). As well, he finds this idea to be "common to the whole of late classical and medieval philosophy" (ibid.). From these statements, he decides that:

I cannot, therefore, discover anything fortuitous in these visions, but simply the revival of possibilities of ideas that have always existed, that can be found again in the most diverse minds and in all epochs, and are therefore not to be mistaken for inherited ideas. ("Structure of the Psyche," 320)

We have gone into such detail here, quoting so often, because Jung saw this case as definitive proof of the existence of archetypes. However, upon further investigation of its particular details, this case falls apart. Aside from the obvious fallacy involved in inferring from the particular to the general, it is interesting to note that even the editors of the *Collected Works* have had problems with Jung's reasoning here. Later in his life, Jung learned that the version of Dieterich's work that crossed his desk in 1910 was not the first edition as he had claimed (ibid., 319), but actually the first revision of an original 1903 printing. Although the example is saved from total refutation by the fact that the patient was committed before 1903, it is nonetheless possible that the patient had heard of the idea and was simply repeating it when Jung stumbled across it. However, it is rather improbable that a patient in a mental institution, no matter how intelligent, would have access to translations of obscure religious manuscripts (institutional libraries being what they are). So we can grant Jung the liberty of assuming that the patient had never encountered Dieterich's work before.

However, we will not grant Jung the liberty of assuming that the patient had never before encountered the entire idea expressed in his hallucination. Jung himself makes the connection between this vision, the story of the Pentecost (Acts 2:1–4), medieval paintings, and philosophy. North Americans sometimes lose track of the pervasive influence of earlier societies upon those currently existing in Europe, especially as regards such cultural artifacts as art. Maybe Zurich was not an artistic capital, but it may as well have been Florence compared to the vast majority of New World cities. Switzerland is well within reach of such centers as Paris, Munich, and Vienna. All of this should go to show just how possible it is that the patient once saw one of those paintings with the ray or "tube" going down into the Virgin's robe (which, of course, Jung does not cite). This is a common motif in European religious art of the Medieval and Renaissance periods. Moreover, if the patient had undergone a traditional education, as did most people of Jung's era, he would probably have been exposed to philosophy and art history, and just may have encountered the idea therein as well.

It may also be interesting to note one other possible instance of a tube hanging off the disc of the sun. Throughout Egyptian art, a symbol of royalty was the uraeus-cobra hanging off the front of the pharaoh's crown. During the time of the pharaoh Akhenaten, when this king enforced a monotheistic sun worship upon the people of Egypt, the only permissible icon of this sun-god, called Aten, was a disc. It is interesting to note that this disc also exhibits the uraeus-cobra—a clear instance of a disc with a tube hanging off it. As well, the uraeus-cobra often made its way onto discs adorning the heads of gods and goddesses. We know from *Unconscious* that Jung was familiar with Egyptian religion and artifacts. And while we have no proof that his patient had ever encountered the ideas of Egypt, we do know that one of the largest collections of Egyptian art can be found in the Museen Insel in Berlin, and that the turn of the century was when the hottest archaeological investigations were underway throughout the Valley of the Kings, and were even being detailed in newspapers. It is therefore not impossible that perhaps the patient saw instances of the Egyptian art, either in Berlin or in the media, and was remembering this when he produced the vision. Jung himself placed great stock in the idea of cryptomnesia (e.g. "On the Significance of Number Dreams," 199); perhaps we have here an example.

Of course, none of this proves anything. Just because the patient could have remembered the hallucinated idea from other sources does not entail that this is actually the case. That is, in spite of the fact that the patient may well have encountered in his past the books or paintings that Jung cites in tracing the descent of the "sun-phallus," or the Egyptian example we just proposed, we cannot prove that he did. For this reason, we will now assume that the sun-phallus vision was generated by the patient himself, and see if that conclusively proves the archetypes. Jung himself considers the possibility that the similarity between the vision and the hallucination is simply fortuitous, but dismisses it because it had both connections with analogous ideas and inner meaning ("Structure of the Psyche," *CW* 8:319). This prefaces his ideas about synchronicity. Nonetheless, he has not given us grounds to believe that the patient's idea must be related to another. When we presented the actual details of the case, we pointed out that between the years 1906 and 1910, Jung must have encountered hundreds of hallucinations. Yet when he found this one duplicated in a book, he became convinced of there being a connection. In *The Logic of Scientific Discovery*, Popper makes the point to which we have repeatedly returned in this inquiry, that a subjective feeling of the truth of an idea is no support for its being accepted as a hypothesis (Popper p. 47). This is one sure category to distinguish legitimate methods of inquiry from quackery. However, Jung bases his idea on exactly such a subjective feeling of truth. It is significant that nowhere in his "proof" of the archetypes does Jung ever give a breakdown of how many visions he encountered during the four-year interlude that did not contain an archetype, because by the time he recorded this particular vision, he had come to see every delusion and every vision as expressing the archetypes. Nor does he ever tell us how many medieval paintings do not depict a tube from heaven to Mary's robe, nor does he tell us from what text he derives the quotation about the spirit descending through the disc of the sun, and not because this knowledge would disprove his theories. If, as Jung says, "there are as many archetypes as there are typical situations" ("Instinct and the Unconscious," *CW* 8:280), a painting without the tube does not challenge the unversality of the tube symbol. Rather, it presents a second archetype, complementing rather than contradicting the first.

Besides these enumerative difficulties, this case contains many inaccuracies and fallacies of fact. First of all, while the first conception of the Holy Spirit in the book of Acts is as a wind, this is not the first occurrence of the Holy Spirit in the entire Bible. The four gospels agree only rarely in terminology; one of these instances is the event of the baptism of Jesus.

> And John testified, "I saw the Spirit descending from heaven like a *dove,* and it remained on him. I myself did not know him, but the one who sent me to baptize with water said to me, 'He on whom you see the Spirit descend and remain is the one who baptizes with the Holy Spirit.' " (John 1.32–33, emphasis added)

This passage and the other three gospels (Matt. 3.16, Mark 1.10, Luke 3.22) all say in no uncertain terms that the Holy Spirit first appeared to the Christian world as a dove, not a wind. And while the book of Acts does open with Jesus' saying that the apostles will be baptized with the Holy Spirit, referring to the Pentecost (Acts 1.5), the book also makes quite clear that it is not even the first volume by its author. If the author of the two books is actually the same person, as the text purports him to be (Acts 1.1), then we can assume that he was familiar with his own writing of the Holy Spirit as coming in the form of a dove (Luke 3.22). If the authors are different, and the device in Acts

1.1 is merely stylistic, this does not imply that the second author did not know that the Holy Spirit had been presented as a dove in the first author's work; the second author does admit to being second, and therefore must have been aware of the gospel preceding him.

More damaging for the archetypes is Jung's statement that archetypes have been found "in the most diverse minds and in all epochs" ("The Structure of the Psyche," CW 8:320). Certainly, he did later go on to produce instances of archetypes in other cultures. However, the case of the sun-phallus was his acid test, so to speak, and in it his line of proof follows a very direct line: Mithraism—classical philosophy—Medieval/Renaissance art—patient. Ignoring the fact that these four time periods hardly represent "all epochs," we should instead concentrate on the fact that they hardly represent "the most diverse minds." Even Jung's staunchest supporters are willing to concede that, because Jung's parallels are mainly from Indo-European cultures, we cannot rule out culture and early learning in forming the archetypes (Samuels, 35). The four instances Jung cites in his line of descent of the idea have all inherited more or less the same cultural setting. So it would seem that Samuels' concession applies here, and that we cannot write off the possibility of common experience being the cause of the idea in the patient's mind, rather than archetypes.

However, in a pattern that we have come to see repeatedly in the *Collected Works,* the fact that we have just utterly demolished the universal nature of Jung's first proof for the archetypes would hardly faze him. Once he had determined that archetypes exist, using the case we have just lambasted, Jung went on to find them everywhere he looked. While there is some justification to saying that disproving the first instance does have ramifications upon all subsequent findings, we cannot say that we have completely destroyed the archetype as a concept. After all, if Samuels (ibid., 35) admitted that early learning and culture could be instrumental in forming the archetypes, but he still saw the archetypes as valid, then we have a long way to go. Unfortunately, we cannot indulge in the luxury of considering each instance of the archetypes in as much detail as we did above; this would require the proverbial million monkeys and take the proverbial million years. However, an analysis of the development of the archetypes in Jungian theory will provide several points where we can focus our attention.

When Jung first enunciated his ideas on the archetypes, he presented them in a form radically different from that which they would come to take in his later works. Not that he ever posited that they were not universal; far from it. However, while he never limited the scope of the archetypes, he did come to limit their relative applicability. In the beginning of his career, he saw archetypes as a sort of unconscious counterpart to the conscious instinct—"the instinct's perception of itself"—existing even in moths ("Instinct and the Unconscious," *CW* 8:277). By the end of his life, the concept had become refined into what came to be called the racial memory. At the same time, however, Jung's actual concept of exactly what it is to be an archetype never fundamentally changes from the early works to the later. We can say that Jung always firmly believed in the following statement:

> Archetypes are typical modes of apprehension, and wherever we meet with uniform and regularly recurring forms of apprehension we are dealing with an archetype, no matter whether its mythological character is recognised or not. (ibid., *CW* 8:280, emphasis removed)

The last portion of the above quotation definitely has implications for one defense of archetypes, namely that they are mechanisms comparable to Tinbergen's Innate Release Mechanisms, or IRMs (Samuels, 36). Tinbergen came up with the concept of the IRM partially in response to the problem which motivated Jung in "Instinct and the Unconscious," that of the yucca moth. IRMs are meant to motivate the animal by triggering a pattern innate in the animal's brain, thus producing behavior. Jung himself supported such a line of reasoning, both in "Instinct and the Unconscious" and elsewhere:

> Inherited possibilities of ideas, "paths" . . . have been gradually developed through the cumulative experience of the ancestors. To deny the inheritance of these paths would be equivalent to denying the inheritance of the brain. To be logical such skeptics would have to maintain that the child is born with an ape's brain. ("On Psychical Energy," 60)

As this whole line of reasoning makes clear, archetypes more than any of Jung's other concepts bring up the specter of teleology—from a purely causal perspective, there seems to be no way the yucca moth could have learned to feed and lay eggs in that particular tree on that particular day. There must be an end toward which the moth is working. We will deal sufficiently with the general concept of teleology in chapter six, but we can simply deal with the specific instance now.*

Through a series of experiments, neurophysiologically based psychology has been able to come up with explanations for many perceptual phenomena which hearken back only to the brain. Theories as to how and why we perceive color, movement, and other visual effects are constantly advanced, refined, and falsified (cf. Goldstein). Working with these and other data, cognitive psychology has been able to advance tentative models to describe how and why we think and remember (cf. Glass and Holyoak). The perceptual data have to a large extent been localized in the brain. For example, we now know enough to say that the visual cortex of the normally developed brain can be found in the occipital lobes (Goldstein, 45). In fact, neurological inquiry can explain several phenomena that psychoanalytic theories cannot, such as phantom limbs. Results such as these have played a large part in the experimental psychologists' decision that a theory of memory becomes unsatisfactory "because of not having a behavioristic foundation, of not being an outgrowth of that simpleminded S-R formulation that . . . is the starting point, the germ from which the theory of learning springs" (Hebb: 1967, 119). As far as the cognitive models go, they have not been so successful in localizing memory and other, higher cognitive functions. However, steps are being made in this effort, and some success has come out of them. For example, using results derived from studies on patients with posterior aphasia, a difficulty in comprehending language, it is now believed that representation of speech categories is localized in the left temporal cortex and parietal cortex (Glass and Holyoak, 480). Hebb, with his cell assembly hypothesis, provides a tentative link between perceptual data and cognitive structures—two people may well be looking

---

*Having said that, we must add that there is no way we can here deal with teleology sufficiently to be able definitively to assert that it does not exist. The best we can do is to say that, in order for a subject to be empirically testable, it must select only those items within its domain. Ends and goals are not in the domain of empirically testable facts, so they cannot be empirically tested, and since Jung claimed to be an empiricist ("Psychology and Religion," 11:2), he should limit himself to this sort of criterion. He has not done so, and we can challenge him on this, but as soon as we do so we step onto shaky ground. When confronting teleology, which we cannot empirically falsify (in spite of the good reasons we have for believing that only highly evolved brains can picture or conceive goals, we cannot hook ourselves up to the brain of a flatworm or a sponge and ascertain this for certain); we have either to concede the existence of something we cannot understand or to find a way around it. In this respect, experimental psychology has shown us a route for the latter option.

at the same thing, but they will perceive it differently. This difference is a function of past experience, of each observer's having a different set of cell assemblies recording a different set of memories. Such an explanation is reminiscent of both Skinner's work on superstition, as well as the theory of religion we derived from it in the last chapter, and Sontag's distinction between the primary experience and the interpretation, which would necessarily be colored by past experience.

With the archetype, Jung allows himself to make a leap of Bergsonian intuition, which proposes to understand universals and transcend the limits of what can be objectively proven. In fact, Bergson says, to try to understand human psychology as the repetition of a single type of state is a logical fallacy. "There are no two identical moments in the life of the same conscious being. . . . A consciousness which could experience two identical moments would be a consciousness without memory" (Bergson, 1912, 12). By this reasoning, no two perceptions of the color blue are the same, because the second is influenced by the first. The concept of the archetype preserves this fluidity by allowing one archetype to take on various symbols in different contexts. On the other hand, insistence on concrete, replicable data demands that not only must the one subject be able to produce identical moments, but that other subjects must be able to do so as well. Jungian psychology can make Bergson's "intuitive leap," positing itself inside the subject as the archetype and acquiring absolute knowledge. Experimental psychology, because it will not attempt to be perfect and infinite but rather falsifiable and finite, can only attain relative knowledge. For that reason, Bergson would say, only Jungian psychology can truly understand the self. "A truly intuitive philosophy would realise the much-desired union of science and metaphysics" (ibid., 74); through the archetypes, Jung tries to make exactly that union.

However, Jung cannot accept Bergson's intuitive leap. The fact that Jung induces from particulars to universals runs directly contrary to Bergson's conception of the intuitive leap. When discussing the principles which govern eternal movement, the Heraclitean way in which he perceives all things, Bergson gives a list of points. One of these is worth repeating here:

VIII. Intuition, once attained, must find a mode of expression and of application which conforms to the habits of our thought, and one which furnishes us, in the shape of well-defined concepts, with the solid points of support which we so greatly need . . . exactitude and precision, and also the condition of the unlimited extension of *a general method to particular cases.* (Bergson 1912, 73, emphasis added)

However, one very telling critique of the archetypes gives four criteria for something to be deemed an archetype. For something to be considered an archetype:

1. it must be specific but occur in different people
2. it must appear in different cultures at different times
3. it must have a similar meaning whenever and wherever it appears
4. it must not show any possibility of being acquired

(summarized in Samuels, 33)

These four criteria are nearly impossible to fulfill in any specific sense. Jung attempts to overwhelm us with examples, in the hope that we will then make the inductive assumption that a great number of cases supporting his point means that his point is universally true. However, counter-examples can always be found. The post-Jungians have realized the difficulty in trying to discover irrefutable specific archetypes, and therefore have advocated abandoning discrete archetypes for an omnipresent numinous body, from which energy is used by the archetypes (Samuels, 53). But at this point, the archetype cannot provide the "solid points of support" that Bergson demands.

We are left with a discrepancy—either accept the specific archetypes and attempt to work around the critique summarized above, or abandon the specific archetypes and, with them, the support for Jungian theory provided by Bergson's intuitive leap. Fortunately, we are spared any choice in this matter. Right to the end of his life, Jung continued to see archetypes as specific symbol-related structures rather than the vague sort of numinous body postulated by the post-Jungian modifications. For that reason, we will look only at Jung's approach to the problem and leave the post-Jungians behind—with one aside: if we limit experience of the archetypes to those who have had a numinous experience, analytic psychology becomes indistinguishable from religion.

Throughout his life, Jung saw the archetypes everywhere he looked. Art, literature, mythology, even human behavior all gave him fodder for this sacred cow. However, he was always very adamant that no literal one-to-one relationships could ever be established between a symbol and an archetype. Even in "Instinct and the Unconscious," when he seems to be saying that animals have visual archetypes that cause their behavior (*CW* 8:277), he does not say that they must manifest themselves in one particular way. He would eventually refine this concept to say that archetypes have no exactly determinable form, but are indefinite structures that assume forms according to personal experience. In a rare concession to materialism, Jung posits that the inherited brain structures in an infant meet incoming sensory information with specific responses, which are instinctual and therefore archetypal ("Concerning the Archetypes," *CW* 9[i]:136), and that they are possibly localized in the brain stem ("Schizophrenia," *CW* 3:582). This deftly sidesteps the great thrust of the critique detailed in Samuels by positing that the archetypal brain structure is the same and becomes expressed in different ways. At the same time, Jung does not make the same conceptual leap as his followers; his idea does ascribe specific meanings to specific images, but it does not stipulate that these images must be the same from individual to individual.

To accurately respond to that, we should look at the development of an image through history and see whether Jung's theory helps us understand this change in meaning any more than it would be understood if we did not consider Jung. In the last chapter, we discussed several aspects of Greek mythology and how Jung's theories did not stack up against them in the religious context. Here, in dealing with the archetypes, we have perhaps relaxed our standards a bit, but we shall nonetheless find again that Jung's ideas will not bear the comparison with Greek culture. We will investigate the Greek *ketos,* or sea monster. Through time, this creature developed from its traditional role as transporting beast of the Nereids to encompass such ideas as the fish that swallowed Jonah and the Jaws of Hell (Boardman, 74 and 83). While the ketos looks like the Babylonian sea monster, Tiamat, it did not originally, its appearance changing over time (ibid., 78); on the other hand, the Indian *makara* adopted the form of the ketos after the time of Alexander the Great (ibid., 83). Certainly, we have to ascertain that every possible source agrees with us when we attribute identity to any creature or being in any Babylonian picture (cf. Lambert, Hansen), because Babylonian artists did not subject their figures to the same sort of iconographic stereotyping as did, for example, the Egyptians. Nonetheless, while we cannot say with certainty that a specific monster represents Tiamat, we can comfortably assert that it does represent a sea monster. For our purposes, that is enough. If "wherever we meet with uniform and regularly recurring forms of apprehension we are dealing with an archetype, no matter whether its mythological character is recognised or not" ("Instinct and the Unconscious," 8:280, emphasis removed), then we can expect archetypes to show the traditional elements ascribed to them by myths.

In that light, we can expect that the figure of the sea monster will always look the same, while allowing for influences from other nearby cultures (e.g., the Babylonians on the Greeks, or the Greeks on the Indians), and that the sea monster will always have more or less the same meaning. We will allow the role of the image to vary (its embodying the Jaws of Hell to a Christian and a horrible, devouring monster to a Hindu is a variation), but for the idea to take on a whole new meaning steps beyond the boundaries Jung has delineated for the archetype.

Even with the relaxed criteria he espoused in "Concerning the Archetypes" (CW 9[i]) Jung would have to agree with us here. While he was willing to allow that for some people, because they did not grow up in a Western society, Christ would not be an adequate symbol of the self, he would not allow the figure of Christ to take on the meaning of some other archetype such as the trickster. If the end of every trickster myth hints at a savior ("Psychology of the Trickster-Figure," CW 9[i]:487), and Christ symbolizes this savior-figure, we cannot allow him to symbolize the trickster as well; by the same token, Coyote could never be a savior.

For that reason, it is significant to note an ancient artistic form taking on an entirely new meaning. This happened to the ketos to a certain extent when it became the fish that swallowed Jonah. However, we need not examine such specific sources for examples of this phenomenon; the entire period of rococo art will serve us well here. As time passed, the frightening satyrs and centaurs of the Greeks became the playful sprites of the rococo period. Coincidentally, these forms were "tamed" just at the time when people first became able to manipulate nature to suit their own needs, and at the same time as a general renaissance of all things Greek. When assimilating the old Greek forms, the Europeans did not feel the same fear and awe of the forces that the forms represented because of their newly discovered control over the natural world. For this reason they depicted the forms as playful rather than the fearful. The world of rococo was the world of the Enlightenment, which everyone knew was the best of all possible worlds. And in the best of all possible worlds, nature is nothing to be afraid of; rococo art reflected this sentiment (cf. von Blanckenhagen for an exposition of this idea).

In the above explanation, we did not need to invoke the archetypes.

Certainly, Jung could do so, saying that just as nature became manipulable and friendly, so too did its archetypal forms, and this was reflected in art. However, that statement does not explain anything more than ours, and in fact carries quite a lot of excess baggage. The transformation of the ketos and the rest of the Greek natural monsters did not happen overnight; it progressed through time. In that light, Jung would have to postulate a similar progression for the archetypal structure that bore them. That is, in order to use the archetypes to explain this change in the meaning of the monsters, Jung would have to allow for the structure of an archetype to change over time. However, this would cause him irreducible problems: it would effectively bar him from any discussion of past archetypal forms. Accepting change in the archetypes would leave him powerless to argue against the view that, if particular archetypal forms such as those of the Greek monsters could change, so too could the others, and therefore all of the "archaic psychic structures" to which he repeatedly hearkens need not actually exist. If a scant 2000 years is enough for an archetype to fundamentally change its meaning, and Indian records predate the Greek by at least another 1000 years, he could not logically support making any positive claims about them.*

This should go to show that, if Jung was to call the structure of the archetypes mutable over time, he would not be able to say anything about either the archetypes of past cultures or those of present cultures alien to his own. We last encountered this problem in our consideration of relativism, and we can now see why unequivocal acceptance of relativism would cause Jung such problems. A wholly relativist view does not allow for global developmental assertions (Sperber, 158). If cultures are totally relative, we cannot ever definitely know anything about a culture to which we do not belong. It would seem that Jung knew this, and for that reason he never adopted a totally relativist stance. As far as our consideration of the ketos is concerned, Jung's approach is still acceptable. However, when we consider the transition of such creatures as the satyr, Jung's position becomes far more tenuous. When nature as an external object is subdued by the advent of science and

---

*It is probably also worth asking why, if the archetypes are archaic structures ingrained in the psyche, none of them pertains to any event in the millions of years of human evolution. That is, the archetypal hero shoots a bow or wields a sword, but never a hand axe or other stone tool. Even arguing that such realism is out of place for an archetype, which deals with mythical content, would not dispel this contention. Archetypes represent collective experience; what experience is more collective than having evolved?

technology, Jung would have to posit that nature as an internal object should become even more wild and unruly. If the unconscious compensates for conscious attitudes, and the conscious attitude espouses the belief that nature is coming under human domination, then the unconscious would have to create horrifying natural forms, to restore the imbalance. However, rococo art shows the exact opposite process.

Certainly, that last discovery has important ramifications for archetypal theory. However, the theory comes under even more fire when we consider another point that becomes raised in the context of the ketos, namely that the archaic psychic structures need not even exist. "Instinct and the Unconscious" showed us that, from the very beginning of the idea, Jung saw archetypes as being mythological in form and content. In the last chapter, when we considered Veyne's ideas about Greek myths, we saw another way of looking at them. Both Jung and Veyne share one particular point of view; both consider that the Greeks and others saw their myths and legends as exactly that— mythical and legendary—and therefore not based on actual fact. Even this way of looking at legends is not universal among the "research" community. For example, more than one person has taken the legends of Atlantis to refer to an actual continent that vanished into the sea several thousand years ago. "Pyramidology," a "science" based on measuring the dimensions of the Great Pyramid and finding other global measurements to which they correlate, has recently enjoyed a great explosion and has been detailed in a plethora of books. Certainly, any "science" that incorporates the visions and statements of Edgar Cayce into its proofs is more than a bit suspect. Nonetheless, pyramidological books are helpful in one very important way. For example, Herodotus reported that from the time of the first king of Egypt to about 700 B.C., 11,340 years elapsed; a similar time period is also detailed in other ancient sources (Fix, 108). This is taken by some pyramidological writers to mean that Herodotus and these other writers had access to or knew of even more ancient sources, showing that this period of over 10,000 years was not legendary but actually a fact. From this, they assume that the ancient writers' statements about Atlantis and other such "legends" actually refer to factual events.

Needless to day, we will not get involved in this debate. For our purposes, it is enough to note that the idea has been proposed whereby the ancient writers were not recording myths but actual facts. That is, the writers were not recording "Vanishing Hitchhiker"-type legends but were rather transcribing older factual historical sources. In Jungian terms, the legends of Atlantis would be archetypal, and Atlantis itself would probably refer to the unconscious contents, which were once above the archetypal water (i.e., conscious) and are now submerged in the unconscious waiting to rise again at the appropriate time. Fix, on the other hand, would argue vehemently with Jung's interpretation, protesting that the legends were actually historical, dealing with an actual civilization and actual events. Thankfully, we need not be concerned with whether or not Fix's hypothesis is correct. The fact that it has been proposed shows that alternative explanations to Jung's can be presented without need of the archetypes. Fix would say that for Jung to believe Atlantis sank into the waters of the unconscious is ludicrous; without agreeing with Fix's general theories about Atlantis, we can agree with his assessment of Jung.

This reference to the water being a symbol of the unconscious brings us back directly to the archetypes, and Jung's conception of them. As we have seen, the post-Jungian conception of the general archetypal pool was a break from orthodox Jungian theory. Although Jung repeatedly made the point that he did not believe in a literal "X=Y" equation for his symbols, he very often called an image "a symbol" for an unconscious content, and he does seem to have accepted a sort of "X,Y,Z=A,B,C, etc." relationship. For example, in one work Jung delivers an exposition on the symbol of the horse and relates it to the unconscious, the devil, sexuality, light, fire, wind, and many other ideas ("The Battle for Deliverance from the Mother"). In the same book, we find Jung calling mythical images such as the wood-demon and soothsayer symbols of the mother ("The Dual Mother Role," 213).

This does not contradict what we said above when discussing the ketos. Everything Jung describes in *Unconscious* lends credence to the idea that, while the idea of the horse as a symbol is universal, the horse as symbol for a specific something is not—it takes on different meanings in different contexts. That is, when a horse is depicted in two different ways, such as the horses ridden by the Four Horsemen of the Apocalypse and the Trojan Horse, the one image refers to two different things. The Trojan Horse is categorically different from horses in general, in that it has a specific meaning and specific connotations. Jung himself makes this distinction, clearly referring to the Trojan Horse as a symbol of the mother ("The Battle For Deliverance from the Mother," 174) while refusing to be so specific about the horse in general. Each different interpretation Jung provides for the horse symbol comes from a different source; throughout each source, the symbolic meaning is internally consistent. As for the confluence of many images around one archetype, Jung explains this by saying that symbols "do not afford the same satisfaction of desire . . . as reality, so that the unsatisfied remnant of the libido must seek still further symbolic outlets" ("The Dual Mother Role," 220). This is really just a high-blown way of getting across one of the major concepts of twentieth-century philosophy, that language is inadequate for expressing the totality of any idea. While a metaphor is internally consistent, it is not always consistent with other metaphors of similar structure. For example, it has been proposed that two metaphors pervading Western culture are that *unknown is up* and *finished is up* in the statements "That's up in the air," and "I'm finishing up" (Lakoff and Johnson, 21). The two concepts are internally consistent but do not relate to each other in exactly the same way—the experiential basis of *unknown is up* is very different from that of *finished is up* (ibid., 21). Jung reflects this idea with his physical concession; in Jungian terms, the archetype would be "up," and experience would constellate the ideas of "unknown" and "finished" around it. Since the archetype has no exactly determinable form, but is an indefinite structure that assumes forms, it can assume any form that experience demands ("Concerning the Archetypes," *CW* 9[i]:136). Just as "up" can take the implication of "finished" and "unknown," depending on the connotation of the sentence, so too can "horse" take on "fire" or "mother" depending on the mythical setting in which it is found.

Again, we can see how the concept of the archetype becomes an extra layer that Occam's razor easily slices away. The idea we proposed in the first chapter will find refinement here, in that we should not say that no literary or artistic image is ever symbolic, but that if the artist did not mean for the image to be a symbol, then any interpretation that assumes a symbolic meaning for the image is adding something to the art object. That is, if Melville had actually meant for the whale in *Moby Dick* to be a symbol of God, and he was on record as having said this, then we could read the story in that light. He did not, and although we can still read the story in that light, we must admit that our reading of the story is different from Melville's conception of it. If we do not, and if we continue in the same vein, relating *Moby Dick* to other stories such as Biblical narrative, then we compound the error. It is bad enough that Jung makes what may be the first error, reading the horse as a symbol, but for him to then relate one particular instance of the horse forces him into the second error. Looking at the horse as simply metaphorical and looking at it to say of what it is a metaphor both seem to have the same implication; however, the difference is epistemological. We are willing to grant that perhaps the Trojan Horse is a symbol of something—perhaps it is not, and we must leave that possibility open as well—but in any case we should not go so far as to say of what it is a symbol. Jung makes that second step, and must posit the archetype to do so. In seeing literary images as simply metaphorical, we can account for the confluence of different images around a single idea in a way categorically different from Jung by allowing them to be experientially formed.

In his *Fear and Trembling,* Kierkegaard relates the story of "Agnes and the Merman" to his reflections upon the story of the sacrifice of Isaac (Gen. 22.1–19).

> The merman is a seducer who shoots up from his hiding-place in the abyss, with wild lust grasps and breaks the innocent flower which stood in all its grace on the seashore and pensively inclined its head to listen to the howling of the ocean. (Kierkegaard: 1848, 144)

This myth has very little to do with the Genesis story, and Kierkegaard admits as much, proposing three alterations to it. First of all, he creates a scenario whereby the innocent Agnes (the flower) voluntarily submits to the merman, but instead of dragging her down to the depths he finds he cannot, so he lets her go, telling her he only wanted to show her the beauty of the sea (ibid., 145ff). This makes the myth into a personal allegory and reifies it in terms more appropriate to the context in which Kierkegaard wants to develop it. However, this one revision does not capture the full extent of the breadth of feeling that Kierkegaard wants to convey, so he creates another reinterpretation. This time, the merman does not want to seduce Agnes, but the sight of her beauty inspires him to overcome his fear of women and lures him out from the placid lake wherein he lived. She loves him, but only because she sees in him the raging ocean, which is not there—he is humble, not proud. But she awakens his pride with her implicit Beauty-and-the-Beast promise of deliverance from his present state. She cannot deliver him, and he tires of her, returning to the water from which he had emerged (ibid., 146n). Again, this revision presents an angle of Kierkegaard's response to the original myth implicit in neither the original story nor its first revision at his hands, that each party expects from the other something it cannot deliver. At this point, Kierkegaard posits and dismisses as the "customary coquetry" of aesthetics a third reinterpretation of the myth, where Agnes saves the merman and lives happily ever after (ibid., 150n).

Kierkegaard himself draws an analogy between his versions of this story and the Abraham story, but does not expand much upon it—he equates the merman and Abraham only in the most circumstantial ways, such as calling both "individuals." Lowrie, in a note to this section, equates Regina, the woman Kierkegaard loved but had to leave, with both Agnes and Isaac. We are not in a position to debate the merits of this assumption—Lowrie not only had access to Kierkegaard's journals but had translated them—but whether or not it is true is irrelevant. In either case, it would provide us with yet another example of how one metaphoric example is never enough; if it were, it would not then be metaphor but equivalence. Lowrie posits the whole of *Fear and Trembling* as an allegory for Kierkegaard's feelings about Regina. However, the Abraham story does not capture the true breadth of emotion that Kierkegaard felt for Regina, so he may have been forced to draw in a second story, to elucidate those details he felt unexplored by the first. "Agnes and the Merman" fills this role in Lowrie's hypothesis, just as the several retellings of the story do in ours. Also worth noting is the fact that not only does Kierkegaard present several reinterpretations of the story to elucidate his point, but he also retells the story in a way that does not suit his needs (the third revision), then promptly tells us of this and discards it. The idea of Agnes and the merman living happily ever after does not strike Kierkegaard as being possible, so he posits it in order to strike it down.

We would do well to remember that, throughout the passage (Kierkegaard 1848, 144–57), Kierkegaard never makes any literal relations between any characters from the Agnes story and the Abraham story. Although he does hint at a connection between Abraham and the merman, the different alterations show that he did not conceive of the two as literal equivalents. It makes more sense to say that Kierkegaard meant the Agnes story to amplify a certain aspect of the Abraham story, rather than to retell it allegorically. If our hypothesis about Lowrie's interpretation is correct, then both Abraham and the merman are meant to elucidate certain characteristics of Kierkegaard himself rather than to symbolize him; if Lowrie's interpretation is incorrect, this does not damage our ideas about the relation between the Agnes and Abraham stories. In any case, this example shows us that the confluence of symbols around one central idea is more likely to be an attempt to reflect different aspects of a central concept than to find "further symbolic outlets [for] the unsatisfied remnant of the libido" ("The Dual Mother Role," 220).

If "a metaphor in a variety of ways places into juxtaposition two terms that are, or can be, thought of as both similar and dissimilar" (Sapir, 6), then to adequately elucidate one item in terms of another, we must in fact have several others, so that the different similarities between the object for comparison (the *continuous term*) and the comparative objects (the *discontinuous term*) complement each other. For example, if we say of a man named George that he is a lobster, we are saying something categorically different than that he is a banker, but neither term is contradictory (Fernandez, 11). To call George a banker, while describing his profession, also brings to mind certain cultural stereotypes surrounding the concept of "banker." To call George a lobster does not imply that he is an arthropod, but it does call to mind a similar body of associations around the idea "lobster," such as that he is snappish, soft-centered, and rigidly defensive (ibid., 12).

This is all well and good, but how does it relate to the archetype? The relationship should be clear; the discontinuous terms (symbols) surrounding the continuous term (central idea which Jung calls "archetype") all elucidate different aspects of it in the same way as a metaphor. The indefinite structure that Jung posits ("Concerning the Archetypes," *CW* 9[i]:142) need not be an archetype. Rather, it could simply be memory, which although slightly more nebulous than vision has nonetheless been localized to a certain extent. This also reduces the archetype to a neural process. For that reason alone, Jung would not want to consider this a valid counterpoint to his archetypes, which he was willing to localize but not to reduce ("Schizophrenia," *CW* 3:582). However, we have seen our idea explain just as much as the concept of the archetypes without carrying their excess baggage. For example, seeing archetypes as memory structures does circumvent the problem of the specific archetypes in a way preferable to that of the post-Jungians. In addition, this removes the problem of whether or not early learning plays a role in formation of archetypes by answering firmly in the positive. Such a role for early learning receives strong support in the writings of Jean Piaget, whose theories reinterpreted in Jungian metaphors say that archetypes are not inherited ideas but inherited potentials for ideas. As his career progressed, Jung began to lean in this direction. However, once he is willing to make this step, it would seem much simpler for Jung to place the structure that bears the ideas firmly in the brain, the existence of which can be empirically verified, rather than in the mind, whose existence cannot be. Jung clings to the collective unconscious and the psyche; it took Hebb's idea of the cell assembly to ground such developmental structures firmly in neurological material.

Unfortunately for Jung, this knocks out much of his theory. One major aspect of Jung's concept of the archetypes, as we saw when we considered the sun-phallus case, comes from the fact that he sees in them forms and ideas that the subject had never before encountered. This is precisely the reason he will not situate the archetypes in the personal unconscious: because their contents are more than personal. If psychology is dependent on neural structure, he asks, then how can the collective material exist ("Constitution and Heredity," *CW* 8:227)? Because of this, we must now look into the entire concept of the collective unconscious and whether it can be definitively proven to exist. Certainly, our treatment of the sun-phallus case did do some damage to the idea that the particular patient whose hallucination we investigated was actually describing a collective belief. Nonetheless, we did not hammer the final nail into its coffin. We must do that now.

> The longer one studies life and literature, the more strongly one feels that behind everything that is wonderful stands the individual, and that it is not the moment that makes the man, but the man who creates the age. Indeed, I am inclined to think that each myth and legend that seems to us to spring out of the wonder, or terror, or fancy of tribe and nation, was in its origin the invention of one single mind. (Wilde, 71)

In a way, Jung has helped us here, by introducing the idea of the racial unconscious into his later works. Certainly, he does report analyzing the dreams of African-Americans from the Southern States and finding themes from Greek myths. "This dispelled any doubt [he] had that it might be a question of racial inheritance" ("Constitution and Heredity," *CW* 8:228). He did in fact make it quite clear that he believed archetypes to be determined by ethnic and geographical differences, dedicating a special essay to "The Complications of American Psychology." Perhaps the original title of the essay, "Your Negroid and Indian Behavior," better explains Jung's views on this topic. For example, he posits that the unconscious of Americans contains a Heroic Ideal, because of psychic influence from the aboriginal inhabitants ("Complications," *CW* 10:976). In fact, he saw Americans as influenced by the habits and psyches of other races to the point where he posited "an x and y in the air and in the soil of a country, which slowly permeate and assimilate him [i.e., "man"] to the type of the aboriginal inhabitant, even to the point of slightly remodeling his physical features" (ibid., *CW* 10:968). The "inferior side" of the American personality is the African, but the unconscious symbols are all aboriginal ("Mind and Earth," *CW* 10:99). In Jung's eyes, this made American behavior a combination of European and African behavior, with an Indian soul (ibid., *CW* 10:103).

In a moment, we will deal directly with whether or not we can consider Jung to incorporate his own prejudices into his views (though these passages should give some clue); for now, they serve our purposes by showing that he posited special elements in the American psyche with which he did not credit their European ancestors. For example, he believed American athletes trained so hard because of the psychical influence of Indian rites of initiation (ibid., *CW* 10:100). Leaving aside the great East German and Soviet sports dynasties that rose during Jung's lifetime, we should look at the basis for Jung's statements about the physical and psychical makeup of Americans. In "The Complications of American Society," he tells the story of visiting a factory in Buffalo, New York, where he saw a group of workers leaving the factory and was struck immediately by what he saw as their aboriginal facial characteristics ("Complications," *CW* 10:948). This reminded him of some writings by Franz Boas, which he combined with these observations to produce his theories about American psychology. That is, he based his theories on a subjective feeling of conviction, which we have repeatedly said is no criterion for proof.

However, this belief that different bone structures belie different ways of looking at the world has parallels in other literature of Jung's time—that of Alfred Rosenberg, a chief ideologue of the National Socialist movement, for example. The debate over whether or not Jung was anti-Semitic is long and somewhat tired by this point, with one side citing the fact that his books were burned in France after the Nazi invasion (reported in the "Epilogue to Essays on Contemporary Events," *CW* 10:464), and the other that in "The Role of the Unconscious" he makes some statements that could be considered anti-Semitic ("The Role of the Unconscious," *CW* 10.18–20). However, this debate is wrongly centered. Jung should not be considered an anti-Semite, but rather a Nordic supremacist. Certainly, some support for this view could be derived from his exhortation of the "blond beast" and its readiness to "burst out" of its "underground prison" ("Role of the Unconscious," *CW* 10.17), and its similarity to Rosenberg's views:

> That old, despised hypothesis which stated that once, from a Northern
> creative point . . . swarms of warriors spread out . . . might explain
> the continuously recurring Nordic longing to conquer distant lands:
> this hypothesis seems probable today. (Rosenberg, 39)

Granted, similarity of ideas means nothing more than that the two
men were exposed to the same ideological fathers, such as Fichte and
Hegel. However, this seems less of a coincidence when we consider Jung's
views of Rosenberg's primary influence, Houston Stewart Chamberlain's
Foundations of the Nineteenth Century.

Jung mentions Chamberlain three times in the entire *Collected
Works,* once in reference to Chamberlain's study of Goethe, once as
to his general theory, and once in the matter of his *Foundations.* The
last two of these three are most relevant to this portion of our inquiry,
and are both worth listing below:

> Asceticism occurs whenever the animal instincts are so strong that
> they need to be violently exterminated. Chamberlain (*Foundations of
> the Nineteenth Century*) saw asceticism as a biological suicide caused
> by the enormous amount of racial interbreeding among the Medi-
> terannean peoples at that time. I believe that miscegenation makes
> rather for a coarsened joie de vivre. ("The Song of the Moth," 5.119n)*

> Houston Stewart Chamberlain is a symptom which arouses suspicion
> that other veiled gods may be sleeping elsewhere. The emphasis on
> the Germanic race (vulgarly called "Aryan") . . . Jesus as a blond and
> blue-eyed hero . . . the devil as an international Alberich in Jewish
> or Masonic guise, the Nordic aurora borealis as the light of civilisation,
> the inferior Mediterranean races—all this is the indispensable scenery
> for the drama that is taking place and at bottom they all mean the
> same thing: a god has taken possession of the Germans and their
> house is filled with a 'mighty rushing wind.' " ("Wotan," *CW* 10.389)

The opposite of "a coarsened joie de vivre" would be a refined one,
and if we take such a statement at face value, it sounds like Jung is
advocating a view that mixed marriages lead to degeneration of culture.
This mirrors Rosenberg's belief that, in order to understand art, one
must understand the "*volkish* will" of the people who created it

---

*This note was not present in the original edition of *Unconscious,* but was added
for the *CW* version.

(Rosenberg, 126). The idea that Christ was Aryan, which Jung attributes to Chamberlain, is mirrored in Rosenberg as well (ibid., 70n, 115). This parallel does not mean that Jung was anti-Semitic. However, it is curious to see that in such a long passage dealing with Chamberlain's *Foundations,* Jung never takes advantage of the privileged position his theories give him to offer the Germans a route out of their "possession." Rather than contradict Chamberlain's belief that asceticism was "biological suicide," Jung chooses to make light of it. It is not enough for him to go back later and claim that he saw a tide rising in the German unconscious, as he did in "The Fight with the Shadow" (*CW* 10:449). He blames Nazism on "the existence of an abnormal state of mind" (ibid., 476) but never asks what could have caused this. More importantly, he never considers the possibility that his own ideas might have been touched by it as well. The parallels between his writings and Rosenberg's, as well as his soft treatment of Chamberlain, both point to the very strong possibility that his own beliefs were, although less extreme, quite similar.

We see in Jung's statements about American psychology a definite tendency to group unconscious contents by race or geography; for example, the heroic ideal that he posits in the American unconscious ("Complications," *CW* 10:976). His basis for positing "the Heroic Ideal" probably comes in part from his "discoveries" about Miss Miller in *Unconscious.* However, he took these items, which he found in Miss Miller's psyche, and extended them to universal statements about the collective unconscious. Although this position is logically inconsistent for several reasons, such as its inductive leap on the basis of content that Jung himself called limited, these reasons cannot totally destroy the concept of the collective unconscious in the manner that we require. We could take a Humean approach, discarding the collective unconscious strictly on the grounds that we cannot enumerate its every instance and therefore cannot assert its universalism. Unfortunately, Jung has not subjected himself to those criteria. And while we can make judgments about different ideologies on the points where they are incommensurable (C. Taylor, 104), Jung has deliberately opted out of the scientific framework. However, in the third chapter we showed that the collective unconscious is unnecessary even in the instances from which Jung derived its existence. That is, when we looked at those cases that Jung saw as proving the collective unconscious, we were able to explain them by means that did not require such universal statements as does the collective unconscious.

However, if we explain every instance of the archetypes by hearkening back to subjective experience, they are no longer archetypes in the Jungian sense. Jungian analysis centers around examination and interpretation of the archetypes precisely because Jung saw the archetypes as universal and therefore suitable for interpersonal discussion. If a married man talks to an unmarried man about fighting with his wife, the unmarried man may well say, "I know what you mean." But does he? Certainly, he can postulate himself in a married state, postulate that he has had a fight with his wife, and imagine how he would feel in these circumstances through analogy with other fights he has had with other people in the past, but he cannot actually know how the other man feels. The experience is qualitatively different. To Jung, the fight with the wife is the archetype, which is latent in everyone. In this analogy, the married man translates to the man who has experienced the archetype, and the unmarried man becomes the man who has not. To Jung, the unmarried man can actually experience the same feeling as the married man, because the potential is within both of them. The relationship is one not of analogy, but of equivalence.

Jung preserved the archetypes because he felt them to exist and saw them borne out by experience. Given the same evidence, we have not seen the archetypes, but perhaps that is because we are not looking for them. This does not say anything about whether the archetypes exist, but it does say a lot about how, if people look hard enough, they can find anything in anything. Jung took his ideas into experiential phenomena such as Miss Miller's dreams, found support for those ideas, and thus considered them proven. We did not have the same ideas, so we did not find them. When presented with the sun-phallus case, we were not convinced by the evidence cited by Jung in its favor, because we were not convinced of the assumptions that his argument took as implicit. For this reason, when we looked at the specific archetypes and found them wanting by Jung's own standards, we were able to postulate the physical substrate that Jung could not allow. Having discarded materialism in his method, Jung could not allow it to be derived in his conclusions. He was therefore forced to abandon scientificity in his theories, thus removing the problems it had caused him. However, we were able to discard science as well and still find Jung's theories to be inconsistent on purely logical grounds. Now, the only recourse he has left is to appeal to the subjective feeling of truth he entertains in regard to his theories.

In appealing to the subjective to prove the archetypes, Jung must see them in himself; to make the inductive leap from individual to general, non-Bergsonian as it may be, Jung must first be able to conclusively prove the individual. In this example, Jung will be the married man, and we the unmarried, and we will look to see if we can also feel his pain, or at least make an analogy with it. Jung's individual experience of the archetypes would be enough for both him and us at least to assume that he believed they applied in his case, whether or not they applied to anyone else. For that reason, we should look into those archetypes that Jung saw as applying directly to the self and determine exactly what they are. From there, we can look at the experience of others as well and see if the archetypes of the self find expression therein, or if they too are excess baggage. Do we need the concept of the archetype to explain personal experience? If not, we have struck a very serious blow to this, a cornerstone of Jungian theory.

4

The Archetypes of the Self

In spite of one claim to the contrary coming very late in Jung's life ("The Conjunction," *CW* 14:672), Jungian theory posits the archetypes of the self as discrete, individual personalities inhabiting the psyche. Certainly, they are not individual in that they behave similarly from person to person, but rather in that they have their own aims, interests, and behaviors, which are distinct from those of the ego. In fact, Jung saw the archetypes of the self as so distinct from the ego that he felt himself able to argue with them ("Confrontation with the Unconscious," 186). This admission on his own part leads us to the door through which we can enter into an investigation of the archetypes of the self. As we said at the end of the last chapter, if Jung found the archetypes of the self in himself, his methodology would lead him from there to induce that these archetypes must actually inhabit every psyche and to search through various sources until he found evidence for them. As such, we look at the archetypes of the self through Jung's own personal discovery of them and determine what exactly his experience actually entailed.

The most important information we have about Jung's life and thoughts is found in *MDR,* a work that has often been called his autobiography. However, we should refer to this work more as an "autoanalysis," because in it Jung does not simply describe the events of his life; he interprets them in light of his theories. In this respect, one of the most important chapters of the book for our purposes is the sixth: "Confrontation with the Unconscious," where Jung tells of the events immediately following his celebrated break with Freud. Characteristic of the book, he relates not the events of his life but the stirrings of his unconscious, his dreams and his fantasies, and, repeatedly, these dreams and fantasies have mythical contents. In them, we find the usual cornucopia of symbols such as scarabs and rainstorms, duly interpreted, but we also find people. Characters such as dwarves, young girls, old men, sages, whores, and many more appear in these dreams. Such characters came to populate Jung's conception of the self and to play a categorically different role in Jungian psychology than the normal archetypes. The archetypes we discussed in the last chapter are typical situations symbolizing a type of transformation as opposed to the archetypes of the self, which are personalities ("Archetypes of the Collective Unconscious," 89).

Before we discuss the characteristics of these archetypes, one point is worth noting. Earlier, we referred to *MDR* as an "auto-analysis." This was not a random decision, though perhaps a bit of a misnomer. Work on the book was not begun until Jung was over eighty years old and was not totally done by him. Jung worked in conjunction with one of his followers, Aniela Jaffé, who is credited on the cover as having "recorded and edited" the work. These points become important for two reasons. First of all, they shed some light on the nature of the descriptions, especially in "Confrontation with the Unconscious," which Jaffé herself admits to having compiled rather than recorded ("Introduction" to *MDR*, vii). Looking back on a dream of more than forty years before, with the benefit of interpretive hypotheses developed through those many years, Jung is able to make statements about their contents that he would not have made at the time. In fact, at the time of the dream he might have described them completely differently. Certainly, these dreams and visions led Jung to the formulation of his theories. However, he is recording the dream or the vision decades after it happened, with those theories having colored his thoughts for every day in between. It is not impossible that his efforts to recall the significance of a character such as "the small brown-skinned savage" were colored by his later works on similar archetypal "savages."

Moreover, we cannot forget Jaffé's role in the formation of this section of the book. Certainly, respect for her mentor may have limited the modifications she would have made to his actual content, but she does admit that "the further the book progressed, the closer became the fusion between his work and mine" ("Introduction" to *MDR*, vii). Since she did not indicate clearly which sections of "Confrontation with the Unconscious" were Jung's original content and which were her additions, we cannot blindly accept the entire passage as Jung's own words or even Jung's own thoughts. While she states that Jung approved the manuscript, she also admits having taken his comments upon it and incorporated them into the work, making it a process rather than a fiat. As such, the best we can say for "Confrontation with the Unconscious" is that it reflects Jung's final interpretation of the archetypes —with the help of one of his favorite pupils. This puts us into a position analogous with that of reporters and students of Jesus or Muhammad, who have no firsthand record of how their lives actually progressed. But we are better off than students of those two holy men, because our primary source was at least overseen by its subject while he was still alive. Because of that, while we cannot take the contents of "Confrontation with the Unconscious" as actual events recorded by Jung, we can see them as retranslated news reports, which, though not ideal, are satisfactory for our purposes.

It is worth keeping those limitations in mind as we look into the archetypes of the self. It is difficult to say whether the self is composed of four archetypes or of three. Certainly, Jung's conception of the self is based upon four units, but he never states definitively whether or not the ego is an archetype. Calling it the "complex factor to which all conscious contents are related" ("The Ego," *CW* 9[ii]:1) does nothing to help us decide, nor does the statement that the relationship of a psychic concept to the ego determines its consciousness (ibid.). That is, although the ego is the point of reference for the field of consciousness (ibid., 5) and is individual (ibid., 10), it is still a universal concept inasmuch as every person is said to have one, and archetypes are universal concepts.

In the absence of any definitive statement on Jung's part as to whether or not the ego is to be perceived as an archetype, we will tentatively assert that it is not. We do so on the basis of the order in which Jung purports the archetypes are discovered during analysis ("Conclusion" to *Aion, CW* 9[ii]:422). In this list, the discovery of the ego is not detailed, which makes sense. If the ego is that component of the personality that average people mistake for the self, each person must by necessity be aware of his ego's existence in order to misinterpret it so. As well, when discussing the arrangement of the self concepts that compose the archetype of the self, Jung calls the self a combination of two personal aspects and two collective aspects ("The Syzygy," *CW* 9[ii]:42). One of these personal concepts is the ego. On these grounds, we can propose that the ego is not meant to be archetypal. Granted, we fall guilty of the same offense of which we accuse Jung if we do not acknowledge that our statement is interpretive, and therefore fallible. In fact, Jung makes statements which can be interpreted as contrary to ours, such as talking of a fourth "missing" archetype when, by our definition of the ego, he has not posited three to begin with (ibid., 42). However, he also says that, although it does have "traces of personalities," there is nothing like the ego in the unconscious ("The Meaning of Individuation," 16). In short, the preponderance of the evidence points toward defining the ego as non-archetypal, and while we cannot make a definitive statement as to its status, we can make a probable one. Hopefully, we have done exactly that.

Having dealt with the ego and Jung's ambiguity as to its status, we can now get down to those components of the self that require psychoanalysis to be discovered. Following the order in which Jung claims they are discovered, we will first discuss the shadow. This statement that the shadow is the first content to be discovered through the psycho-analytic procedure seems somewhat tautological in light of Jung's belief that the shadow's contents can be largely inferred from the personal unconscious ("The Shadow," *CW* 9[ii]:13). In spite of its personal nature, Jung calls it an archetype. Later, he rescues himself somewhat by positing that the shadow is both a personal content and an archetype and that these two are distinct, discrete entities (ibid., 19), but this embroils him in another problem. When we discussed the ego, we cited Jung as attributing four dimensions to the archetype of the self—two personal, two collective. This was the problem with our definition of the ego as nonarchetypal; if the two collective aspects are the syzygy and the Wise Old Man/Chthonic Mother, which we will get to later, the personal contents must be either the shadow and the ego or two categorically different shadows. Not only does this cast doubt on our tentative assertions about the ego, it renders the shadow logically absurd. If the personal shadow and the archetypal shadow are different, but the shadow component of the self is personal and an archetype, then either the archetypal shadow is the same as the personal shadow or the archetypal shadow is a personal content and the personal shadow is archetypal, but these are two different concepts. Certainly, we have limited the extent to which logic can be used against Jung, but to let this slip by would give Jung too much of a concession. No other archetype is doubled. When Jung posits the trickster or the hero or any other psychic content, he settles for just one of each. On these grounds, we can demand that his logic be at least internally consistent and that there be only one shadow.

However, Jung could not allow there to be only one shadow. If forced to call the shadow either personal or collective, various elements of his theory would lose vital support. If the shadow is personal, then it is not archetypal. While Jungian theory allows for the contents of archetypes to be determined by personal experience, their actual structure must be collective. However, if the collective structure is categorically distinct from the personal content, then it describes a different thing. That is, if the collective structure of the shadow is a bowl the contents of which can be different from person to person, this bowl rendered into Jungian discourse is the archetype of the shadow. Either the contents as found in the collective "bowl" are duplicated in the personal unconscious, or the personal contents are the same actual contents as the collective ones.

At this point, we can reintroduce logical rules. If the personal contents are the same as those contents that populate the collective structure, it would make more sense to refer to the two sets of identical objects as one single set. Unfortunately for Jung, this would require definitively placing this single set in either the personal or the collective half of the unconscious. If the contents are personal, then their existence is contingent upon personal experience—if a person has never seen a walrus, then the concept of the walrus is absent from that person's past; and since Jung defines the unconscious as all past concepts ("The Transcendent Function," 8:132), the walrus will not be found in that person's unconscious. Making the shadow such a personal content would entail that, if a person has no experience with a personality trait, it does not exist in the personal unconscious and therefore it does not exist in the shadow.

Unfortunately for Jung, this means that the unconscious cannot compensate for the conscious attitude—people who are wholly altruistic by definition have no experience of greed, and although Jung's definition of the shadow would include greed, his definition of the unconscious makes that impossible. Jung gets around this by placing complementary emotions such as greed in the collective unconscious, making them elements of the archetypal shadow. This is no solution; it just makes personal experience into a mere epiphenomenon of collective contents and engulfs Jung in the problem of the two identical but different shadows. If everyone is greedy, then personal expression of avarice is irrelevant. Certainly, the personal expression of greed could serve as a guidepost to show its collective nature, and by this, Jung could maintain the distinction between the personal shadow and archetypal shadows. This would be consistent with other symbols, which are not equivalent to archetypes but represent them. However, besides the fact that Jung himself has differentiated the archetypes of the self from those of transformation ("Archetypes of the Collective Unconscious," 89), it is one thing to say that the tree is a symbol of growth and development ("The Philosophical Tree," *CW* 13:350), and another thing entirely to say that the personal expression of greed is a symbol of greed in the abstract.

Jung repeatedly refers to literary symbols to elaborate his points; we can steal a page from his workbook and do the same in the context of emotion to show how it is categorically different from a symbol. When Nietzsche says of the virtuous that "they were playing on the sea-shore—then came a wave and swept their playthings into the deep: now they cry," (Nietzsche, "Of the Virtuous," 1885), we do not take this statement at face value, but rather believe that he meant it to be a symbol. That is, the sea-shore, the wave, and the playthings can be considered allegorically, as symbols of other concepts; we need not be concerned with what other concepts they may symbolize to Nietzsche and to his readers. However, when Nietzsche says of the virtuous that "some want to be edified and raised up and call it virtue, and others want to be thrown down—and call it virtue too" (ibid.), we can interpret the raising up and the throwing down symbolically, but we do similarly interpret the wanting. While the particulars of wanting could well be interpreted as symbols, the emotion itself is taken at face value. In the same vein, while Jung could call greed for money and greed for possessions and lust merely psychological expressions of the same emotion—greed— he would not interpret the greed as a symbol for loathing. That is absurd.

We have gone to such lengths to show the difference between contents that Jung normally ascribes to the archetype and those contents that he puts in the shadow to show how categorically different is the shadow compared to other archetypes. In his own experience, as well as that of his patients and in his literary sources, Jung finds symbols of the shadow such as his "small, brown-skinned savage" ("Confrontation," 181). This is the archetypal shadow. The personal shadow, being those aspects repressed out of the conscious personality, must by necessity change from person to person. The shadow of greedy people will be altruistic, that of altruistic people, greedy. As such, the symbols of the archetype will differ from person to person. That is, the expression of the collective is dependent on personal experience. First of all, this should by rights prohibit Jung from making any categorical assertions about literary symbols of the shadow. For him to call a particular literary figure a symbol of the shadow, he would have to know the personal unconscious of the author. Without this knowledge, the best he could do would be to say that a particular character expresses a particular character trait, which may or may not be in the shadow, depending upon the personal unconscious of the reader. The 1988 film *The Thin Blue Line* depicts the case of Randall Adams, a hitchhiker who had been wrongly convicted of murdering a Dallas policeman in 1976 and placed on death row. Upon release of this film, the case was reopened, and Adams' conviction was overturned. Once out of prison, Adams turned around and sued Errol Morris, the director of *The Thin Blue Line,* because Morris did not give him royalties from the film's distribution. Colloquially, this is called "biting the hand that fed you." For someone who would do this, the character of Mercurius from Grimm's "The Spirit in the Bottle" would hardly symbolize the shadow. Upon being freed from his prison at the roots of the oak, Mercurius attempted to kill the boy who had freed him. It takes no great mental leap to construct an analogy whereby Mercurius could symbolize Adams and the boy could represent Morris. As such, from Adams' point of view, Mercurius would not be equivalent to the self as symbolized by the opposite of Christ (as is claimed in "The Spirit Mercurius," *CW* 13:295). That is, the Antichrist, whom Jung has called both the opposite of Christ and a symbol of the shadow ("Christ, a Symbol of the Self," *CW* 9[ii]:76), would embody those traits that Adams actually displays, making Mercurius in Adams' case a symbol of the self. As such, Jung's calling Mercurius a symbol of the shadow must have a limiting clause applied to it—that Mercurius is a symbol of the shadow as Jung perceives it. But if Jung starts to limit the application of his symbolic interpretations in this case, he has to allow for alternate interpretations in other cases as well. This would knock the foundation out of a great portion of his theories. Nonetheless, he must either allow for the alternative interpretations or embroil himself in an inconsistency that is not only logically indefensible but, as we have just shown, cannot be defended on empirical grounds either. Having chosen the latter, Jung leaves himself open to criticisms such as ours.

Having exhausted the archetype of the shadow, at least for our purposes, we will now turn our attention to the first of the two "collective aspects" of the self: the syzygy, which cannot be discovered until the shadow has been integrated ("The Syzygy," *CW* 9[ii]:42). One phenomenon of the shadow that we did not point out is that, in dreams and fantasies, its symbols are always the same sex as the subject, and that when the symbols begin to refer to the opposite sex, this is no longer the shadow ("The Shadow," *CW* 9[ii]:19). These symbols of the opposite sex are called either the anima, for a man, or the animus, for a woman. Jung uses the word "syzygy" as a collective noun for both the anima and the animus. Of all the symbols and archetypes he discovered in "Confrontation," the first one he presents as having any capacity to interact with him, rather than just exist in him, is the anima. He tells a story of how one day he had been sitting, recording his fantasies, and had come to wonder what exactly he was doing, because it bore no resemblance to any science of which he had ever heard. At that point, a woman's voice said to him, "It is art." Eventually, he came to have an interactive discussion with her, which he summarizes quite succinctly in "Confrontation":

> I was greatly intrigued by the fact that a woman should interfere with me from within. My conclusion was that she must be the "soul," in the primitive sense, and I began to speculate on the reasons why the name "anima" was given to the soul. Why was it thought of as feminine? Later I came to see that this inner feminine figure plays a typical, or archetypal, role in the unconscious of a man, and I called her the "anima." The corresponding figure in the unconscious of woman I called the "animus." ("Confrontation" 186)

This passage tells us several things about the nature of the syzygy. First of all, we should be wary of Jung's instant conclusion that this feminine voice represented the soul, especially in light of his admission that she spoke in the voice of one of his patients (ibid., 185). More interesting is Jung's decision that this "inner feminine figure" was not unique to him, but rather was common to all men—it was the maternal Eros ("The Syzygy," *CW* 9[ii]:29). We say "men" quite deliberately; Jung placed a different figure in the unconscious of women—the animus, which, according to Jung, is equivalent to the paternal Logos (ibid.) and is both deductively and empirically justified (ibid., 27).

That Jung would call the syzygy empirically justified indicates that he saw it as more than simply an inductive concept. In fact, as far as Jung was concerned, the anima was the archetype of meaning, of life itself ("Archetypes of the Collective Unconscious," 82). As such, he could not ascribe something such value in a man and expect to justify its existence in a woman on purely logical grounds, especially in light of how totally he has eschewed logic elsewhere. So, in spite of his avowed antiscientific bias, Jung does appeal to biology to demonstrate the existence of the syzygy. However, his biology is utterly incorrect: "biologically speaking, it is only the greater number of masculine genes that tips the scale in favor of the masculine sex," and because the number of feminine genes in a man is smaller than the number of masculine genes, this forms a feminine personality that is inferior to that of the masculine and therefore unconscious (ibid., 77). We can contrast that with the definition of "Sex Chromosome" in the *Penguin Dictionary of Biology,* which tells us that "the presence or absence of a Y-chromosome determines sex in mammals." That is, there is no biological reason for a feminine principle in men, and even less for a masculine principle in women. This totally contradicts Jung's assertion that "a man contains female-producing elements, a woman male-producing elements" ("The Meaning of Individuation," 18). Certainly, men do produce estrogen, and women do produce testosterone, and Jung would be correct on this level. However, he did not say that, for example, women contain "masculinizing" elements. He said "male-producing," and that gender was determined by a relative proportion of these compared to the female-producing elements. If gender is determined solely by the presence or absence of a genetic component, there is no question of greater or lesser numbers, especially in the feminine context. The Y-chromosome is specifically male—women do not have it and thus are not male; men do have the female component (the X-chromosome), but they have the Y-chromosome, which determines their gender as well.

This recourse to genetics has very important ramifications for Jungian theory. As much as Jung may have wanted to eschew science, it has shown him up here. We have already seen that Jung used the argument that, during development, the human fetus resembles that of a fish and a chicken and expanded upon it to assert that so too does the human psyche start out undifferentiated, then it individuates and becomes fully human ("Approaching the Unconscious," 66). He uses a similar argument in the case of the syzygy; just as women grow moustaches and men develop hips as they grow older, so too do the animus and anima assert themselves around middle age ("The Stages of Life," *CW* 8:780). This entails one of two things—either a physical substratum for the syzygy or a locus of interaction between the psyche and the body. By now we have shown that the latter possibility is no possibility at all, and our comparison of Jung and genetics should discount the former as well. A hormonal explanation would make sense, but, as we have just shown, this was not Jung's intent. As such, the syzygy cannot be shown to interact with the body at all, and these biological justifications for its existence cannot be considered adequate proof.

Of course, Jung never stakes the existence of the syzygy to something so falsifiable as biology. The passage between Jung and his anima from *MDR* shows well the process by which Jung determined the nature of this universal feminine element. First, he determined that the feminine voice represents the "soul." Then, he speculated on its nature—in particular, why it was conceived of as feminine. From these reflections, he derived a theory that he applied, found justified, and therefore invoked as universal, making the necessary revisions to include women as well as men in its scope. We will look at this procedure, not to find out what it tells us about the soul, but to see what it tells us about Jung.

First of all, this sort of reasoning is absolutely typical of the Jungian method. Jung was definitely a child of his times; anyone with any experience studying German philosophy should by this point have realized how much Jung owes to Hegel, the post-Hegelians, and the phenomenologists. They approached questions, as did Jung, through reflection. Even a cursory glance through the *Collected Works* shows the respect Jung held for the German idealist philosophers, especially Nietzsche. In that light, we can expect that Jung, just as Nietzsche, would "no longer want to hear anything of all those things and questions which do not permit experiments" (Nietzsche 1882, §51). Granted, Nietzsche's ideas about experiments are somewhat different from ours. Nonetheless, in light of this statement we can ask whether or not Jung's conception of the anima stands up to experimentation. Overwhelmingly, the answer is no. In fact, the soul has not always been "thought of as feminine"— for example, "soul" in Hebrew is espressed as having both masculine and feminine aspects; and English, the language of our discussion, has only a rudimentary concept of gender, which does not extend over "soul." The fact that, in some Indo-European tongues, words such as *die Psyche* and *l'ame* and *anima* do take the feminine articles does not mean that this is a proper attribution, if we can even speak of such a concept. This statement does show that, for whatever reason, these three languages have conceived of the soul as a feminine object. As such, Jung would not be remiss in saying that speakers of these three languages have conceived of the soul as a feminine object, when they have even pondered such intricacies as what, if anything, underlies linguistic gender. However, Jung has not limited himself in this way; the anima is meant to be a universal concept, and as such must meet the criteria of all people, in all places, at all times. If Jung is going to support his idea that the soul is an "inner feminine figure" by the fact that "the soul was thought of as feminine," the least he can do is to demonstrate unequivocally such a universal feminine conception of the soul. Since he himself has chosen to prove by induction, by appeal to enumerating instances, if we can show an instance that runs contrary to Jung's induction, we have disproven his claim. We have shown such an instance, and therefore can consider that we have disproven the claim.

Now that we have shown Jung's claim not to be universal, we are left with a problem. Proven or not, the anima is one of the cornerstones of Jungian theory. Thankfully, we do not have the problem of trying to justify its existence in order to preserve the theory. However, we should not discard our inquiry into the anima at this point. The fact that Jung placed such stock in the existence of the anima should show us how certain he was of its existence. At this point, we should ask ourselves why. Fortunately, Jung himself helps us with this problem, and through investigation of it we learn something very important about Jungian theory.

Before allowing his anima to speak, thereby producing the statement by which we examined it, Jung was in a quandary as to this unconscious voice that spoke to him and called his work "art." In his discussion of the voice, Jung drops an aside that tells us much about his conception of the anima.

> Obviously what I was doing wasn't science. What then could it be but art? It was as though these were the only alternatives in the world. *That is the way a woman's mind works.* ("Confrontation," 185, emphasis added)

Perhaps it is a phenomenon of the 1990s that, in our current drive to purge gender from English thought and speech, to talk of "the way a woman's mind works" sounds as out of place as a kazoo in a concert hall. For this reason if no other, we must look at the anima in a whole new light. Having shown that the idea of a feminine soul is hardly universal, we are still left with the fact that Jung himself conceived of it in such a manner. And, although this comes dangerously close to analyzing Jung's own thought processes, an examination of Jung's writings on the anima will show that, in fact, they reflect his own opinions and those of his society rather than a set of factual, empirically justified statements

The whole concept of the syzygy seems like a post hoc justification for Jung's own sexist views. If we say that conceptions of masculinity and femininity are psychically ingrained, inherited structures, then we justify Jung's statements such as "a man should live as a man, and a woman as a woman" ("Woman in Europe," 170). For Jung, a woman who follows "a masculine calling" introduces into any discussion

> a whole host of argumentative biases which always go a little beside the point in the most irritating way, and which, furthermore, always inject a little something into the problem that is not really there . . . [which] can even grow into a downright daemonic passion that irritates and disgusts men . . . [and] smother[s] the charm and meaning of femininity. . . . Such a development naturally ends in a deep, psychological division, in short, a neurosis. (ibid., 171)

The reason for this sort of reaction, as far as Jung is concerned, is that a woman who moves into society is the same as a woman assuming a masculine psychology (ibid., 169), a view that becomes understandable if we assume, as Jung does, that notions of masculinity and femininity are ingrained not only in the psyche but in the genes. Because of this view, that a woman who does not remain entrenched in her traditional place in the world is denying her femininity, Jung sees it as the man's responsibility to keep her in line, and that "often the man has the feeling— and he is not altogether wrong—that only seduction or a beating or a rape would have the necessary power of persuasion" ("The Syzygy," CW 9[ii]:29).

In light of his holding beliefs like these, we could be excused for asking why many of Jung's most prominent followers were women— Marie-Louise von Franz, Aniela Jaffé, and Jolande Jacobi, to give three examples. In fact, the post-Jungians have had to deal with the fact that both Jung and analytic psychology are hopelessly wrapped up in the patriarchy of the Swiss society in which Jung lived (Samuels, 229). One way they have dealt with this is to strip such concepts as Logos, Eros, animus, and anima of their genders, which they claim leaves them with "superb tools" for psychoanalysis (ibid., 207). However, gender is inextricable from Jung's conception of the syzygy, as we saw in the quotation from MDR as well as the biological claim for its existence. As such, any conception of gender-specific objects utterly denuded of gender is absurd, and no longer Jungian.

Samuels uses the fact that the animus seems to be a post hoc construct instituted merely to balance the anima as one reason to remove the idea of gender from the syzygy (ibid., 214). Certainly, Jung claimed that the animus was demonstrated empirically ("The Syzygy," *CW* 9[ii]:27), but in an attempt to explore the validity of this claim, Samuels' statement is worth keeping in mind, as it helps us draw a distinction of more than a purely semantic nature. If we show that the animus has not in fact been empirically justified, we do not by extension support Samuels. That is, in the event that we do not find a masculine element in the feminine psyche, this does not entail that a universal syzygy exists in a form devoid of gender. Rather, it would support our claim that the syzygy was merely a construct to provide a basis for Jung's own sexist views. If he could propose an anima, with corresponding animus, Jung could support a claim that sexism is actually a fault of human nature in general, that it is inevitable, and that therefore any attempts to eradicate it are futile.

Keeping this intent in mind, we will now look for some of that empirical justification for the animus that Jung claims to have found. It seems odd that Jung would assert universality for the animus in light of his own statement that a woman cannot describe it. "On the biological level a woman's chief interest is to hold a man, while a man's chief interest is to conquer a woman, and because of his nature he seldom stops at one conquest" since the unconscious compensates for the conscious attitude, men can describe their anima, because it is one woman, but the animus is many men and therefore is harder to describe ("Mind and Earth," *CW* 10:81). Again, this seems awfully post hoc. In his appeal to genetics to support the idea of the syzygy, Jung demonstrated that his views of biology are more than a bit skewed. This instance is no exception. Women today can be just as promiscuous as men, and the same was true in Jung's day. However, in the social circles in which Jung lived, women were not promiscuous. We saw Jung's own views on sexuality when we discussed his "A Contribution to the Psychology of Rumor"—views that are representative of his society. Brides wore white to show their virginity; the same "purity" was not expected of men, and for this they were quite fortunate. But the fact that, in society, men can have many lovers while women have been expected to be faithful to one is hardly due to biological influences. As such, Jung's appeal to this as a support for the concept of the animus through the idea of the compensatory unconscious is not persuasive.

Jung also uses the Eros/Logos dichotomy by which he has defined the syzygy to assert the existence of the animus. The argument by which he makes this assertion is circular, but since it can be questioned on other grounds, they too are worth pursuing. Since the animus is equivalent to the masculine principle, which is thinking, it must therefore embody thinking; but in an unconscious, therefore stunted manner. If we substitute "feeling" for "thinking," the same goes for the anima. "If the anima is irrational feeling, the animus is irrational thinking" ("Mind and Earth," *CW* 10:80). Of course, if such a statement cannot be made of the anima, the modus ponens relationship cannot be established, but again, we will not settle for arguing on logical grounds when we can invoke Jung's own writings against himself. Jung's rationale here is reminiscent of a distinction we will explore when we look into his personality theories— that when he discusses the extraverted feeling type, he can never picture men who embody it, only women. This is because "feeling is, incontestably, a more obvious peculiarity of feminine psychology than thinking" ("General Description of the Types," 448). We will not enter into an examination of the types here; let it suffice to say that perhaps the only reason Jung cannot enumerate any instances of men who fit the extraverted feeling description is because historically men have been told not to show their feelings. The sensitive Woody Allen-type male image that emerged in the 1970s helped break the centuries-old mindset that said men do not show emotion. The chivalrous knight pined for his lady fair, but he did so in an abstract way—he wrote romantic poems on her behalf, but he did not cry himself to sleep over her. We will leave aside the various sociobiological hypotheses, because that whole field reeks of Lamarck, and instead we will propose how much more likely it is that this prejudice, that men think and women feel, is due to social, not biological, causes. When the prejudice is removed, so too is the distinction. This last fact could have inspired Samuels' assertion that the syzygy becomes useful when we purge all ideas of gender from it. In fact, without gender, the syzygy becomes irrelevant; when we discuss the types, we will see that the thinking and feeling types suffice to explain the undeveloped, irrational thinking and feeling that would populate a neutered and spayed syzygy—without its excess archetypal baggage.

In short, Jung's empirical justification for the animus does not exist. Furthermore, his whole idea that men conceive of the soul as feminine is unsupported. Discarding the syzygy leaves Jung with no tool to explain the presence of the opposite sex in dreams and fantasies, but he never makes clear why this needs to be "explained" at all, except the general psychoanalytic hypothesis that dreams convey a message, which must be decoded. If we do not feel the need to decode the dream, then we do not need the syzygy to help us do so.

In that case, let us no longer flog a dead horse, and move on in our investigation to the second of the two "collective aspects" of the self. This archetype is also distinguished by gender into the concepts of the Wise Old Man and the Chthonic Mother. It is somewhat puzzling that Jung does not devote an essay to this aspect of the self as he has done for the others, especially since he sees it as so integral to the individuated personality. At the end of his discussion of the syzygy Jung refers to it, but does not go into any detail ("The Syzygy," *CW* 9[ii]:42). Instead, we are referred to another paper where this archetype is described in the masculine context using terms reminiscent of Nieztsche: beyond good and evil, both the father and son of the soul, a superior master and teacher best epitomized by the magician ("Archetypes of the Collective Unconscious," 86).

As with the anima, it is fruitful to look to Jung's own "discovery" of his own wise old man, a character whom he named Philemon.

> Psychologically, Philemon represented superior insight. He was a mysterious figure to me. At times he seemed to me quite real, as if he were a living personality. I went walking up and down the garden with him, and to me he was what the Indians call a guru. ("Confrontation," 183)

This character, a pagan, brought with him "an Egypto-Hellenistic atmosphere with a Gnostic coloration" (ibid., 182). Jung's response to Philemon is very interesting, as are the lessons that this character "taught": psychic objectivity and the reality of the psyche. "Through him the distinction was clarified between myself and the object of my thought" (ibid., 183). Jung admits that, at the point when Philemon appeared to him, he had been feeling personally devalued by the new personalities that had taken form within him, and that he "could have wished for nothing better than a real, live guru, someone possessing superior knowledge and ability, who would have disentangled for [him] the involuntary creations of [his] imagination" (ibid., 184). For Jung, Philemon played this role, along with another spiritual being, *Ka,* who he equated with the Anthroparion or the homunculus and "who made everything real" (ibid., 185).

We cannot underestimate the strangeness of the fact that Jung wrote so little about the Wise Old Man, especially in light of how important he claimed it was in his own individuation. Fortunately, he does give us one route into exploration of this archetype—through a work he produced in 1916, when he "was compelled from within, as it were, to formulate and express what might have been said by Philemon" (ibid., 190). This work, published only privately during Jung's life, was the "Septem Sermones ad Mortuos," now included as an appendix to *MDR*. In keeping with the rule of Philemon that Jung himself was independent of his thoughts (ibid., 183), which happens to be a principle of post-Hegelian thought in general, Jung wrote the "Septem Sermones" pseudonymously, attributing the work to a second-century Gnostic named Basilides. We will not cite this work at length here; let it suffice to say that if this is how Philemon spoke, then he spoke both incoherently and to the converted. Stylistically, the work resembles Kierkegaard or the medieval mystics at their worst—rambling, ranting, and generally unable to form a cogent thought. But we are not concerned with style. Rather, the content of the "Septem Sermones" should intrigue us, especially in light of Philemon's telling Jung to dissociate himself from his thoughts. For if we remove the obfuscation from the following statement, we will see a basic tenet of Jungian theory couched underneath:

> Spirituality conceiveth and embraceth. It is womanlike and therefore we call it MATER COELESTIS, the celestial mother. Sexuality engendereth and createth. It is manlike, and therefore we call it PHALLOS, the earthly father.
>
> The sexuality of man is more of the earth, the sexuality of woman is more of the spirit.
>
> The spirituality of man is more of heaven, it goeth to the greater.
>
> The spirituality of woman is more of the earth, it goeth to the smaller.
>
> Lying and devilish is the spirituality of the man which goeth to the smaller.
>
> Lying and devilish is the spirituality of the woman which goeth to the greater.
>
> Each must go to its own place. ("Septem Sermones," 387)

Strip away the style, and we are left with "a man should live as a man, and a woman as a woman" ("Woman in Europe," 170). Now, if Jung looks at this not as a product of his own psyche but as independent, objective productions of an independent, objective portion of the psyche (consistent with "Confrontation," 183), this goes a long way toward explaining why he saw the archetypes of the self as universal. If an independent observer were to come up with writings such as the

"Septem Sermones," such statements would support Jung's hypothesis about the syzygy. This could have a lot to do with why Jung rejected the neural hypothesis, instead insisting on a noncorporeal psyche. If we posit that the psyche is really an epiphenomenon of the brain, then this statement and all the other "Septem Sermones" must come directly from Jung. All of his thoughts would be grounded in his body, and any claim of objectivity for the psyche from the ego would become ludicrous. At one point, Jung was willing to make such a claim ("The Basic Postulates of Analytical Psychology," 206), but his later work posits the psyche as categorically distinct from the body.

After such a diversion, we return to the archetypes of the Wise Old Man and Chthonic Mother still unable to say why Jung wrote so little about them. Throughout his later works, the anima, the shadow, and the self become the subject of countless symbols and investigations; the Wise Old Man and Chthonic Mother are curiously abandoned. Jung never tells us why. In such an absence, and in light of certain other facts, we can advance here a tentative, interpretive hypothesis. We can propose that Jung never dealt specifically with this fourth archetype because he actually did explore it, almost ad nauseam, in his discussions of alchemy and Gnosticism. The alchemists and the Gnostics themselves symbolized the Wise Old Man for Jung, and their works, which provided the other symbols that led to the process of individuation, were inexorably linked to themselves. Certainly, this sort of statement is risky, but in the absence of any other reason for his abandoning this fourth archetype, it at least bears investigation. At least it could explain why he agreed so strongly with the statement from *The Secret of the Golden Flower* that "everything depends on the man and little or nothing on the method" ("Commentary," on *The Secret of the Golden Flower,* Wilhelm, 83). If the method were practiced by someone who did not himself have the characteristics of the Wise Old Man, the rest of the archetypes from the alchemical process would not find expression.

Here, we cross the bridge into the most obscure branch of Jungian theory, Jung's writings on alchemy, without having finished our discussion of the archetypes of the self. However, such a transition is justified at this point in our inquiry. If, as Jung proposes, the alchemical expression is actually the process of individuation rendered into symbolic terms, it should lead us inexorably to a discussion of the self. Therefore, we will now look into alchemy and discuss the archetypes and archetype of the self as they arise in that context.

5

Alchemy, the Occult, and
Other Cultural Fashions

When we discussed Jung's frequent appeals to the study of comparative religion, we made a note that such justification could well scare off even the bravest philosopher. Even those hardy souls who have managed to follow us this far would be excused for taking one look at alchemy, throwing up their hands, and running away. In fact, if we tried to argue with Jung on his own grounds, we would find ourselves starting from a horrible disadvantage. Jung had access to rare alchemical manuscripts and the benefit of years to interpret them. We will not try to debate with him the validity of his translations from Greek and Latin. This makes our job much easier, but at the same time it does not grant him any concessions, because we need not be interested in whether or not Jung's interpretations of the alchemical manuscripts are correct. That is, even if Jung interprets every facet of every alchemist's writings entirely in accordance with the intent of the writings, this does not detract from the criticisms with which we will level him. Certainly, as we explore, we will find grounds to suspect that, occasionally, Jung has misinterpreted a text or two, but this is a secondary goal. Our primary intent is, as before, to undercut Jung's assertion of universality for the alchemical phenomenon as he interprets it. Even if the alchemists did mean exactly what Jung says they did, this makes absolutely no progress toward asserting the universality of the process that Jung claims their writings describe.

Jung traces the descent of his theories through Gnosticism and alchemy, which by extension says that the alchemical ideas are the direct

inheritors of the Gnostic tradition ("The Meaning of Individuation,"
28). These ideas pass from Gnosticism to alchemy through the person
of Zosimos ("Adam and Eve," *CW* 14:627). As even Samuels is forced
to admit, the examples from alchemy and mysticism that Jung cites
may simply show that groups of people with similar reasoning processes
have lived in different ages (Samuels, 34), and that because his parallels
derive in the main from Indo-European cultures, we cannot rule out
cultural influences in the learning of archetypes (ibid., 35). In fact, if
we see a direct link between Gnosticism and alchemy, a role Jung posits
for Zosimos, we have even more reason to suspect cultural influences
rather than expression of archetypes. Therefore, every time Jung invokes
a parallel between alchemy and Gnosticism, we should keep in mind
these caveats, which even the post-Jungians have had to consider.

Without further ado, we will now look into the alchemical experiment
proper and Jung's interpretations of it. He describes seven steps to the
alchemical experiment:

1. the unknown *prima materia* is in a state of blackness, which state
   is called the *nigredo;*
2. the contradictory principles are joined in a union (*coniunctio*) often
   spoken of in terms of masculine and feminine;
3. the prima materia undergoes a stage of disintegration, often referred
   to as a "death" (the *putrefactio, mortificatio,* or *calcinatio*);
4. the prima materia is washed off (*ablutio*);
5. the white stone or white earth is produced (*terra foliata alba*), which
   is an extract or a sublimate of the opposites;
6. the stone or earth is reddened (*rubedo*), projection upon which
   produces gold or silver from the base metals;
7. the rubedo is yellowed (*citrinitas*), producing solid, coagulated, or
   fluid gold.

("The Idea of Redemption in Alchemy," 208)

With this procedural description out of the way, Jung introduces more
familiar alchemical concepts. The Philosopher's Stone (*lapis philosophorum,* or simply *lapis*) is either an instrument in the procedure (the
rubedo) or the end itself (a winged hermaphrodite with body, soul, and
spirit, ibid., 209). Mercury comes into the picture as an analogous concept
to the prima materia—the *aqua permanens,* or eternal water (ibid.).
The Hermetic vessel (*vas Hermetis*) has a particular relationship with
the prima materia and the lapis (ibid.); in it, one becomes the other.
Finally, the whole process was conceived of as cyclical and referred

to as a wheel (*circulatio, rotatio,* or *rota*) (ibid.).

Although it really need not be said, Jung points out that this description bears very little resemblance to chemistry. Since the ancients knew chemistry, he proposes, they must have known that this was definitely not chemistry. "The fact is that the alchemists had nothing whatsoever to divulge, and least of all the secret of manufacturing gold" (ibid., 211) We will discuss this claim later. However, Jung proposes, the fact that the alchemists worked so hard at building up a body of knowledge over such a long period of time cannot be explained by calling their field of study a fraud. According to Jung, the true root of alchemy is not in transmitting philosophy, but in experiencing psychological projections via chemical experiments (ibid., 213). Our accepting Jung's interpretations of alchemy hinges upon our accepting his idea that the relationship of alchemy to Christianity is as a dream to consciousness ("Introduction to the Religious and Psychological Problems of Alchemy," *CW* 12:26). That is, Christianity is a conscious attitude and therefore must be compensated by an unconscious attitude, which finds expression through alchemy. The alchemical experiment is a concrete symbol for unconscious projections, and the conclusion of the experiment represents the reconciliation of the unconscious content ("Rex and Regina," *CW* 14:446). This explains why Jung interprets all alchemical symbolism in metaphors reminiscent of unconscious symbolism; if, as the *Rosarium Philosophorum* says, certain psychic factors are absolute requisites to find the lapis ("The Idea of Redemption in Alchemy," 216), and these psychic factors find expression through hallucinations and visions during the alchemical experiment (ibid., 215), then Jung's method would say that these psychic factors would be unconscious. In fact, he calls alchemy a bridge integrating the conscious and unconscious psyches ("The Conjunction," *CW* 14:779). For this reason, we will explore Jung's interpretations of one particular alchemical factor, not to see if he has interpreted them "correctly" (though we will not be able to help questioning his interpretations), because if we remain consistent with the ideology stated in our first chapter, the interpretation is irrelevant to the primary fact, which is the alchemical manuscript. Instead, we will concentrate on two points: whether or not Jung's interpretations aid his assertions of universality for his concept, and whether or not the alchemist necessarily thought along the same lines as Jung.

In this respect, the symbol of the lapis will serve as an excellent springboard into our investigation of alchemy. As we have already said, Jung has found instances where the lapis is symbolized as an element in the alchemical procedure and other instances where the lapis represents the product of the procedure itself ("The Idea of Redemption in Alchemy," 209). We will now clarify this statement on Jung's behalf. While sometimes he cites alchemists for whom the lapis is an element of the procedure and sometimes he cites those for whom the lapis is the product, he never gives an example of one alchemist who conceives of the lapis as both an element and a product of the alchemical experiment. That is, each alchemist is internally consistent in the application of his own symbolism. This point will be worth our keeping in mind as we continue to look into Jung's interpretations.

Jung explains the tenacity of seventeen centuries of alchemists by the numinous nature of the archetype of the Anthropos, which they sought ("The Conjunction," *CW* 14:748). That is, the alchemist was working toward perfection of the self, and the lapis is the self ("The Fish in Alchemy," *CW* 9[ii]:194). Unequivocally, this sets the lapis as the alchemist's goal, rather than an element in the procedure, and also explains why we were able to avoid talking about Jung's conception of the self until now. In fact, the prominence of alchemy in Jungian theory is explained by this analogy between the lapis and the self—just as the process of assimilating the unconscious is accomplished through individuation, so too is the process of alchemy resolved through production of the lapis, that is, the self. In fact, one of Jung's studies of the phenomenon of individuation led him to his work on alchemy ("A Study in the Process of Individuation," 51), because his patient dreamed in obviously alchemical symbols in spite of her having "no knowledge of alchemy" (ibid., 46). We could question this assertion. This patient spontaneously invoked a connection between silver, quicksilver, and Mercury as both god and element (ibid., 37); later, she is said to have identified a silver band in one of her paintings with the wings of Mercury and told Jung that he would "call it the animus;" (ibid., 46). Jung admits she had been influenced by Swedenborg, who had in turn been influenced by alchemy, but he protests that "anyone with a sufficient knowledge of Swedenborg's chief writings will know that it is very unlikely that he could have infected my patient with alchemistic philosophy or that she could have reproduced it by cryptomnesia" (ibid., 47). This is no place to discuss Swedenborg in any depth; let it suffice to say that Jung's categorical statement in this regard could do with some revision.

From his work with this woman, Jung became very interested in alchemy in general and came to the decision that unconscious use of alchemical symbolism today is "almost . . . a regular occurrence, though it is little known. . . . My patients would have produced 'alchemistic' symbolism even if alchemy had never existed" (ibid., 50, abridged). We can be excused for being somewhat unconvinced. As we have seen, the patient has experience with alchemistic ideas, such as the equation between silver, quicksilver, and Mercury; even if she has never read any alchemy per se, her attempts to think symbolically could well elicit such alchemical language. We know from Jung's own admission cited above that she was in the habit of interpreting her own symbols, and that she had interpreted these symbols in alchemistic terms. Therefore, Jung's assertion that his patient had no knowledge of alchemy rings quite hollow.

This is worth keeping in mind when we consider that, as Jung well admits, this case led him into his alchemical studies. He believed his patient to have no knowledge of alchemy; in light of this, we cannot be surprised to see him say that "the most sensible way" of explaining its occurrence in her dreams and paintings is by resort to the collective unconscious, and for this reason he places alchemistic symbolism therein ("A Study in the Process of Individuation," 50). This means Jung went into alchemy looking for something he had already found—"the ground which underlay [his] own experiences of the years 1913 to 1917" ("Travels," 209). Like a broken record, we are back to the idea of Jung's subjective feelings of certainty. He found in alchemy a system that mirrored his own experiences with Philemon and the anima and the other characters that came to populate his unconscious after the break with Freud. Thus, he explored it. If, as he admits, he makes alchemy sound like a Gnostic myth because the one descends from the other and they both come from the collective unconscious ("Introduction to the Religious and Psychological Problems of Alchemy," *CW* 12:28)—and, as the *Septem Sermones* have shown, Jung's own writings can resemble those of the Gnostics—then Jung may see alchemy as well supported because of its strong correspondence with his own experience. As such, his equation of the lapis with the self and the alchemical experiment with the process of individuation would be grounded in his own experience of each psychoanalytic concept.

As a symbol of the self, the lapis is indistinguishable from the quaternity. As a mandala, the circle is the most important figure "because of its perfect form" ("The Structure and Dynamics of the Self," *CW* 9[ii]:351n). As such, the quaternity is "the minimum number of parts into which the circle may naturally be divided" (ibid.) and therefore represents an attempt to categorize the chaos of the universe (*CW* 9[ii]:381). The logic of this argument is, in a word, abysmal. First of all, we will look at the concept of the mandala; then we will discuss why such a definition leads so "naturally" into division into four.

> "Mandala," a Sanskrit word, means circle or magic circle. Its symbolism embraces all concentrically arranged figures, all circular or square circumferences having a center, and all radial or spherical arrangements. ("Archetypes of the Collective Unconscious," 95n)

> The mandala is the center. It is the exponent of all paths. It is the path to the center, to individuation. ("Confrontation with the Unconscious," 196)

If there are four components of the self, and the mandala is the path to the self, then the mandala will necessarily have four sections. As well, we must keep in mind that perhaps the circle splits so "naturally" into fours because the ancient world conceived of so many fours. Jung saw these as expressions of the archetype of the quaternity; perhaps he has the relation backward. Four not only happens to be the number of the elements, and the cardinal directions, and everything else fundamental to ancient science, but it also happens to be the number of fingers on the hand (excluding the thumb), and the number of appendages (excluding the head), as well as the smallest number by which we can state more than one quality of an object. Perhaps the perception of the relation came first, then came the logical structure of the quaternity to explain it. For example, when Aristotle spoke of the different qualities of the four elements: four, he called fire hot and dry, air hot and wet, water cold and wet, and earth cold and dry (Aristotle, *De Generatione et Corruptione*, 330b5). These two pairs of characteristics, hot and cold and wet and dry, seem to be the basic differences Aristotle perceives in the elements. Certainly, fire is hot, and nothing wet stays wet for long when in a fire. By the same token, water, when unheated, is cool and wet, and earth (when unmixed with water—this would be mud) is cool and dry. In this relationship, air seems to be a construct invoked to balance off the pairs of opposites rather than due to any intrinsic elemental qualities of its own. Jung could not consider such a hypothesis because it destroys the quaternity of the elements: four upon which so much of his theorizing rests. Nonetheless, it is a possibility.

Instead, Jung supports his idea of the quaternity through recourse to the alchemists. In this respect, his favorite quotation is one attributed to one Maria Prophetissa: "One becomes two, two becomes three, and out of the third comes the one as the fourth" ("Introduction to the Religious and Psychological Problems of Alchemy," *CW* 12:26). This idea crops up throughout Jungian thought, supported by some of his claims (e.g., personality theory) and supporting others (e.g., the doctrine of the Trinity). This "one" Jung calls the Gnostic "spark" of enlightenment, and it is the point at which the four elements of the quaternity meet, that is, the self ("The Paradoxa," *CW* 14:42). Needless to say, if quaternities are not archetypal, this whole statement, and any doctrines based upon it, become ludicrous. This is why Jung must place so much stock in quaternities. However, he never gives any reason why these structures should exist. Rather, he enumerates many examples in an attempt to show that the quaternity is an archetypal structure. As such, if we can show examples where fundamental structures do not reflect quaternities, we knock out much support for Jungian theory in this regard. When discussing Jung and Taoism, we saw him ignore the Chinese five-element theories. Now we know why. The list could continue ad infinitum— the fact that we use a base ten numerical system, the fact that there are twenty-four hours in a day, the fact that the hieroglyphs that comprise the Egyptian Eye of Horus actually add up to sixty-three sixty-fourths— but the fact that we can enumerate even this many shows that the quaternity is not the fundamentally unifying principle which Jungian theory demands.

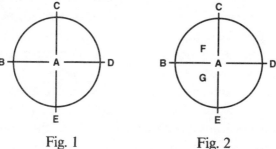

Fig. 1   Fig. 2

However, in characteristic fashion, Jung provides himself an escape route. Figures 1–4 all represent permutations of the quaternity (B,C,D,E). Figure 1 is a quaternity, with the added "spark" of the self (A) ("The Paradoxa," *CW* 14:36). Figure 2 is the "hidden magical Septenary" that unites the four (B,C,D,E) and the seven (A,B,C,D,E,F,G) into one (A) through the spark ("The Components of the Coniunctio," *CW* 14:10). Figure 3 is an ogdoad, a double quaternity (B,C,D,E; F,G,H,I) and therefore represents totality (ibid., 8). Figure 4 represents the ogdoad (B,C,D,E,F,G,H,I) united with the Gnostic spark (A), which, if the other three figures represent totality, must represent totality as well. When we unite these figures with the statement of Maria Prophetissa, we show that every number below ten is reducible to the quaternity. And if the four and the seven are united into one, then eleven (4+7) becomes reducible to one as well. From there, we could go on forever; if we allow Jung to use this sort of logic, every number becomes reducible to one, which is four, which is three and one. . . .

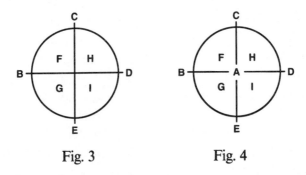

Fig. 3   Fig. 4

Let us go back to more sturdy ground. Hopefully, we have shown that Jung, if we let him, will invoke absolutely any example, process it through his interpretive numerological hypothesis, and produce a response in keeping with his theories. In the process, we should have by now shown that the quaternity arrangement is not so archetypal as Jung might hope. Nonetheless, Jung does base major portions of his theories upon the quaternity, and seeing as we have allowed the archetypes to stand up to the same empirical comparison as the platypus, we must examine at least some of the quaternities empirically as well. In that regard, the quaternity must still be explored, especially in the symbolic expression Jung finds for it as the lapis. From his analogy between the alchemical four-in-one (the lapis) to the four arms of the cross ("Introduction to the Religious and Psychological Problems of Alchemy," *CW* 12:41), Jung raises one very important question: Is Christ equivalent to the lapis? That depends upon where we look. In *Aion*, Jung certainly makes no bones about saying that he is, going so far as to title one chapter "Christ, a Symbol of the Self" and, in it, to say that "in the world of Christian ideas Christ undoubtedly represents the self" ("Christ, a Symbol of the Self," *CW* 9[ii]:115). Since, as Jung admits, the alchemists were convinced of the veracity of Christian truth ("The Conjunction," *CW* 14:772), this would put them squarely in the world of Christian ideas. Logically, therefore, Christ would symbolize the self in the alchemical context. As such, if the alchemical experiment is equivalent to the process of individuation, and the process of individuation culminates in the production of the self, then the alchemical experiment would have to culminate in the production of the lapis. Traditionally, this production has been represented through the artistic form of a winged hermaphrodite with body, soul, and spirit ("The Idea of Redemption in Alchemy," 209). But this hermaphrodite is Mercurius, who Jung has called "the self, the individuation process, [and] the collective unconscious" ("The Spirit Mercurius," *CW* 13:284). However, Mercurius is also an opposite to Christ and therefore not the self (ibid., 295). The role of this strange figure depends strongly on who is doing the talking. That is, when comparing alchemical descriptions Mercurius can simultaneously symbolize the self and its opposite. So either the lapis is Mercurius and the self is the shadow, or, by contrasting the symbols of two different alchemists in the same way as does Jung, we have shown a pitfall in Jung's method. Jung's post hoc explanation that Mercurius is all conceivable opposites (ibid., 284) cannot hold here— no matter what the value of the paradox, Mercurius is addressed as an individual throughout the alchemical process, and he is its goal. If the goal of the alchemical process is anything other than the self, and Jung persists in drawing the analogy between it and his own process of individuation, he then says that his own process to its fruition need not necessarily lead toward discovery of the self, which is a step not even he would be willing to make.

But Jung is not disturbed by this—he is willing to call Mercurius both the shadow and the self. And even if we suspend our critical faculties for a moment and allow him this paradox, he promptly embroils himself in another inconsistency from which the paradox is no escape. Jung turns his own logic around and expands upon it to say that if a painting depicts the hermaphrodite Mercurius, it necessarily depicts the lapis. Through this parallel, he is able to expand the influence of the alchemical symbol. That is, because of the existence of androgynes such as the Siva/Parvati representation from the Hindu tradition, the idea that he sees as coming to light through the alchemical experiment must be universal, and therefore archetypal.

The androgyne is popularly regarded as a universal, archetypal symbol . . . [and] though it is widespread, beyond any single culture, many religions, particularly the "primitive" ones, have managed to survive without it . . . we are dealing with a symbol that has meanings—different meanings—for several independent cultures. (O'Flaherty 1980, 285)

By calling it a symbol of the self, Jung proposes that the androgyne represents the quaternity in balance, the masculine totally reconciled with the feminine.

[Although it] dangl[es] before us the sweet promise of equality and balance, symbiosis and mutuality, the androgyne, under closer analysis, often furnishes bitter testimony to conflict and aggression, tension and disequilibrium, between female and male and between the human and the divine. (ibid., 334).

That is, if Jung insists that the alchemical experiment and the process of individuation both produce the same result, which is a harmonious androgyne, either he has missed the mark, or his conception of the self is fundamentally flawed.

It was for this reason that we left our discussion of the self until this chapter. Only through an exposition of the alchemical procedure can we show how Jung's most important archetype is so fundamentally inadequate. Certainly, we must consider Samuels' points that, if individuation is the quest to replace dominance by others with self-dominance, no one can tell someone else to do it (Samuels, 104), and that Jungian theory does not tell us whether or not the "self" is the whole personality or merely a central archetype of it (ibid., 105). However, the real problem with Jung's conception of the self is that his principal example of its expression, through the alchemical experiment, does not actually lead to it at all! Of all pictures of the Hermetic androgyne that Jung provides in any of his books, or even in any other book sympathetic to alchemy (e.g., de Givry), not one displays an androgyne with a vagina. "Female genitals are seldom if ever depicted; the breast, not the vagina, is the emblem of the woman that contrasts with the phallus" (O'Flaherty 1980, 331). This conflicts with Jung's idea that the Hermetic androgyne represents equilibrium between the genders, but not with O'Flaherty's. Jung has sought support for his own experience and found it in alchemy. Usually, we could fault him on these grounds alone. Now, however, we can see that in his appeal to alchemy he has quite possibly misinterpreted its contents as well.

As we have said all along, we are not in a position to propose an alternative interpretive hypothesis to Jung's. However, this does not mean we must allow Jung the moral high ground here; he has not supported the idea that alchemy must be "explained" at all beyond the general reason that, as far as he is concerned, every phenomenon has an explanation, and if that explanation is not instantly clear, it must be decoded ("Dream Analysis in its Practical Application," 14). As such, we will now look to Paracelsus, one alchemist about whom Jung wrote extensively, to see if this demand for interpretation is justified.

Perhaps the strongest argument against Jung's interpretive strategies comes from Arthur Edward Waite, the translator of some of Paracelsus's most important works. In the introduction to the first volume of *The Hermetic and Alchemical Writings of Paracelsus the Great,* Waite enjoins us to take Paracelsus at face value and not symbolically—if the alchemist says he has produced a homunculus, then he has actually produced a tiny gnomelike creature (Paracelsus: 1894, vii; this statement is mirrored in "Paracelsus as a Spiritual Phenomenon," *CW* 13:158). Certainly, Paracelsus did create an analogy between the "philosopher's mercury" and "quick mercury," and man and woman (Paracelsus: 1656, 23), and between the alchemical experiment and the sexual relationship (ibid., 24). Nonetheless, when Paracelsus describes copper as a mixture of sulphur and salt (Paracelsus: 1894, 7), and equates it with Venus, which has the power to heal wounds (Paracelsus: 1656, 8), he does not sound like he is discussing a psychological transformation. Even Jung is forced to admit that Paracelsus was first and foremost a doctor, who seems to have seen alchemy as a purely physical process ("Paracelsus as a Spiritual Phenomenon," *CW* 13:158). It is significant to note that, while Paracelsus does explicitly state that the setup of the alchemical experiment should mirror that of the physical world (Paracelsus 1656, 17), he says nothing about whether it should reflect the psychological state of the experimenter.

This state of repeatedly insisting upon physical states, while at the same time ignoring mental ones, seems to conflict with Jung's belief that "the alchemists sought for that affect which would heal not only the disharmonies of the physical world but the inner psychic conflict as well" ("The Conjunction," *CW* 14:674). Jung claims that, at first, alchemists were so unconscious of their own symbols "that they understood their own symbols as mere allegories or—semiotically—as secret names for chemical combinations," but later alchemists knew better (ibid., 677). The example of Paracelsus has given us grounds to question this, but we will do better if we can not only describe this phenomenon but explain it. As such, we must now challenge Jung's interpretation, not with the intent of supplanting it, but rather in hope that we will provide a plausible alternative.

Repeatedly throughout his alchemical works, Jung admits that the alchemists wrote in deliberately obscure language in order to keep their knowledge within a small, privileged community. He has challenged the idea that the symbols that they used were merely secret names for chemical compounds. Certainly, Paracelsus used alchemical notation and terminology throughout *The Archidoxes of Magic* to record medical recipes, but even Jung admits that Paracelsus' writings are very obscure, "which makes interpretation even more hazardous than usual" ("Paracelsus as a Spiritual Phenomenon," *CW* 13:213). As such, we will take the words of an avowed scientist of Paracelsus's time—Robert Boyle, discussing "a Place in England, where, without petrifying Water, Wood is turned into Stone"—and render them into alchemical language so as to examine the resulting passage.

First we will quote directly:

> I was a while since visited by a gentleman, who tells me, that he met with a place in these parts of England, where, though there be no petrifying spring (for that I particularly asked) wood is turned into stone in the sandy earth itself, after a better manner than by any water I have yet seen: for I had the curiosity to go look upon pieces of wood he brought thence, and hope for the opportunity of making some trials to examine the manner a little further, than I have been yet able to do. . . .
>
> I was lately making some trials with the petrified wood I told you of, which I find to be a very odd substance, wonderfully hard and fixed. If I had opportunity to reprint the History of Fluidity and Firmness, I could add diverse things about stones, that perhaps would not be disliked; and I hope, if God vouchsafe me a little leisure, to insert several of them in fit places in that history, against the next edition. Here is a certain stone, that is thought to be petrified bone, being shaped like a bone, with the marrow taken out; but with a fit menstruum, I found that I could easily dissolve it, like other soft stones: and possibly it may prove as fit as osteocolla, for the same medicinal uses. (Boyle, vol. 2, pp. 736–37)

Now let us make him sound like an alchemist:

I was a while since visited by a gentleman, who tells me, that he met with a place in these parts of England, where, without Adam,[1] the tree is brought to life[2] as the lapis[3] inside of Eve[4], after a better manner than by any spirit[5] I have yet seen: for I had the curiosity to go look upon that tree he brought thence, and hope for the opportunity of making some trials to examine the manner a little further, than I have been yet able to do. . . .

I was lately performing the opus with the tree of life[6] I told you of, which I find to be a very odd substance, wonderfully hard and fixed. If I had opportunity to reprint the History of Fluidity and Firmness, I could add diverse things about this lapis, that perhaps would not be disliked; and I hope, if God vouchsafe me a little leisure, to insert several of them in fit places in that history, against the next edition. Here is Adam, that is thought to be no more than fuel for the Art,[7] being shaped like that fuel, with the life taken out . . . I found that it was amenable to the water, like other stones . . . and possibly it may prove as fit for medicinal uses.

Certainly, we have not proved by this diversion that the alchemists were actually chemists. Jung may well be right in his interpretations. However, we can hope that all this work has not been for naught, and that we have provided an alternate hypothesis to Jung's.

As well, views expressed of alchemists from medieval and Renaissance writings could tell us a thing or two about how alchemists were perceived by their peers. Jung has explored *Faust* ad nauseam, so we will look to other sources. First and in passing, we can take note of René Descartes' statement that, through application of his method, he had learned "enough of the disreputable doctrines not to be taken in by the promises of an alchemist" (Descartes 1637, 8). But more important for our purposes are the words of Geoffrey Chaucer in his *Canterbury Tales*. This collection of medieval anecdotes, one of the most famous works of English literature from the fourteenth or any other century, contains one story of an alchemist—"The Canon's Yeoman's Tale." This

---

1. "Adam and Eve," *CW* 14:545—we will footnote in this case, so as not to break the continuity of the passage.
2. "The Philosophical Tree," *CW* 13:350.
3. "The Idea of Redemption in Alchemy," 209.
4. "Adam and Eve," *CW* 14:545.
5. "The Visions of Zosimos," *CW* 13:102.
6. "The Philosophical Tree," *CW* 13:350.
7. "The Visions of Zosimos," *CW* 13.

tale hardly paints a picture of the noble alchemist questing for individuation. Rather, the Yeoman tells that "[His] eyes are bleared with work on preparations,/ That's all the good you get from transformations." (Chaucer, 472). From Chaucer's descriptions, which are said to be "accurate and reliable in so far as they can be checked" (ibid., 473n), the ingredients of the alchemical experiment, which Jung is so quick to symbolize, were actually literal—the alchemist actually poured burnt bones and iron filings and trisulphide of arsenic into a pot and tried to make mercury out of it (ibid., 473).

Given the choice between accepting Jung's post hoc interpretations of alchemy or those of Chaucer, whose statements may reflect a firsthand knowledge of—and anger at having been fleeced by—an alchemist himself (ibid., 473n), we should at least lean toward those of the medieval era. Jung might allege that Chaucer did not have the benefit of psychological theories, but Chaucer had something better—firsthand experience. Chaucer was hardly uneducated; he could read Latin, French, English, and Italian and had done so quite widely in each language (ibid., 13). He had high posts in the English Court and waited on the Duke of Lancaster (ibid., 11). In short, Chaucer was no country bumpkin, and while his opinions of alchemy may not have been those of the alchemists themselves, he is far more likely to have known their machinations than someone looking back over a chasm spanning hundreds of years.

However, Jung did not tie his fortunes solely to the alchemy of the West. Rather, he believed that he had found alchemical symbolism throughout Tibetan and Chinese thought. We have already beaten the *Bardo Thödol* into the ground, so we will concentrate on Jung's other major source for Eastern parallels to alchemy— China. Certainly, this claim for parallel thinking seems somewhat odd in light of Jung's claim that a book like *The Secret of the Golden Flower* "never would have originated in European brains" ("Commentary" on *The Secret of the Golden Flower*, Wilhelm, 83); if he is going to assert similarity for the symbols the book describes but also say that no one who thinks in Western symbols could have produced the Eastern book, he does seem to contradict himself slightly. However, to help us through this disadvantage he claims we will have, Jung has decoded the book for us and found that it actually teaches us to understand the unconscious and thereby free ourselves from it (ibid., 122). We are to do this through yoga, which trains us for death (ibid., 125) and which makes us immortal by showing us how to assimilate the unconscious (ibid., 131).

Any Western reader who explored *The Secret of the Golden Flower* might well read the whole book without coming to the same realizations as Jung. However, this would not mean Jung was wrong. On the contrary—taking the book literally would be wrong in Jung's eyes because Oriental philosophy is symbolic (ibid., 129). Now we are back at John Smith's ideas about symbolic thinking. *The Secret of the Golden Flower* makes no literal sense—we can admit that much—so Jung tries to make sense out of it by looking for analogies between the new story and old facts (J. Smith, 202). As such, we can see the reason that "light on the nature of alchemy began to come to [him] only after [he] had read the text of the *Golden Flower,* that specimen of Chinese alchemy which Richard Wilhelm sent [him] in 1928" ("Travels," 204). It is worth noting that he had read the work of Herbert Silberer, which looked for links between alchemy and theories of the unconscious, as far back as 1917 ("Epilogue" to *Mysterium Coniunctionis, CW* 14:792). That is, Jung had been introduced to the theories before, and when confronted with this new and unfathomable work, he began to look for similarities; his own phenomenon of cryptomnesia came back to haunt him. He later found similar ideas in alchemy, and although he had seen these concepts before and merely forgotten about them, he based his later suspicions about the universality of alchemical symbolism in no small part upon his having found "original" instances of it in China.

Jung makes one other very large comment about Chinese "alchemy" in one other work, which will shed some light on exactly what he found in China. In a discussion of Chinese "alchemy" in "The Philosophical Tree," we see Jung ignore points of conflict between the Chinese thought and his own systems while adding symbols to relate Chinese ideas to Western ones.

> For the latter [i.e. he who will perish] will employ the "false method;" he will direct himself in all things by *the course of the sun and the stars,* in other words will lead a rationally ordered life in accordance with the rules of Chinese conduct. ("The Philosophical Tree," 13:433, emphasis added)

Jung himself often invoked proofs which were based on astrology. Many chapters of *Aion* detail the astrological constellations at the time of Christ's birth, and throughout the "Synchronicity" papers (*CW* 87), he refers to astrology as a manner of proof. He points to the fact that even Paracelsus's astrological sign "showed" that he would be a great physician ("Paracelsus," *CW* 15:1). Of course, we can use Jung's own writings against him; at one point he says words to the effect that it does not matter if people who conduct themselves by "the course of the sun and the stars" are using "the false method," because "everything depends on the man and little or nothing on the method" ("Commentary" on *The Secret of the Golden Flower,* Wilhelm, 83). The passage in "The Philosophical Tree" is meant to show that Chinese philosophy understood the "importance" of alchemy. But if the method is irrelevant, how can one be "false?" Jung does not refer to Chinese thought very often; as such, we can be glad the contradictions in his interpretations are so easy to find.

> If the adept at this point orders his life according to rules traditionally regarded as rational he brings himself into danger. "Danger will come to the black mass." The black mass is the *massa confusa,* the chaos or nigredo of Western alchemy, the prima materia, which is black outside and white inside, like lead. ("The Philosophical Tree," *CW* 13:433)

Here, the Chinese source simply refers to "the black mass," which could be nearly anything, particularly in translation.[8] Certainly, Jung's theories parallelling Chinese and Western ideas of "alchemy" are supported if he can back up this claim that this "black mass" actually is an equivalent concept to the prima materia. He does not even try. Rather, he just makes the statement then moves on, leaving no justification in his wake. Presumably, by this point in the work we should have bought into Jung's interpretive hypothesis, so he does not try to preach to the converted.

In short, given the choice between believing that the first alchemists were mistaken when they referred to their symbols as semiotic metaphors or that they meant them to be such metaphors, we should choose the latter. Jung himself admits that "it is characteristic of Paracelsan thinking, and of alchemy in general, that there are no clear-cut concepts, so that one concept can take the place of another ad infinitum, [but] at the same time every concept behaves hypostatically, as though it were a substance that could not at the same time be another substance" ("Paracelsus as a Spiritual Phenomenon," *CW* 13:178). Despite what Jung has said about Paracelsus, examinations of the writings of this alchemist show that he applied his symbols consistently—and literally. Jung has given us no reason to believe any other alchemist acted differently.

---

8. Jung could not read Chinese—he was dependent upon Wilhelm's translations.

6

Proof in Jung

In philosophical circles, the words "proof" and "proven" can almost become battle cries or loaded words carrying values far beyond the purely logical. After all, if something is "proven," it must then be accepted by any rational mind, and philosophers, considering themselves of rational mind, must then agree upon it. Who has ever heard of philosophers agreeing on anything? Even such seemingly obvious subjects as the existence of physical objects become topics for debate when philosophers get at them. In accordance with this, different people have different criteria for proof than do others. It takes far less evidence to remind the priest that God exists in the world than it does to persuade the skeptic. In a similar vein, Jung's criteria for proof are substantially diminished in comparison to those of Popper, and this brings us to a problem in our investigation.

In a nutshell, the problem we have when looking into Jung's proofs is the same as we have encountered and will encounter repeatedly. Can we judge Jung and his version of proof by standards he himself eschews? That is, if Jung does not submit himself and his work to Popperian criteria and then he and his work do not meet Popperian criteria, is this necessarily a strike against his theories? Certainly, it would be if he had purported to be scientific. This is why Freudian analysis has been the subject of so much debate—it does claim scientific status and therefore can be expected to meet the established criteria. But Jung did not claim that his works formulated any sort of science. In fact, not only did he claim not to be scientific, but he considered this a point in favor of his theories, not a strike against them. In light of this, we must approach Jung and his "proofs" from a different angle, first of all asking ourselves whether Jung should have to justify his work at all.

If Jung were only a philosopher, we could judge him according to different standards. Hume could never prove that the sun might not rise tomorrow, but he was able to propose it as a possibility, and although the preponderance of physical evidence weighs against his theory, this does not mean his theory is worthless. Certainly, our knowledge of planetary movement shows that, without something to stop it from happening, the sun is going to rise tomorrow. However, Hume could say that we cannot prove that the something will not happen and continue from there. That is, he is dealing explicitly with hypothetical constructs, and as such he forces us to alter our standards. If Hume had purported to be dealing with empirical evidence and had provided some objective, external reason why the sun would not rise tomorrow, we could criticize his reason using our own knowledge of physical reality. But he does not provide such a reason—his theory is logical, not empirical, and for that reason does not rely upon physical evidence. It is in a different category of proof, if we can use such terms, and must be disproved by its own criteria and on its own terms. Jung, however, repeatedly insisted that, "although I have often been called a philosopher, I am an empiricist and adhere as such to the phenomenological standpoint" ("Psychology and Religion," CW 11:2). This statement implicitly carries the method for its own refutation. We cannot use rules of logic to disprove the theories of someone who, in his own words, has eschewed them—while it is useful to be able to say that some element of Jungian theory makes no logical sense, that is not enough for our purposes. Any attack on Jungian theory must come from the empirical standpoint and refute Jung's tenets point by point according to empirical criteria. If Jung claims that a phenomenon exists, and it does not, then that element of his theory based upon the existence of the phenomenon becomes unsupported. At that point, we can refute.

In this light, it can now safely be said that Jung should not have to justify his proof, in that the justification should be readily apparent. He set up his own theories as universal for all of humanity, and for that reason the evidence upon which he based them should be both accessible and definite. That is, if Jung has based a tenet on a fact that does not exist, or that exists but not in a universal form, then that portion of his theory becomes unjustified on empirical grounds. This is the battlefield that he himself has delineated, and this is the battlefield on which he and his theories must be ready to fight. Logic, although a useful tool, is not a weapon here. For example, when discussing the anima, Jung points out that, because this feminine principle exists in every man, there must logically exist a corresponding masculine principle in every woman, but he then says this was borne out empirically ("The Syzygy," *CW* 9[ii]:27). We can criticize this statement on logical grounds: to say some principle exists in a man does not entail that it exists in a woman. Nonetheless, if Jung can prove that the animus exists, the fact that it need not is made irrelevant by the fact that it does. George Berkeley has shown us that physical objects need not logically exist, but experience tells us that, at least on an empirical level, they do. Our difficulty here is not with Berkeley, but with Jung.

> Philosophical criticism will find everything to object to in [the archetypes] unless it begins by recognising that they are concerned with *facts,* and that the "concept" is simply an abbreviated description or definition of these facts. Such criticism has as little effect on the object as zoological criticism on a duck-billed platypus. ("The Self," *CW* 9[ii]:63)

The most obvious point to attack Jungian theory is through one of its most basic tenets, the idea that the unconscious compensates for the activity of the conscious mind. In fact, we should look to cast aspersions upon it from Jung's own writings. Success in this attack would truly undercut Jung, because the compensatory relationship is absolutely central to his thought, underpinning such diverse theories as archetypal activity, the inferior function of personality, and his whole interpretation of alchemy. Since he has placed them in such a prominent position in his theories, it is important that we know exactly why Jung considered the unconscious and the conscious compensatory, and we should see if his reasoning is sound. In his most concise treatment of the subject, Jung gives four reasons why this relationship must be compensatory; we will examine each of them separately to enumerate their weaknesses.

> 1. Consciousness has a threshold of intensity its contents must have reached—everything else is unconscious. ("The Transcendent Function," *CW* 8:132)

This statement is tautological. If we define the unconscious as everything that is not conscious and call everything over a certain threshold "conscious," by necessity everything else has not reached that threshold and is therefore not conscious, i.e., unconscious. However, we have already decided that logical reasons are not enough if we want to defeat any of Jung's assertions. Therefore, we must find empirical justification if we want to call this statement incorrect. Fortunately, Jung provides us with such justification in his assertion that unconscious contents can become conscious. Repeatedly, in his attempts to justify that archetypes are universal, he emphasizes that they have emerged spontaneously from the unconscious of his patient (e.g., "Dream Symbols of the Process of Individuation," 97). That is, they had not been prompted by any events in the patient's conscious life, nor by any suggestion from the psychoanalyst. For the patient in the "Dream Symbols" study, the mandala was supposed to be totally unpredicated in his experience. Whether or not this was in fact the case, Jung assumed that it was, and, therefore, we can use some anomalies in the facts of the case against him. If the mandala was an unknown symbol, we can ask what caused it to attain that "threshold of intensity" demanded of conscious contents. That is, if the symbol emerged to consciousness, it must have done so as the result of an expenditure of psychical energy upon it.

However, Jung's whole concept of attention and association runs contrary to this idea. He believes that ordinary, directed thinking is "tiring," while fantasy thinking is "non-exhaustive" ("Concerning the Two Kinds of Thinking," 11). That is, the expenditure of psychical energy produces conscious thought, and once exhaustion sets in, unconscious contents emerge. But for something to become apparent to the conscious mind, it must become conscious—by definition, the unconscious is not conscious, i.e., not known. For any unconscious content to attain a "threshold," psychical energy must be expended upon it, which makes it the product of directed thinking. However, if thinking can only be directed at conscious contents, the object of reflection is a conscious, not an unconscious, thought. Therefore, unconscious contents can never become conscious—this would be like trying to think about nothing. To think about nothing, we must reify it, which makes it something. So too is thinking about an unconscious content impossible. If we can conceive of it by the expenditure of effort, it is conscious, but for it to accumulate enough psychical energy to break the threshold of consciousness, the energy must be expended upon it.

The truly ludicrous nature of this last point will become clear when we consider the second of Jung's proofs as to why the unconscious should compensate, rather than oppose, the conscious.

2. Consciousness is directed, so it inhibits all incompatible material, which becomes unconscious. ("The Transcendent Function," *CW* 8:132)

To inhibit something is to expend psychical energy upon it, which runs contrary to the spontaneity Jung finds in unconscious material. If we direct psychical energy upon one item, we will soon become tired, and by Jung's own statements we can then expect that unconscious contents will become conscious ("Concering the Two Kinds of Thinking," 11). By this logic, directing psychical energy upon one item should actually cause more items to become conscious. This runs contrary to the idea that items can be repressed into the unconscious. In fact, it will soon become impossible for anything to be unconscious at all. If expending psychical energy on items raises them over the "threshold of consciousness," as Jung asserted in the first example, and if inhibiting requires the expenditure of psychical energy, as he has claimed in the second example, then those contents that Jung would like to inhibit in this second instance must actually become conscious by the psychical energy of inhibition. And if concentration produces fatigue, which allows still more unconscious contents to rise to consciousness, the unconscious will soon be left with nothing at all. We know that psychical energy can be transformed into symbols and rituals ("On Psychical Energy," 47), but in order for that psychical energy to be transformed into the symbol or the ritual, it must have been in another form to begin with. This other form is the unconscious content. However, if psychical energy used to inhibit the unconscious content inheres in the object, then that object tautologically carries energy, which should propel it over the "threshold of consciousness" from Jung's first statement. If the energy used to inhibit the unconscious content is not enough to propel it over the threshold of consciousness, then the directed attention cannot be enough to propel the other content into consciousness either. Certainly, Jung has contended that "we cannot prove scientifically that a relation of equivalence exists between physical and psychic energy" (ibid., 15). However, we can at least assume that, because psychic energy is a "relatively closed system" (ibid., 18), if we take energy from one object, we give it to another. This is inherent in the definition of a "closed system." If we have taken enough psychical energy away from the first content that it falls below the "threshold of consciousness," giving the energy to the second object makes it conscious. However, taking away the energy from the first object is not the same as inhibition, which is an expenditure of psychical energy. Rather, expending the psychical energy on the second object will eventually tire the conscious mind, allowing the first object to come to consciousness as well. Inhibition is an expenditure of psychical energy and is directed thinking; if fantasy is spontaneous, as Jung has said it is ("Concerning the Two Kinds of Thinking," 11), then inhibited contents cannot emerge in fantasy. If inhibited material is unconscious, then fantasy cannot contain unconscious material. Again, Jungian theory has no answer.

Before we leave this point entirely, it is worth pointing out one more problem with psychical energy. If, as we have just seen, Jung calls psychical energy a "relatively closed system," then we can expect it to at least accord with other closed systems, or else it loses any value it could possibly have as a theoretical construct (in accepted science, there is no such thing as a "relatively closed" system—systems are either closed or open). More precisely, we can demand that psychical energy be subject to the Second Law of Thermodynamics. But if psychical energy does follow this law, which says that all closed systems will eventually degenerate to entropy, then we cannot predict the behavior of the psyche. If energy is expended upon items to repress them into the unconscious, then at the moment of entropy all items will become conscious. However, if psychic energy is expended upon objects to keep them conscious, then at the moment of entropy all items will sink into unconsciousness. Jung considers neither possibility.

> 3. Consciousness is the momentary process of adaptation, while the unconscious contains material of the personal and collective past. ("The Transcendent Function," *CW* 8:132)

Once more, Jung has made a logically circular statement. If we define consciousness as all psychic activity occurring at the moment and define the unconscious as containing everything not in consciousness, we must therefore posit that the unconscious contains everything in every past. However, the two categories overlap when we consider memory. Memory is a past element, but the act of remembering occurs in the present. Thus, the content is both conscious and unconscious at the same time, which for Jung is an impossibility. Memory is an empirical fact, so we can use it to discount this statement outright. As well, Jung himself says that dreams can be anticipatory ("Dream Analysis in its Practical Application," 9). The very idea of "anticipating" carries inextricable connotations of future activity—only a fool waits for something that has already occurred. Here again, Jung contradicts himself.

4. The unconscious contains all fantasy combinations not yet conscious. ("The Transcendent Function," *CW* 8:132)

This assertion directly correlates with the third statement, that the unconscious contains past contents. Here, Jung makes a normative claim—that the content of all future fantasy will come from events in the past. Definitions such as this necessitate the collective unconscious in that fantasies containing material that has not occurred in the subject's experience must have come from somewhere. Certainly, the entire phenomenon of science fiction fantasy jars with this view in that it attempts to predict the future—societies in films such as *Metropolis* and *Blade Runner* bear little if any resemblance to any society that has ever occurred in the past, and if fantasies depict past contents, no such predictions of the future can ever be made. However, this is not the definitive refutation we require here—Jung could concoct an "archetype of bleak future" or some other construct. However, if we take Jung's second of these four "proofs" at face value, ignoring our refutation of it, we can then put Jung into a quandary here. If an unconscious content becomes conscious and is then repressed back into the unconscious, it is not covered by this statement. Certainly, the content was unconscious by this definition before it became conscious, but what about after? "Not yet" means something categorically different than "no longer"— "not yet" implies that the content has not been conscious but will be, whereas "no longer" means that the content has been conscious and may or may not do so again. Under this fourth definition of the conscious-unconscious relationship, previous fantasies go into limbo.

Jung himself also defeats this fourth proof in another paper that bears looking into here because it will lead us nicely into another question about the relationship between the conscious and the unconscious. When discussing dreams, Jung has repeatedly made the point that they and their contents derive from the unconscious and as Jung's career progressed, that unconscious became the collective unconscious. However, even he had to admit that some dreams seem to pertain directly to current events. For example, if a woman has to present her Ph.D. dissertation, we can expect that her dreams the night before may be of her presenting that dissertation. This is obviously not a collective content, and Jung admits as much.

I do not in any way deny the possibility of "parallel" dreams, that is, of those whose meaning falls in with the attitude of consciousness,

> or reinforces it. But, in my experience at least, these are fairly rare.
> ("Dream Symbols of the Process of Individuation," 100)

If we, along with *The Concise Oxford Dictionary,* define "fantasy" as "image-inventing faculty, esp. when extravagant or visionary," it quickly becomes clear that, while the word carries the connotations of "extravagant" and "visionary," they are not integral to the definition. That is, central to the idea of "fantasy" is that its contents must not be an actual record of fact; not that it must be unrealistic. The woman's dream about her dissertation is fantastic not because it is extraordinary, but because it is not actually occurring. If we compare this statement with Jung's fourth proof for the compensatory relationship, we see that the two are incompatible. The dream content is fantastic in that more specific sense ("Concerning the Two Kinds of Thinking," 17). For this reason, it must come from the unconscious to fit with Jung's general theory. In the case of the Ph.D. student, it comes from consciousness. She therefore provides a falsifying instance for the theory.

In the case we have just detailed, the concept of the collective unconscious was shown to be logically inconsistent. However, we can extend this to a more general problem with the collective unconscious, namely that it is not necessary at all. At one point, Jung asks himself "are these inclusive concepts after all necessary?" ("Spirit and Life," 86), but he does so in the context of discussing spirit and living beings. We can stretch this question to encompass a far greater portion of Jungian theory—the collective unconscious itself. Jung places much stock in the existence of the collective unconscious, both proving it and basing proofs on it countless times. If we can take some proofs for its existence and produce other explanations that fall more in line with accepted scientific knowledge, then we can question the need for it to exist at all.

> The classic examples of unconscious psychic activity are to be found in pathological states. Almost the whole symptomatology of hysteria, of the compulsion neuroses, of phobias, and very largely of schizophrenia, the commonest mental illness, has its roots in unconscious psychic activity. We are therefore fully justified in speaking of an unconscious psyche. ("The Structure of the Psyche," *CW* 8:297)

From this statement, one of the most succinct in the *Collected Works,* we can see that Jung makes his proof of the collective unconscious contingent upon our accepting his hypotheses about mental illness. He "proves" the universality of the archetypes by appeal to the collective unconscious, more precisely by "the psychopathology of mental disturbances that are characterized by an irruption of the collective unconscious" ("Instinct and the Unconscious," *CW* 8:281). In his mind, these sorts of mental disturbances are best exemplified by schizophrenia, a topic on which he wrote extensively throughout his life (though in most of those writings he called it "dementia praecox"—we will use the more common term). In his last writing on the subject, he made quite clear the link between schizophrenia and his conception of the collective unconscious:

> It was this frequent reversion to archaic forms of association found in schizophrenia that first gave me the idea of an unconscious not consisting only of originally conscious contents that have got lost, but having a deeper layer of the same universal character as the mythological motifs which typify human fantasy in general. ("Schizophrenia," 3:565)

In light of this admission, it is no wonder that after years of waffling on the subject, Jung comes out in the same paper to say that although he leaves open the possibility of a biological cause for schizophrenia, he believes "the psychogenic causation of the disease is more probable than the toxic causation" (ibid., 570, emphasis removed). If he was to admit a biological cause for schizophrenia, as he did in other papers (e.g., "Recent Thoughts on Schizophrenia," *CW* 3:548), then he would have to allow for a biological substratum in which the archetypes could be found. This, for the most part, he is unwilling to do. Granted, he does admit that "if there is any analogy between psychic and physiological processes, the organising system of the brain must lie subcortically in the brain stem" ("Schizophrenia," *CW* 3:582). However, he does not say whether or not this analogy must exist, and he is on record as saying that "the microscopic lesions of the brain often found in schizophrenia [he] would, for the time being, regard as secondary symptoms of degeneration, like the atrophy of the muscles in hysterical paralyses" ("Mental Disease and the Psyche," *CW* 3:503). As such, he has boxed himself into a corner where he is forced to accept the psychogenic element as the cause of schizophrenia. As for the nature of this psychogenic element, he sees it as more probably a particularly strong affect than a weakness of the ego-complex ("Schizophrenia," *CW* 3:580), though the end result is the same—diminished capacity to form associations. Schizophrenics, according to Jung, associate very superficially, through such similarities as sound ("The Psychology of Dementia Praecox," *CW* 3:23), rather than along more meaningful grounds.

This criterion for schizophrenia brings us to Jung's early experiments on word-association. Through a series of tests, Jung elucidated a scheme by which he was able to categorize different word associations by type along such dimensions as internal, external, or sound association; and he could further subdivide in each type, splitting sound association into associations by word completion, sound, or rhyme ("The Associations of Normal Subjects," *CW* 2:111). These experiments, being of the form and content of science, can be criticized on methodological grounds, such as the fact that Jung saw complexes only where response either took a long time or differed from test to test, where it might seem more consistent with psychoanalytic theory that a complex would produce a stereotyped response that would actually be produced the quickest. However, any such criticism, though interesting, would be meaningless; Jung later abandoned the method he himself pioneered, seeing dream analysis as a "more penetrating method" ("New Paths in Psychology," *CW* 7:432).

When he abandoned the method by which he discovered the collective unconscious, however, he did not abandon the collective unconscious along with it. Looking at the chronology of his early papers, we can see a definite progression in which the word-association test would come to be insufficient for his needs, while simultaneously the case material would indicate something more than the simple Freudian notion of the unconscious. "The Associations of Normal Subjects" came out in 1904, and its use flourished around that time. In 1906, Jung made the statement that the complex revealed through the association test is the root of dreams and hysterical symptoms ("Association, Dream, and Hysterical Symptom," *CW* 2:858), also producing his work on "The Psychology of Dementia Praecox"." With his decision in this second paper that schizophrenics have reduced attention, and that reduced attention in normal people produces superficial associations ("The Psychology of Dementia Praecox," *CW* 3:24), we can see the basis for his assumption that schizophrenia is actually an extreme version of a condition that affects everyone to a greater or lesser extent. This combined with his assertion that the material produced by schizophrenics is of a mythological character (ibid., 133) presages the link he will later draw, namely that the reduced attention allows this mythological material to come through. After this "discovery," Jung started to encounter cases such as "Number

Dreams," where the standard association test could not explain the numerological data he felt so strongly was both present and valid. "The Psychology of Number Dreams" was reported in 1911; in 1912, Jung produced "New Paths," where he officially abandons the word-association test in favor of psychoanalysis.

This little diversion has shown us one very important fact—that as he found material that could not be explained by standard Freudian procedures and theories, Jung looked beyond those theories to find other constructs that could explain the material. When he had agreed with the Freudian outlook, he had noted mythological parallels with the material he analyzed and explained them in Freudian terms (e.g., "On the Psychology and Pathology of So-called Occult Phenomena"); once he abandoned Freud, he would abandon the Freudian explanations as well, which would leave this mythical material unexplained. Having embarked on this voyage into mythology, he neglected to consider other routes to the truth, because he subjectively felt that the one he had chosen to follow would in fact lead there. However, Popper makes very clear that subjective feelings of certainty cannot be used to justify a scientific claim (Popper, p. 47). Popper's criteria for a science have little effect on something like analytic psychology, which considers itself not only unscientific but antiscientific, but he does bring to light one point worth noting here. When Jung undertook his mythological studies, the subjective feeling of certainty he entertained was neither questioned nor abandoned in spite of the fact that he had since discarded as useless the avenues that had led to this feeling. As such, he went into the mythological texts looking to find something and found it. He then related the mythological material back to the assertions he had made in "The Psychology of Dementia Praecox" without considering that he had discarded the methodology that had led him to make those assertions. It is as if we were to throw out the Qur'an upon publication of a commentary upon it, because this commentary explained the original book. The fact remains, the original Qur'an could and has led to hundreds of different conclusions as to what it "really" means; so too could Jung's word-association tests. Keeping the interpretation, Jung discarded the primary fact. If it is not rational to hold an interpretive representation as a factual belief (Sperber, 172), it is even less rational to cling to the interpretive representation while consciously discarding the factual beliefs that led to it.

In short, Jung threw out his method but kept the conclusions, which were not even all that sound to begin with—to say that reduced attention in normal people is the same as the attention of schizophrenics requires more justification than simple induction from the results of a simple test. But even if these conclusions were sound, they could not be divorced from their method any more than quantum theory can be divorced from Newtonian mechanics. Newton's theories were a necessary antecedent to quantum theory, and the discoveries of the latter can be reduced to the former. Jung has done the equivalent of discovering quantum theory, then reasoning that because Democritus posited the atom, we can use Democritus's writings rather than Newton's theories to predict particle behavior. Not only by the standards of science, but by the standards of logic, this will not do.

This brings us back to our original reason for looking into schizophrenia in such detail. Since schizophrenics have observed the same phenomena as Jung, can their existence be explained by other means than the collective unconscious? When we come to deal with the archetypes, we will discuss the specific case from which Jung formulated his concept of the collective unconscious; for now, it is enough to look at schizophrenia in general. Jung saw the neural lesions in the brains of schizophrenics as secondary to the psychogenic cause for their disease. This runs directly contrary to other opinions as to the genesis of mental disease, which have circulated for over 100 years (Andreason, 1381). Schizophrenias are divided into two broad categories, those showing positive symptoms and those showing negative symptoms. Positive symptoms are aberrations of normal functioning, such as hallucinations and delusions, while negative symptoms are displayed as a loss of normal functioning, such as obsessive-compulsive disorder and anxiety (ibid.). By these standards, Jung's patients seem to have always displayed positive symptoms, and these are harder to locate in the brain than negative ones (ibid., 1382). Nonetheless, in spite of the fact that failure to locate lesions visible to the naked eye was enough to convince some early psychiatrists that these lesions did not exist (ibid., 1381), other techniques have been developed that lend support to the neural hypothesis of schizophrenia. These techniques have been successful in examination of both positive and negative symptoms, though again, positive symptoms have shown more conclusive results. Nonetheless, results such as these strike a very serious blow to Jung's theories about schizophrenia.

At this point, we may ask ourselves, so what? Jung never purported to be a neurologist; if his theories are not compatible with neurology, can we hold that against him? In a word, yes. We can criticize anyone who justifies the existence of the collective unconscious, a mental and not physiological phenomenon, on the basis that "almost the whole symptomatology of hysteria, of the compulsion neuroses, of phobias, and very largely of schizophrenia, the commonest mental illness, has its roots in unconscious psychic activity," ("The Structure of the Psyche," *CW* 8:297). That is, Jung has staked the collective unconscious on disturbances in the psyche, which, when they become pathological, express themselves as schizophrenia. However, modern science proposes that the schizophrenias can be located in the brain, and quite probably have something to do with the dopamine pathways (Andreason, 1384). At this, Jung runs into a dilemma. Either he has to locate the archetypes in neural material, and not simply in the brain stem but rather throughout the cerebrum, or he has to posit a locus of interaction between the brain and the collective unconscious and a mechanism by which this occurs. As we saw in the last chapter, Jung does neither. Certainly, to posit a locus of interaction could leave him sounding like Descartes and his pineal gland, but if Jung is not willing to tell us how the mind and the body interact, he should not be surprised to see us look for explanations that circumvent this problem. Accepting a purely neural origin and degeneration as responsible for schizophrenia and the other so-called "mental" diseases does exactly that.

However, if we accept a neural origin for the hallucinations and delusions of schizophrenia, and if the collective unconscious is not a neural phenomenon, then these hallucinations and delusions cannot come from the collective unconscious. For that reason, Jung could not accept any neural hypotheses about schizophrenia. However, attributing mental disease to the brain and not the mind is not only more consistent with science in general, but it discards certain extraneous assumptions that Jung's views require. For us to accept Jung's ideas about mental disease, we must also accept the collective unconscious and the archetypes. But, as we have already seen, the archetypes are logically and empirically inadequate concepts. Neurology has found a more plausible nonmental explanation for mental disease than that of the collective unconscious.

In his discussion, Jung again grasps at the explanation that corresponds with his nonmaterialism rather than acquiescing to the simpler, physicalist explanation.

We have briefly discussed synchronicity in our discussion of Mithraism, and will not repeat what we said there, but here it is worth looking into the reasons Jung thought synchronicity to be so solidly supported that he later used it as proof to support such conclusions as that being itself is composed of one unitary aspect ("The Conjunction,"

14:662). That is, Jung felt synchronicity strongly enough supported that he was willing to base metaphysical, not just empirical, claims upon it. This is in spite of the fact that he claimed his works on synchronicity itself were not final proof of his views but rather conclusions from empirical evidence and that they were merely submitted for our approval ("Synchronicity," *CW* 8:947). They themselves were not considered metaphysical, but they soon supported metaphysical claims. This shows that he considered them well-supported, so we will look at the two different circumstances on which Jung based his conclusions and see how they stack up.

In more discussions than simply that of synchronicity, Jung places quite a bit of stock in the experiments of J. B. Rhine into the phenomenon of extrasensory perception. On the basis of these experiments, which alleged that people could discern the contents of various random containers (e.g., a deck of cards), Jung determined that a tense emotional state leads to the activation of a preexisting, correct, but unconscious image that enables the conscious mind to get more than the chance level of hits ("Synchronicity," *CW* 8:857). We are not interested in Rhine's methodology, although it leaves much to be desired; as D. O. Hebb points out, Rhine's results defy physiology and physics, and even if Rhine were right, he would have to show very overwhelming reason for us to restructure the nature of scientific inquiry (Hebb 1951, 5). Rather, we are interested in how Jung interpreted Rhine's results and what conclusions he based upon them. Jung saw Rhine's results as "irrefutable" ("On Synchronicity," *CW* 8:981), and as proving that synchronistic events were not merely coincidental.

> Synchronous phenomena . . . prove that a content perceived by an observer can, at the same time, be represented by an outside event, without any causal connection. From this it follows that the psyche cannot be localised in space, or that space is relative to the psyche. The same applies to the temporal determination of the psyche and the psychic relativity of time. (ibid., 996).

Saying that the psyche transcends space and time are fairly substantial claims for someone who claimed not to be a metaphysician ("Christ, A Symbol of the Self," *CW* 9[ii]:122). Certainly, Rhine's results suggest this (although Rhine's work has been conclusively refuted—see Hines pp. 82–84 for details). Nonetheless, whether or not extrasensory perception extends independently of space and time, we cannot empirically test this. If, as Jung says, our predicting a coincidence in advance shows that it is not due to chance ("On Synchronicity," *CW* 8:974), then in every instance where what Rhine might determine to be extrasensory perception, we actually have proof of extrasensory perception. However, if we predict that the coincidence will not occur, then we have not disproved synchronicity, but merely this instance of it.

Again, we find John Smith's ideas about symbolic thinking to be useful here. "Concepts of randomness and of symbolic thinking are incompatible" because if nothing is due to chance, then every event is a reflection of a great cosmic order (J. Smith, 204). Jung himself admits this view, calling Taoism and Leibniz's theory of pre-established harmony synchronistic because in them no event is caused—rather, everything is preordained, with an illusion of causality grafted on top ("Synchronicity," *CW* 8:922; *CW* 8:937). In addition, Jung believes "any unprejudiced observer will admit" that divination is synchronistic, because its coincidences cannot be meaningfully explained if we assume "that they really are what they appear to be," that is, that they are meaningful coincidences (ibid., 866). But perhaps the most significant example of preestablished harmony Jung invokes is that of astrology. Jung spends a good part of "Synchronicity" detailing an experiment looking into synchronicity between marital status and astrology (ibid., 872–915). One aspect of Jung's conclusion is particularly interesting. When presented with the fact that no statistical relationship could be asserted between the two variables, Jung says this fact conclusively proves the synchronicity of the relationship—if the statistics had conclusively proved the relationship, the relationship would not appear to be coincidental, and synchronicity explains meaningful coincidence (ibid., 904). That is, astrology and marital status must be related through synchronicity because they are not related statistically, but sometimes good astrological signs and marital status occur in tandem, and this cannot be due to chance. Ignoring the fact that Rhine felt his ESP experiments proved that ESP existed at a level above chance (Rhine, 34), we can instead point out the innate absurdity of Jung's logic. He asserts that the two facts must be related, not because he can objectively prove such a relationship, but because he finds meaning in it. Yet again, the subjective feeling of certainty guides Jung's methodology, showing the most common aspect of pseudo-science—"the nonrefutable or irrefutable hypothesis" (Hines, 1).

We see this subjective feeling reemerge in another support Jung invokes for synchronicity—correspondences. "Synchronicity is a modern differentiation of the obsolete concept of correspondence . . . not based on philosophical assumptions but on empirical experiment and experimentation" ("On Synchronicity," *CW* 8:995). We have already dealt with that portion of the statement after the ellipsis, leaving us only to show that Jung himself was quite ambivalent on the topic of correspondence. Certainly, he admired Paracelsus for basing his treatments on correlations with the stars rather than on dissection, because Jung saw him as healing the spirit, not the body ("Paracelsus the Physician," *CW* 15:22). Whether this analysis of Paracelsus is correct (a facet of Jungian theory proven incorrect in chapter five), it does not sit well with Jung's favorite metaphor in the "Synchronicity" essays. Repeatedly, he draws the analogy we have previously encountered, between his formulation of synchronicity and Galileo's discovery of the moons of Jupiter ("Synchronicity," *CW* 8:861). Jung sees himself in the same position as Galileo; he has uncovered a new phenomenon, but the other scientists will not come look through the telescope, so to speak. It seems rather ironic to see Jung invoke this example to bemoan his own situation, then in the same paper say that such relationships as that between the organs and the stars in which Paracelsus believed are synchronistic (ibid., 931). Perhaps he should have paid some heed to words he himself proposed in an early paper, that "we must always bear in mind that, despite the most beautiful coincidence between the facts and our ideas, our explanatory principles are none the less only points of view, that is, phenomena of the *psychological and aprioristic conditions* under which thinking takes place" ("On Psychical Energy," 4, emphasis added).

In spite of this early caveat, Jung referred to correspondences throughout his life, and he can be criticized on this point as well. Even among his last works, he invokes a correspondence between the development of a human fetus, morphologically resembling those of the other animals and then becoming specifically human, and the development of the psychic contents, starting as undifferentiated and then becoming differentiated ("Approaching the Unconscious," 66). This belief in correspondences and the belief in synchronicity both belie a bedrock of finality in thinking. Jung himself admits as much, calling the concept of finality "not only logically possible [but] also an indispensible, explanatory principle, since no explanation of nature that is purely mechanistic suffices" ("On Psychical Energy," 2). "A purely causalistic approach is too narrow to do justice to the true significance, either of the dream, or of the neurosis" ("Dream Analysis in its Practical Application," 7). Just as the fetus develops through the animal stages to the uniquely human, so does the psyche develop from the most unconscious to the most individuated; for both of these statments to make sense, their subjects must be developing toward some goal. However, without the goal, the concept becomes ludicrous.

While this sort of a non-goal-oriented standpoint may not be too popular with Jung or biological theorists or fundamentalist Christians, its utility quickly becomes clear when we explore one instance where Jung invokes finality to explain a concept. In the first chapter, when we discussed "Number Dreams," we saw Jung's concept of the unconscious take on a categorically different nature from Freud's simple wish-fulfilling psyche. The elaborate number symbolism must mean something, and something that relates to the patient's problem. We will not repeat the description of the number symbols from the first chapter, but we will once again pause to point out that, in one dream, the number "152" was broken down into the different addresses at which the patient's mistress had lived ("On the Significance of Number Dreams," 193). Certainly, the fact that this symbol exists at all fulfills a wish even in the Jungian interpretation, namely that the man should reconcile his personal difficulties. However, the fact that the number can be interpreted to indicate the addresses shows that the wish fulfillment has more than just a purpose but a meaning, which is only described by this interpretation. Otherwise, Jung reasons, the patient would not have dreamed it—no dream content is irrelevant, and this interpretation is the only one that gives relevance to the number. Joseph Jastrow has shown in a quite amusing manner that when gematria (the technical term for numerology) is itself interpreted numerologically, we prove that it "is all bunk" and "is all bible" at the same time (Jastrow, 271–72); and, if we try hard enough, we can divine that "Alphonse Capone" has such traits as universal love, artistic genius, and selfless service (ibid., 280). Jung would discard these concerns with a wave of the hand and a reminder that, as far as the patient is concerned, Jastrow's points would not mean anything. The numerological interpretation Jung provides is true because it provides an interpretation that means something to the patient and his current condition.

In the end, every instance we have enumerated in this chapter reduces to one simple difficulty we have with Jung's proofs. They are not supported by overwhelming evidence, but rather by Jung's own opinions. By no means are they totally unsupported in the empirical realm— quite the contrary. Repeatedly, Jung takes a symbol, enumerates several other instances of it, and induces a universal conclusion that he feels to be right. But even when his conclusions or premises come under attack by experts in the field, as they did in the case of Lévy-Bruhl, he clings to them. When he could not find any objectively testable criterion to support his subjective beliefs, he created synchronicity rather than discarding them. In short, Jung was unconcerned with actually proving anything he said. Rather, he felt his proofs to be self-evident, and he stuck with them even when he was wrong.

7

Personality Theory

Having weighed in the balance and found wanting every one of Jung's theories we have looked into so far, we would be remiss in not considering that area where he actually made a reasonable contribution to the advancement of scientific knowledge. Certainly, we purport to be exposing what is wrong with Jung, but if we were to gloss over his achievements, concentrating only on his fallacies and mistakes, we would be guilty of no less an offense than that of which we accused Jung in our chapter on religion. And for all of his strange statements and his forced logic and every other problem we have had with his works so far, Jung did make a substantial contribution to the field of personality theory. *Psychological Types* is not the definitive book on the topic, and certainly there were both problems and oversights in his approach, but this section of the *Collected Works* is definitely seminal in the field. All investigators after Jung in both the psychoanalytic and experimental psychology branches of psychology have had to at least consider his thoughts on personality theory, whether they accept them or not.

That Jung should play such a role on any stage, especially that of experimental psychology, seems rather odd in light of the problems we have had with him so far. However, as we examine Jungian personality theory, we will find that most of the difficulties we have enumerated with Jung's works in general will vanish, and those that remain do not impede acceptance of the theory. For example, when Jung invokes the archetypes to support his typology, he does not do so in the absence of any other supporting evidence. *Psychological Types* is an anomaly in the *Collected Works* in that Jung's feet stay firmly planted on the ground, although occasionally his head does voyage into the clouds.

For once, his categorical disdain for empirical evidence does not rear its head, and because of that he has come up with quite a solid base upon which later researchers have been able to build. Nonetheless, personality theory provides us with a unique opportunity; with Jung's work being at the forefront of both the psychoanalytic and experimental psychology fields, we have the potential for a partial reconciliation between the two schools. Unfortunately, that has not occurred; while psychoanalysts have spent their time elucidating descriptions of the various types, experimentalists have worked on tests to determine the type of a particular individual. Both have been "successful" by their own standards, the psychoanalysts in producing long essays telling of the "inner psychic state" that drives each type, the experimentalists in devising complex tests in order to classify individuals. We will deal with one of these tests, the Myers-Briggs Type Indicator, in due course. However, it does bear repeating here that Jung did not expressly dictate either approach to his typological theories. He simply produced the book, and once it was over, he looked back very rarely, almost as if it had been a labor rather than a pleasure to write.

With that last statement, we skirt the boundaries of the limits we have set for ourselves. We cannot know whether or not Jung enjoyed writing *Psychological Types,* nor should we try to decipher it from the manuscript. To do this would be to fall victim to a similar interpretive fallacy as that into which we have accused Jung of falling. However, we can say that the works on typology do seem to form quite a concise unit in Jung's larger corpus. Unlike the archetypes, the personality types do not crop up repeatedly in different forms. Although it could conceivably be said of an image that it symbolizes extraversion, or even an extraverted world view, Jung never chose to look at symbols in that light. This could shed some light into how Jung saw the types, that they were not items for self-discovery but rather clinical tools that he used in practice. Jung saw the different types as different filters through which a person would look at events in the world. The extraverted thinking type sees the world and its affairs in a categorically different way from the introverted feeling type, and Jung is forced to consider these empirical realities in his consideration of the types. Certainly, he does talk of dreams being empirical facts, but he treats them as a categorically different sort of fact than he does the personality type.

The personality type, unlike the dream, is not subjected to the interpretive hypothesis. "In so far as we judge others only by affects, we show that our chief, and perhaps only, criterion is affect" ("Psychological Types," 296). To put it another way, while Jung will occasionally see archetypes being perceived better by a certain personality type, he does not look to the personality type in order to find the expression of an archetype. Perhaps this viewpoint is forced upon him because personality types are categorically different and therefore do not belie any sort of universalism. If there is an archetype of extraversion, then is the introvert living in privation of that archetype or expressing a different archetype of introversion? If Jung was to say that the introvert lives in privation of the archetype of extraversion, then he might be seen as making a value judgment that introverts are wrong in their outlook and must work to adopt the extraverted outlook. This, as we saw when we considered the problem of relativism, Jung would not do. On the other hand, if he were to say that there are archetypes of both introversion and extraversion, then he would be postulating a conflict in the archetypal world, which would be impossible to assimilate. The alchemical paradoxes, as we have seen, were set up in opposition in order to illumine, not to conflict—they are Hegelian, but the type paradox is not. By no means should we interpret this to say that Jung sat down and actively thought out the different ramifications of these two archetypal alternatives. We have no reason to believe that he did. However, it is a happy coincidence that his typological theories do deftly skirt the question of the archetypes in all but purely tangential ways. It would be wrong to believe that Jung avoided all discussion of the archetypes in *Psychological Types;* but when he does bring them up, they arise in such a way that they can be comfortably ignored in considering the theories.

After such a long preamble, it is time to sit down and investigate exactly how Jung perceived the types. We have already mentioned briefly such types as "extraverted thinking" and "introverted feeling;" the conjunction of the two words should tell us something about how Jungian typology works. The personality type is composed of two elements: the "general attitude type;" and the "function-type" ("General Description of the Types," 412). Every person combines one of two general attitude types: introversion or extraversion; and one of four function-types: thinking, feeling, sensation, and intuition. Jung defines pure instances of the four function-types as follows:

> *thinking:* "the function of intellectual cognition, and the forming of logical conclusions"
> *feeling:* "a function of subjective evaluation"

> *sensation:* "all perception by means of the sense organs"
> *intuition:* "perception by way of the unconscious, or perception of an unconscious content"
>
> ("Psychological Types," 305)

We can ignore the reference to the unconscious for now; later we will see it is not integral to the definition of intuition or any other element of typology for that matter.

Either of the two general attitude types can take on any of the four function-types, thus permitting eight combinations of personality: extraverted thinking, extraverted feeling, extraverted sensation, extraverted intuition, introverted thinking, introverted feeling, introverted sensation, and introverted intuition. Jung could not resist a quaternity arrangement here; each of the four function-types is opposed to another, thinking to feeling and sensation to intuition. He calls thinking and feeling the rational types, because they exalt reason and judgment ("General Description of the Types," 452), while sensation and intuition are irrational types because they are primarily based on perception and the empirical (ibid., 468). However, it is significant to note that here Jung limits himself from making a universal claim: "had [he him]self chanced to possess a different individual psychology" the rational types may well have been called irrational types and vice versa (ibid., 453). As well, he admits that while introversion and extraversion may not be the only possible method for classifying the types, he uses it because he sees it as the best ("Psychological Types," 312). Whether or not he is correct in either of these statements, they cut a strange figure compared to the universalist attitude he espouses in his other works.

Jung sees a forerunner to the two general attitude types in nature, saying that they must arise from a "biological precursor" ("General Description of the Types," 414). In his eyes, nature adapts to change in two ways—by increased fertility, providing more offspring to try to survive a stressor if not individually then as a species, or by increased self-defense, attempting to ward off the stressor, individually (ibid., 414). In children, the introvert shows a defensive attitude and a propensity toward a reflective, thoughtful manner; the extravert shows marked assurance and enterprise, quickly adapting to any environmental change ("Psychological Types," 303–304). These statements are rather odd to see in any of Jung's works. Not only do they appeal to external, empirical evidence, but they allow for falsification. Granted, we still do not have the sophisticated techniques for analyzing the behavior of children, which falsifying Jung's statements may require, but if such techniques were to be developed, they could conceivably falsify these claims. This is a pattern often repeated throughout all of Jung's typological works and very rarely outside them. The ideas espoused in *Psychological Types* would have to be falsifiable in order to be adopted by experimentalists; they are, so they have been.

Turning to extraversion in people, Jung says that "if a man so thinks, feels, and acts, in a word so *lives,* as to correspond *directly* with objective conditions and their claims, whether in a good sense or ill, he is extraverted" ("General Description of the Types," 417). Again, this statement is falsifiable—people who do not have this viewpoint simply are not extraverted. After having defined what it is to be extraverted, Jung then takes this general attitude type and applies it to each of the four function-types, defining in observable, falsifiable terms what exactly would constitute each one. Those of the extraverted thinking type orient themselves by objects and objective data; while their ideas are not necessarily concretistic, they must be received, not generated (ibid., 428). To those of the extraverted feeling type, the object determines the type of emotional response to it, such as peer pressure (ibid., 446). For the extraverted sensitive type life is the accumulation of sensory stimuli, inhibiting the subjective element of sensation (ibid., 457). Finally, the extraverted intuitive type displays a perceptive and penetrating vision into the object, but only the result can show how much of the perceived material is actually in the object and how much is "perceived into" it (ibid., 461).

All four of these extraverted types have an inferior function, which is repressed into the unconscious. In this context, the term "unconscious" actually refers to the shadow—the personal shadow—although Jung had not yet devised this terminology when he wrote *Psychological Types.* This limiting factor on the "unconscious" here may go some way toward explaining why Jung's later works do not deal so much with the personality types—because they deal so much with the personal unconscious, inquiry into which Jung chose to abandon quite early in his career in favor of elucidating the contents of the collective unconscious. In any case, the repressed function takes the opposite characteristic to the type that the person usually expresses. For example, the shadow of an extraverted thinking type is characterized by introverted feeling, which being unconscious is necessarily primitive and clumsy. Jungian personality therapy deals with integrating the "superior function" with the "inferior function" in order to produce a complex whole.

But we are jumping the gun here, detailing the inferior function before we have discussed every type. After all, we do not want to imply that extraversion is normal and introversion is abnormal, nor to assert the converse. When discussing the idea of relativism, we saw that Jung conspicuously avoids making any normative statements about general attitude type, exalting neither one over the other. For example, he makes it very clear that activity is uncorrelated with extraversion ("The Type Problem in the Discernment of Human Character," 186). In fact, he sees all eight different types as playing particular roles in society; for example, the extraverted intuitive type he sees as a potential leader, if that person avoids the pitfall of becoming egocentric ("General Description of the Types," 466). In Jung's eyes, no one type could ever replace any other, but merely fill the gap in society until a credible candidate from the most suited type came along. The introvert is just as important as the extravert, but in different ways.

Keeping this in mind, let us look into Jung's ideas of introversion. Unlike Freud, Jung did not see introversion as a maladapted view, simply "one that under all circumstances sets the self and the subjective psychological process above the object and the objective process, or at any rate holds its ground against the object" ("Introduction" to *Psychological Types*, 12). Here, Jung starts to invoke the idea of the collective unconscious in that he sees the introverted viewpoint as being governed by instincts, which he sees as products of the collective unconscious; when introverts become neurotic, this just means they have more or less identified their egos with their selves ("General Description of the Types," 476–77). However, we can remove this reference to the collective unconscious, as Jung does when he also says that the object has too small a role in the introverted attitude (ibid., 477), and we are still left with a cogent theory. That is, to say that introverts look at the world through a subjective filter means the same thing as to say that they project unconscious contents. This is perhaps the best instance of how we are able to remove the contentious points of Jung's other theories from his typology and still be left with a complete set of beliefs afterward.

Those of the introverted thinking type orient themselves at decisive points through subjective data, collecting facts only as evidence or examples of a theory and never for their own sake (ibid., 481). The introverted feeling type is primarily controlled by subjective preconditions which are even more difficult to express than introverted thought, requiring artistic expression for full development (ibid., 489–91). The introverted sensitive type does not report sensations per se but rather subjective impressions given by the object that often, being archetypal, end up sounding like the "demon-in-every-closet" variety (ibid., 503). The introverted intuitive type apprehends the archetypes in perceived objects and reports a prophetic vision, making both the self and external objects symbolic (ibid., 510).

In these capsule descriptions of the introverted types, we have taken great pains to avoid relying upon the collective unconscious. However, as we saw in the very definitions of sensation and intuition, it cannot go without saying that the concept of the collective unconscious does play a very important role in Jung's conception of the types. Granted, even Jung admits that these eight descriptions are "Galtonesque family portraits" (ibid., 513), exaggerating the one type at the expense of the inferior function and secondary functions. However, this does not mean we can ignore the role of the unconscious and the archetypes in Jung's definitions. Because Jung sees the collective unconscious as playing such an important role in every consideration of the subjective, he would necessarily incorporate it into any definition of introversion that posits objects as being perceived through a subjective filter. Nonetheless, if we remove the concept of the collective unconscious, keeping only the second half of Jung's statement, we are still left with a very acceptable definition of introversion. To say that the introverted person forces objective perception through a subjective filter of past experience does not require the unconscious in order to make sense, and Jung's definitions allow for that. By the same token, we can say that the intuitive person makes associations quickly between new and past experiences, and this statement makes sense entirely without the concept of the unconscious. Jung did invoke the collective unconscious to help elucidate the introverted or intuitive types, but this was because he considered the unconscious to be definitively proven. Since disproving the collective unconscious and the archetypes does not disprove his typology, we can still consider the latter.

So let us consider other aspects of Jung's typology, namely the secondary function. As we have seen, Jung readily admitted that his capsule definitions of the types were exactly that, and not at all representative of what these types would look like when encountered in the real world. In the real world, every personality type is modified by secondary functions and the unconscious, inferior function. The primary function would still be most differentiated, but it would be modified by the secondary function as well. The secondary function can never be contradictory to the primary, and it must take the same general attitude as the primary function. Beyond that, Jung places no restrictions. For example, feeling can be supplemented by either sensation or intuition, but not by thinking. Nonetheless, only one function can be absolutely sovereign, because independent intervention of a secondary function would necessarily produce a different orientation that would at least partially contradict the first ("General Description of the Types," 514). Logically, this makes sense, and Jung claims to have tested this empirically and proven it (ibid., 514).

This again shows us how much his typology looks and acts like normal science. As well, the fact that Jung claims to have tested the secondary function supports the view we set forth earlier in this chapter, that the types are not archetypes but simply constructs that he used in clinical practice. Again and again, we have seen Jung say that the archetypes are not suitable for empirical testing in spite of their being derived from empirical evidence. The only elements of his theories we have seen him submit for empirical testing are his clinical constructs, those being the word-association test and his typology. Interestingly, both of these constructs measured items Jung considered to be held in the personal unconscious—complexes and personality—while the contents of the collective unconscious were rendered untestable, and, when he abandoned inquiry into the personal unconscious, he abandoned these tools along with it. Nonetheless, this concession to empiricism rings strangely in the *Collected Works,* and only begins to make some sense with the publication of "Psychological Factors Determining Human Behavior" over twenty years later. For the first time in over two decades, this paper sees Jung hearken back to introversion and extraversion, calling them "psychical modalities," to explain how human functioning can influence behavior ("Psychological Factors Determining Human Behavior," *CW* 8:250). In the same paper, Jung gives a hypothesis for how and why the four function-types develop unequally—because the psyche has an inherent tendency to split, certain parts are isolated and developed at the expense of others (ibid., 256). In this section, he does not make clear whether or not he considers the function-types to be archetypes. Nonetheless, in the concluding paragraphs of this paper Jung does explicitly say that he has attempted to gather together those aspects which, from the standpoint of "purely empirical psychology," play a leading role in determining human behavior (ibid., 261). That is, he saw his typology as empirically testable, and although he does invoke the unconscious and the archetypes in these pages, all this means is that we should consider them in an empirical sense as well. Jung has stipulated that he considers the archetypes to be above empirical testing ("The Conception of the Unconscious," 469); that is, he sees the archetypes as existing whether or not they can be proven to do so. In the absence of any similar statement regarding the types, we can assume that he allows for them to be tested by objective means, because he himself had tested them in this way and found them supported (e.g., "General Description of the Types," 514).

Regardless of how correct Jung happened to be in his theories of personality, we cannot forget that he was working in the scientific era, and for that reason we can expect him to use such tools in his inquiry as scientific method. However, he did not, and for that reason we cannot allow him to escape unscathed by criticism. When he would find in his clinical or scholarly studies such elements as a quaternity, Jung would always attempt to find a justification for it in a mythical source. The function-types turn out to be no exception: "just as, of the four sons of Horus, only one had a human head, so with the four basic functions, only one as a rule is fully conscious and differentiated" ("Psychological Types," 308). By the same token, he goes on to say, only one of the four function-types can ever be developed in any person. For that reason, his theories could never have been used for any scientific purpose in their original state. Science can never be satisfied with sheer poetic insight, no matter how brilliant it may be; if compared to atomic theories, Jung's typology follows more the lines of Democritus than Bohr. We could be excused for thinking that, if Jung had never come up with the concept of the collective unconscious and had remained content with personality theory and word-association, he could have gone down in history in a drastically different way. These ideas, while not scientific in themselves, can be rendered so; no matter how hard we try, we cannot say the same for the collective unconscious.

However, this is not the place to praise Jung, nor should we lament the direction his thought took. Instead, we should now consider how those who came after him took his materials and worked with them, producing radically different results. The psychoanalysts we can deal with almost summarily. To read a work such as "The Inferior Function" (Hillman) is to see how orthodox post-Jungian theorists have taken Jung's writings and worked with them to produce essays dealing with all of the types. These essays have the character of many of the essays Jung himself wrote in *Psychological Types,* such as "The Apollonian and the Dionysian," where he investigates the dichotomy presented in Nietzsche's *The Birth of Tragedy.* Certainly, they make a fascinating read, but as far as scientific tools go, they are totally useless. They require the existence of a subject, whom the psychoanalyst can then examine and, after many hours of investigation, derive a typological analysis, which may or may not be correct.

It took the non-Jungians to come up with a predictive test using Jung's personality types. According to Jung, a person's "real" personality is "partly that which every man distinguishes from himself as distinct from affect, and partly that in everyone which is regarded as inessential in the judgement of others" ("Psychological Types," 300). Characteristic of Jungian discourse, this statement is nothing on which to base an objective diagnosis. For that reason, experimental psychologists took *Psychological Types* and sifted through it, culling those elements that could be assimilated into a test and administered. As a result, two tests emerged: the Myers-Briggs Type Indicator and the Gray-Wheelwright Test. Since the Myers-Briggs is far more widely used in the field, we shall deal with it alone in our investigation. However, before we undertake our examination of how Jungian personality theory is used today, we can permit ourselves the luxury of one aside. It is ironic to note that, just as empirical tests are being devised to objectively test and tentatively support Jung's personality theories, Jungian circles have come to see these categories as controversial and have started to challenge them (Samuels, 68). Certainly, the tests are not infallible, and they are somewhat limited in that they can only measure three dimensions with any great certainty: extraversion versus introversion, introverted thinking versus extraverted feeling, and sensation versus intuition (ibid., 86). Nonetheless, this is the one spot where we can see the potential for a *rapprochement* between experimental psychology and analytic psychology, and just as the experimentalists are starting to build the bridge, the psychoanalysts are burning it at their end.

Having said that, we will now investigate just how Jungian theory has been applied in experimental psychology circles. Perhaps the best place to start is with one of the most vehement critics of psychoanalysis in all of its forms, Hans Eysenck. Eysenck compares the analytic cure to Skinner's "superstitious pigeon" studies (Skinner 1959c, Skinner and Morse), which tell how random application of a reward conditions an unrelated behavior in a group of pigeons. In Eysenck's eyes, the same principle applies in the psychoanalytic context—people who believe in psychoanalysis do so because their improvement reinforces the stimulus, that stimulus being the idea that the psychoanalysis is what made them improve (Eysenck: 1972, 32). This is just one instance of Eysenck's attacks on psychoanalysis; in other settings, he attacks such concepts as dream interpretation and the word-association test. For that reason, to see him advocate Jung's typology is a very great support indeed. Yet he repeatedly does just that. As far back as 1953, he referred to Jungian typology, especially in its correlation between general attitude type and particular mental disease (Eysenck 1953, 24). Jung believed that extraverts were more likely to develop the anxiety state commonly labelled "hysteria," while introverts were more likely to develop the obsessional state categorized as "psychasthenia" ("On Psychological Understanding," *CW* 3:418). Eysenck agreed, and was later able to invoke some experimental evidence to support this view (Eysenck and Eysenck, 50; Eysenck 1957, 257). However, this is not to say that Eysenck agreed with Jung's theories in their entirety. Calling the entire system of Jungian typology difficult to apply "in any rational manner" (Eysenck and Eysenck, 48), he advocated adopting its general framework while ignoring the technicalities (ibid., 49), perhaps because of such obviously psychoanalytic baggage as the archetypes.

Even this support in experimental psychology circles would have been enough to guarantee that Jungian typology would at least never be relegated to the back of the theoretical cupboard. However, the advent of the Myers-Briggs Type Indicator ensured that Jung's ideas would come to the fore in experimental psychology. This test, a 166-item verbal report scale, measures all three of the traditional dimensions of Jungian personality type, as well as a fourth—perceiving and judging—which Myers and Briggs saw as implicit in *Psychological Types* (Hunter and Levy, 379). Using this test, studies have advanced such hypotheses as the idea that there is no interaction between gender and personality type (ibid., 383). Furthermore, this test has suggested a correlation between personality type and imagery on the dimension measuring thinking against feeling (Ireland and Kernan-Schloss, 123), though no difference was found between introverts and extraverts with regard to the vividness of that imagery in the same investigation (ibid., 122). Perhaps because Jung himself was so interested in the paranormal, the Myers-Briggs test has been used to measure the correlation between Jungian personality type and belief in various paranormal phenomena (Levy and Ridley; Lester et al.), and has discovered some very interesting correlations, such as one between intuition and belief in witchcraft, spiritualism, precognition, and pseudo-sciences (Lester et al., 182). Some studies have even gone so far as to attempt to find a correlation between temporal lobe indicators and Jungian personality types (Huot et al., 841).

All of the above studies have agreed that the Myers-Briggs Type Indicator is a valid and reliable measure of Jungian personality types (see especially Levy and Ridley, 420), which runs against one part of Samuels' critique of the test. However, opinions are split as to whether or not the test has predictive validity. Some say it does (e.g., Hunter and Levy), while others are not so sure (e.g., Ireland and Kernan-Schloss). Samuels posits that the polarity of thinking against feeling in the Myers-Briggs test is more a phenomenon of the forced-choice nature of the questions than a true discovery (Samuels, 85), and he may well be right. Nonetheless, this should not lead us to totally discard Jungian typology, as the psychoanalysts have done. On the contrary, if we are presented with any compelling critique of the test, we can then attempt to modify it, so that the criticism will no longer apply, or if a better test is proposed, we should accept it instead. This shows even more how Jung's theories of personality and the Myers-Briggs test based upon them meet standard criteria for a science, in that they can both be falsified and revised to consider also that case that previously falsified them.

At this point, it could well be noted that, in fact, the Myers-Briggs reports are not so falsifiable as might be desired. A brief examination of several personality reports will show how universally applicable these typological analyses are.

1. Succeed by perseverance, originality, and the desire to do whatever is needed or wanted. Put their best efforts into their work. Quietly forceful, conscientious, concerned for others. Respected for their firm principles. Likely to be honored and followed for their clear convictions as to how best to serve the common good.

2. You appear to be a cheerful, well-balanced person. You may have some alternation of happy and unhappy moods, but they are not extreme now. You have few or no problems with your health. You are sociable and mix well with others. You are adaptable to social situations. You tend to be adventurous. Your interests are wide. You are fairly self-confident and usually think clearly.

3. Inquiry into the nature of the universe dominates your personality at this time, but this could change. Your horizons seem somewhat limited, but this limitation is self-imposed and the door could soon open. Sometimes it might seem like forces beyond your control are opposing you, but with enough perseverance you should overcome all obstacles.

4. Good at on-the-spot problem solving. Do not worry, enjoy whatever comes along. Tend to like mechanical things and sports, with friends on the side. Adaptable, tolerant, generally conservative in values. Dislike long explanations. Are best with real things that can be worked, handled, taken apart, or put together.

In fact, only the first and fourth of these reports describe actual Jungian types as determined by the Myers-Briggs Type Inventory. The second description is a "stock spiel" written so as to be applicable to anyone (Hyman, cited in Hines, 38). The third report was produced from a Tarot reading I performed on myself five minutes before typing this segment (September 9, 1991). As for the two Myers-Briggs reports, they are meant to apply to diametrical opposites—the first for the introverted, intuitive, feeling, judging type; the second for the extra-verted, sensitive, thinking, perceiving type. [INFJ] [ESTP]

The purpose of this exercise was not to dismiss the Myers-Briggs Type Inventory nor any other personality test. What it is meant to do is to show the dangers inherent in projective tests, namely that the test administrator may well believe that more has been discovered about the subject than is actually revealed in the description. Nonetheless, the Myers-Briggs Type Inventory reports do not contain so many "multiple outs" as the stock spiel and the Tarot reading. That is, they do make some definite, falsifiable statements as to the personality of the subject. The nonscientific assessments do not. People who do not dislike long explanations should not turn out to be ESTP; if they do, there has been a problem with the administration of the test or with the test itself. The Tarot and stock readings do not provide such falsifying instances. As well, the Myers-Briggs Type Inventory gains some respectability from the fact that its data comes from self-reports. This leaves no room for the suggestive techniques so often used by Tarot readers, "psychics" and others.

In his *Scientific Research*, Mario Bunge gives what he calls five "very obvious" rules of scientific method. It is worth listing them here, both to show how much the personality theories conform to them, and how much other Jungian theories, such as that of the archetypes, do not.

R1. State your problem precisely and, in the beginning, specifically . . .
R2. Try definite and somehow grounded conjectures rather than noncommital or wild hunches . . .

R3. Subject your assumptions to tough tests rather than to soft ones . . .

R4. Do not pronounce true a satisfactorily confirmed hypothesis: regard it as, at best, partially true . . .

R5. Ask why the answer should be as it is and not otherwise.

(Bunge, vol. 1, 10)

Discovering the archetypes has no precise goal, just a vague muddling around to fit the patient's thought patterns into preformed molds. Starting from the assumption that every symbol (that is, every thought that cannot be instantly decoded) expresses an archetype is about the most noncommital statement that could ever be made, and by its very nature does not allow for rigorous testing. Not only are archetypes eternal once found, but they are eternal even before they are found—the goal of Jungian analysis is to determine how they are expressed. However, perhaps most strikingly contrasted with Bunge's rules is the fact that, as far as Jung is concerned, archetypes need not be explained—they just *are* and must be dealt with instead.

On the other hand, discerning personality type has a specific goal—to see which of the eight categories best describes the patient. It starts from empirical evidence, and the secondary function and inferior functions pass for checks and balances against the original assumption; if the primary function is determined to be thinking and the secondary function to be feeling, something has gone wrong in the diagnosis. The fact that a patient can develop the inferior function allows for the diagnosis to be changed over time. But most importantly, grounding the personality type in empirical evidence from tests or even the clinical setting nonetheless provides reasons why the answer to the problem should be as it is rather than otherwise. Personality types are not archetypes; they are not the platypus, which can only be explained because it exists. Logical reasons can be given as to why the personality type must exist, and in support of a diagnosis. Certainly, the arrangement in fours may well be a result of Jung's predilection toward quaternities. Nonetheless, every person can be said to be of some type, no matter how many or how few types we may posit, and because each type is not universal to the human species, bumping up against the limits of our current typology just means we need to add another class, not that the whole idea of classifying is wrong.

This is not to say that Jung, in his personality theories, has come up with the ultimate statement on that topic. One limitation of Jungian theory is that it does not adequately explain the fact that people behave differently at different times. For example, while at one moment a soldier might react to being charged by an enemy by running away, ten minutes earlier the response might have been to stand and fight. This discrepancy in response is not adequately covered in the Jungian context. Has the soldier's personality type changed in the ten-minute period? Jung, even with his concepts of the secondary function and inferior functions, is able to define personality in the abstract, but he cannot account for very much actual behavior. Horowitz and Zilberg, with their construct of the supraordinate self organization, give a tool that can describe why the same person will act in different ways at different times due to differing perceptions of the self from moment to moment. For example, people running a marathon have a different perception of themselves as athletes while they run than they do while lying in bed with a cold, but at all times they remain the same individuals. At present, this idea has no predictive power. Perhaps Jung's typology, applied through the Myers-Briggs test, will in the future be reconciled with the supraordinate self organization or some similar construct to explain away the discrepancies in human behavior. Nonetheless, for now the Jungian theory remains subject to that criticism.

However, in the end we must allow for the fact that even a stopped clock is right twice a day and admit that in this particular instance Jung has shown the correct time. Not only is his personality theory firmly grounded in reality, but it has been picked up by experimental psychologists, who usually will not give the time of day to a psychoanalyst, and turned into an adequate, if imperfect, scientific tool. Before leaving personality theory altogether, it may be interesting to look at one area where Jung's ideas can be applied to explain a very relevant phenomenon. In one of his more famous works, Henri Bergson attempts to explain the nature of the comic. In the end, he comes out advocating an approach to the comic that relies upon typology: "Every comic character is a type. Inversely, every resemblance to a *type* has something comic in it" (Bergson: 1911b, 148). When we look at Jungian types applied to characters from popular fiction throughout the ages, we see this concept come to the fore. For example, the characters in the English comedies of manners that were popular in the time of the Enlightenment so exemplified types that their names actually took on stock characteristics. Charles Surface, from Sheridan's "The School For Scandal," acts exactly as his name implies he would—he is very shallow and easily deceived by appearances. He is so rigorous a stereotype that his every action becomes laughable.

Applying Jungian typology in this respect adds a whole new level to it. Now not only is it a tool for scientific inquiry, but it also explains concepts that have traditionally not been considered subjects for any sort of scientific investigation. In this respect, perhaps it can help us bridge the gap between the sciences and the humanities, however much the psychoanalysts might like to see that bridge burned. However, in order to test the applicability to popular culture of Jung's personality theories, or any of his theories for that matter, we must undertake an involved study of the implications of popular culture on Jung's hypotheses in general. We shall do that now.

8

Against Interpretation

In this chapter, we will embark upon what might seem a bit of a diversion, but it will serve us well when we move on in the next chapter to discuss Jung and popular culture. The title of this chapter reflects the source of the method for this investigation of Jung—an essay by Susan Sontag bearing the same name. In it, Sontag presents an idea that seems to have been passed over by the thirty years of academic work since its publication. Sontag's essay puts our method in a nutshell; she and we both come down quite hard against the idea of interpretation and its cousin, hermeneutics. Sontag's work enunciates many points that will help us greatly in our critique of Jung's theory. The allegation could certainly be raised that Sontag shows no evidence in "Against Interpretation" of being well-acquainted with Jung's thought. Such an allegation would be quite correct. However, this is no reason to discard her ideas out of hand, for while the particular thrust of her essay is in the direction of literature, it attacks ideas that underpin Jung's ideology as well.

Quite simply, Sontag says, the idea of interpretation is a fallacy. In her eyes, artistic interpretation is really a form of translation, where the interpreter attempts to convince others that an element of a work is not what it claims to be, but actually stands for something else. The application to Jung is obvious—in a dream or a book, Jung does not see a lake as a lake but rather as a symbol representing the collective unconscious. The traditional interpretation of *Moby Dick* elucidates this point well. If *Moby Dick* is an allegory where the whale is a symbol of God or the implacable universe, Ahab is equivalent to human will, and Ishmael exemplifies reason and rationality, and the whole novel

157

actually consists of a debate between Ahab and Ishmael (Jones and Wilson, 15), then why did Melville himself not know of the allegory until someone else told him (Jones and Wilson, 16)? That is, why could the novel not simply be one man telling another man about his quest to kill a big white whale, which other people have decided is about God and reason and will? The 1956 film version presents a very literal rendition of Melville's work, and although this comparison brings up the whole issue of making film versions of books, it also points out one very obvious contention with the interpretive hypothesis. If the novel is allegorical, as has been suggested by the vast majority of critics, it would stand to reason that the film version would have to encompass that allegory in order to accurately represent the novel.

At this point, the only reply would be that Huston and Bradbury missed the allegory; that is, in writing the screenplay they missed the point of the novel. But if they missed the point of the novel, then why does the film story bear such a resemblance to the book that no one has accused them of lifting an old title onto a new story (like the James Bond series)? In fact, many high school and even college students partake in the time-honored tradition of watching the movie instead of reading the book, because it is easier for them to follow. These people, while unable to quote *Moby Dick* directly, can allude to the film version as easily as the book, and if any differences between the two categories of reviewers exist, they refer to such mundane details as whether or not Gregory Peck was miscast as Ahab. Leaving aside any questions about the intelligences of Huston and Bradbury, as well as those students who would rather watch the movie version of a book, it would seem logical that, if the novel is truly an allegory, then this would be part and parcel of the framework of its story. That is, it seems far more likely that the allegory was added on by later critics than that it was there originally. If the Ahab/Ishmael conflict is inextricable from the book, as the point of a book should be, then it should be impossible to miss. If it can be separated from the book, and the film version definitely did separate the two, then it is not a part of the book at all. Sontag's message is precisely what we have just said—the interpretive method that posits the allegory does not clarify the text but instead places a new meaning on top of the old one. "Interpretation thus presupposes a discrepancy between the clear meaning of the text and the demands of later readers" (Sontag 1961a, 16). That is, the text as story does not have an explicit "meaning." This meaning is provided by calling the text an allegory.

The true magnitude of this point requires some explanation to become fully clear. Sontag asserts that the text is a primary fact that can be interpreted by any number of methods, producing different conclusions depending on the theory. This strikes a vaguely familiar chord in the psychoanalytic context. One major allegation against the different schools of psychoanalysis is that they can take an event, such as a dream, and produce countless different interpretations of it. Jung himself recognizes this fact: "it is not so very uncommon for two psychiatric diagnoses to reach contradictory conclusions" ("A Third and Final Opinion on Two Contradictory Psychiatric Diagnoses," 1:430). Sontag would say that this results from confusing a secondary level with the primary one. That is, the dream is the fact, and the theory produces an interpretation of it that is no longer primary. This interpretation, coming as it does from a theory, is never accepted universally; if Descartes can find it in himself to doubt the existence of physical objects, then we should not be surprised that critical hypotheses are even more hotly contested. There is room for debate upon whether or not *Moby Dick* contains an allegory, but not upon whether or not it contains a whale.

Certainly, Sontag was not the first to propose this attack on interpretation, which is convenient for us here. If this idea had not arisen until Sontag, who wrote "Against Interpretation", in the year Jung died, we could excuse Jung for not considering the idea. However, the idea is much older than Sontag, and was actually presented by someone whose works we know Jung read. Contemporary with the development of Jungian theory, Henri Bergson expressed a view very similar to Sontag's:

> To analyse . . . is to express a thing as something other than itself. All analysis is thus a translation, a development into symbols, a representation taken from successive points of view from which we note as many resemblances as possible between the new object which we are studying and others which we believe we know already. (Bergson 1912, 7–8)

The similarities between this statement and Sontag's should be instantly apparent, which makes it even more strange to see how Jung repeatedly insists upon the factual status of dreams in his analysis, and how virulently he polemicizes against other theoretical schools for twisting facts to fit theories, when the same criticism can be leveled at his method. For example, in "Dream Analysis in its Practical Application," Jung repeatedly says that dreams are facts and the psychoanalyst must not prejudge them based on any doctrine. This sentiment is by no means isolated in his work. So why do Jung's interpretations often seem so wildly fantastic? A clue to this comes in the same article, when Jung gives a guideline for understanding obscure dreams. If a dream is obscure, the first task of the analyst is not to understand it but instead to analyze its context ("Dream Analysis in its Practical Application," 14). If everything else in the patient's experience is interpreted as one type of symbol, and the dream seems incomprehensible, the dream must reflect the same symbol as the other elements. That is, if the psychoanalyst sees the dream as straightforward, then a straightforward explanation will be forthcoming, but even if the dream seems not to make any sense, it is still telling something. The problem is in the decoding.

Now we are back to Sontag's distinction between the fact and the interpretation. The fact, the dream, sits before the artist, or the psychoanalyst. It simply exists, and will continue to exist indefinitely, so long as no interpretation is applied to it. However, as Eysenck has pointed out, psychoanalysis cannot differentiate between a fact and an interpretation of a fact (Eysenck 1972, 35). Jung is no exception; he calls for a hermeneutic style of investigation to find what caused the symbols and what they mean. In Sontag's eyes, this is worse than interpretation, which simply obscures its object—hermeneutics destroys it entirely by excavating through it for an underlying cause (Sontag 1961a, 16). Jung, in spite of his intellectual posturing, would have us do exactly that—find a cause underlying those facts that we cannot explain. By seeing the dream as an effect rather than an event, Jung effectively denies the factual status of the dream. Like Melville's whale, the dream is simply there. When the whale becomes God and the dream becomes a symbol, then neither can be studied in and of itself any longer. Jung does not want us to look at the dream qua landscape, but rather the dream qua work of an artist. And since, as Jung says in "Dream Analysis In Its Practical Application," every dream produced after the first onset of psychoanalysis is no longer simple (i.e., conscious), but more complex (i.e., unconscious); every dream produced during the course of psychoanalysis requires this hermeneutic investigation ("Dream Analysis In Its Practical Application," 9).

If "we can call someone irrational who affirms both p and not-p" (C. Taylor, 87), and the psychoanalyst can go through a day telling some patients that God exists and some that there is no God, is this rational? Jung would call this question irrelevant. As far as he is concerned, the question is not objective truth but functionality, which is moral or psychological truth. If believing in God is beneficial, then God exists; if it is not beneficial, then God does not exist or is irrelevant to the patient's situation. Jung's equation between Christ and the self is "not to be taken as anything more than a psychological one," not intruding into metaphysics or faith ("Christ, a Symbol of the Self," *CW* 9[ii]:122). Whether or not patients believe that God exists externally, God does exist internally, as part of the collective unconscious, and this has no bearing on his external existence. That is, the supernatural nature of Christ may not be historical fact, but it is eternally true (Strauss, 22).

To anyone who has read *Nineteen Eighty-Four,* this idea should ring a bell. In fact, it is the very underpinning of the society described in the novel, where the Party is the sole arbiter of truth. In the interrogation, O'Brien, the inquisitor, repeatedly impresses upon Winston, the protagonist, that if O'Brien thinks he levitates, and Winston thinks he sees it, then it happened. Whether or not it happened in fact is irrelevant, because objective truth does not exist—all truth is in the mind. That principle underlies everything in *Nineteen Eighty-Four,* from Winston's job changing old newspaper stories to match current world affairs, to the concept of crimestop, where paradoxes are reconciled through elaborate illogic. "[The truth] was merely a piece of furtive knowledge which [Winston] happened to possess because his memory was not satisfactorily under control" (Orwell, 35). In the book, Winston goes from believing that $2+2=4$, through a stage where he can be made to believe that $2+2=5$ by having his brain rescrambled by a machine, to the point where he honestly believes that $2+2=5$. This is an extreme case, of course, but perhaps Orwell uses it precisely for that reason. Even a child can tell us the literal truth of the equation $2+2$, but for Winston the objective truth and psychological truths are different. In his particular society, Winston is better-adapted if he believes that $2+2=5$, and for that reason no psychoanalyst would try to convince him otherwise. That is, the society in which Winston lives has made the equation $2+2=5$ into one of its accepted norms, and for Winston to believe the objective truth would put him in opposition to society. In order for him to lead a better-adjusted life, he would have to be brought to believe that $2+2=5$. In *Nineteen Eighty-Four* it takes O'Brien, a series of severe physical deprivations, and a cage full of rats surrounding Winston's head to bring him to this "realization." In our world, psychoanalysis would suffice.

Are we being too hard on psychoanalysis here, calling it a tool for reinforcing society's norms rather than for helping the individual? Sigmund Freud gives us some insight into this when he discusses " 'Civilised' Sexual Morality and Modern Nervous Illness" (Freud 1908a). In this paper, Freud repeatedly talks of the difficulties people come under when they stray away from natural sexual morality, which he defines as "a sexual morality under whose dominance a human stock is able to remain in lasting possession of health and effiency" (ibid., 33). In fact, when he speaks of civilized sexual morality (the morality of his time), he blames it for nervous illness (ibid., 34), a belief that we should be able to predict from the emphasis he places on the sexual hypothesis. This makes it all the more surprising to see Freud come down so hard against any break from civilized sexual morality. As well, he refuses to comment on the utility of this particular attitude toward sexuality, calling it "certainly not a physician's business" to judge such matters (Freud 1908a, 55). That is, rather than consider the idea that people might be happier if they were able to have free sex, Freud conditions them to accept society's norms instead.

We have dealt with Freud here only because his appeal to and proselytizing of society's views are more blatant than they are in Jung's work, not because Jung is a visionary social reformer. Very early in his career, Jung was called in to a girls' school in a clinical capacity, basically to do some damage control on a rumor spreading around the school ("Rumor"). In a nutshell, one of the students, a girl named Marie, had dreamed a quite extravagant scenario involving one of her teachers, a long swim, a night spent in a barn, and a pregnant woman. In its transmission through her circle of friends, the dream became blown far out of proportion, to the point where some girls believed Marie had dreamed that she was pregnant with the teacher's baby. Jung was called in to examine Marie and discover any reason why she should come up with such a wild dream. Of course, she had not had this dream at all, and Jung promptly found this out; then he provided both a diagnosis of the dream and a resolution of the problem it had caused. Granted, this paper was written before *Unconscious,* so Jung would agree with Freud that dreams play a wish-fulfilling role in life. Nonetheless, Jung was prone to going over his old papers and revising them to accord with his new theories as they came out, and the edition of "Rumor" in the *Collected Works* does not reflect any such revision. That is, from the fact that he did not revise "Rumor," we can at least assume that he never substantially changed his diagnosis of Marie throughout his life—even to his death, he did allow for a Freudian dream interpretation if he thought it justified, and he did write quite a laudatory eulogy for Freud ("In Memory of Sigmund Freud," *CW* 15:60–73). He never came to see Freud's theories as wrong; he merely saw them as incomplete (compare "New Paths in Psychology" [*CW* 7:407–41] to "On the Psychology of the Unconscious" [*CW* 7:1–291]). In any case, Jung attributed the spread of the false report of the dream in "Rumor" to Marie and her friends becoming confused about their attitude toward this teacher, both desiring and despising him, and using the dream as a weapon against him. He treated the situation by confronting Marie with this news and resolved it by having Marie acknowledge that she could not have her teacher sexually.

There was never any question about the two of them sleeping together, even if it was what they had both actually wanted. Swiss society would never hear of a teacher having relations with a thirteen year-old girl because it was what the two of them wanted and because it would be beneficial for her. Neither would Jung—in his eyes, this was a case of Freudian transference, not lust. Instead of resolving the situation by having the two spend a night together and resolving Marie's supposed urge, they instead had to solve the problem inside the norms of society. Whether or not the best cure would be having sex, it was not an option.

This discussion of "Rumor" brings us nicely back to the point from which we have embarked on a rather long tangent. According to Jung's proposal, Marie is assumed to want to sleep with the teacher, and her "cure" is administered based on that assumption. However, "Rumor" nowhere reports that Marie actually voiced a desire for sex. This was an assumption put forth by Jung. This assumption is a frame that Jung postulates around an empirical fact, the dream. In "Rumor," Jung was presented with a series of facts: the dream, the garbling of it in trans-mission, and the effect. His explanation of how the rumor became garbled shows that he understands the phenomenon of interpretation changing fact into a new entity. He assumes that the other girls assumed that Marie wanted to have sex with her teacher and reinterpreted the story for themselves in that light, exaggerating the sexual details and omitting the others.

So far, we have no problem with Jung's idea—that may well have been how the other girls perceived Marie's intentions. However, Jung sees this not as the other girls submitting the dream to a reinterpretation according to their own assumptions, but as the other girls recognizing Marie's unconscious sexual desires. And at some point, Marie may well have wanted to sleep with her teacher. However, it is equally possible that Marie never wanted to have relations with her teacher. We simply do not know and are not given enough information in "Rumor" to find out. In any case, Jung never considers the possibility that the other girls were wrong in their analysis of Marie, because he himself considers them to have been right.

Jung had to make sense out of the dream in order to be able to explain it. John Smith would say that he did this by comparing the new fact to old ones, looking for analogies. However, Smith ignores one very crucial element—the theory. Certainly, analogies between the new and old facts are very important but are found only in light of a theory. No matter what the circumstances of any dream, Jung would never consider it representative of a desire for cannibalism, because he does not consider cannibalism a human goal. People eating people has no place in Jungian theory, at least not as an end in itself. For example, throughout "Transformation of the Libido," Jung draws mythical parallels between rubbing wood to create fire and masturbation, then resorts to linguistic means to create a link between rubbing (*reiben* in German) and breaking (*reissen* in German), to equate masturbation with breaking the apple off the Tree of Knowledge in Eden and the corresponding power produced by this act. That is, he derives *reissen* from *reiben,* as opposed to the other way around. But why could rubbing not come from breaking, and masturbation be interpreted not as an infantile desire for power but rather as an attempt to deal with sexual frustration by breaking off the penis entirely? The argument hinges on the order of derivation of the two verbs, for which Jung has no grounds except his theory.

Jung's predilection for finding an underlying explanation to explain strange phenomena shows up best in his papers on synchronicity ("Synchronicity: An Acausal Connecting Principle," and its shorter companion, "On Synchronicity"). In a nutshell, synchronicity is a meaningful coincidence of two or more events. For example, once Jung was sitting in analysis with a particularly unresponsive patient who was telling him of a dream in which a golden scarab figured highly. At that time, a beetle flew in the window. Jung caught it, presented it to the patient, and asked, "Is this the one?" At this, the patient's resistance broke down, and the analysis proceeded posthaste ("On Synchronicity," *CW* 8:982). Some people might see this event as just a remarkable coincidence, but to Jung the fact that it had meaning says it must be something more ("Synchronicity," *CW* 8:827). That is, there is a difference between the normal coincidence, that is purely random, and the coincidence which actually means something. To draw this distinction, Jung tells a story of a man who notices the number on his streetcar ticket, gets a phone call where the same number is mentioned, and buys a theater ticket that night with the same number ("On Synchronicity," *CW* 8:969). According to Jung, this is not synchronicity because the series of events has no meaning.

Here we see a perfect example of the idea that something that does not make obvious sense must be subjected to a process that will render it in some way sensible. For something with meaning to be the result of a totally random procedure is totally antithetical to Jung's entire philosophy. "Concepts of randomness and of symbolic thinking are incompatible" (J. Smith, 204). Jung has made it his business to find meaning where there seems to be none; in a synchronistic series, he is presented with a group of events that seems to mean something but shows no causal connection. So he posits an explanation which, instead of denying the meaning of the coincidence of the events, denies the role of causality instead. Synchronistic events rest on the simultaneous occurrence of two different psychic states—the normal state, which is causally explicable, and the critical experience, which cannot be causally derived from the normal state ("Synchronicity," *CW* 8:855). The external appearance of the object has become indistinguishable from the internal psychic state.

Let us put synchronicity into terms reminiscent of Sontag (1961a) in order to show how it fits with the general ideas we have put forth in this chapter. Taking his example of the woman and the scarab, Jung is presented with the two primary facts, the woman telling her scarab-dream and the simultaneous appearance of the beetle at the window. On the surface, the coincidental appearance of these two items does not make sense; the fact that the two events occurred in tandem seems to mean something, in a way that the story of the man and his streetcar and theater tickets does not. So Jung constructs an interpretation that assimilates the two events. "After all, the believer in the prophetic nature of hunches or dreams will tell you, these things aren't precise—they must be interpreted to make them meaningful" (Hines, 52). Although no causal relation can be demonstrated between the occurrence of the dream and the beetle, the two events do seem related nonetheless. Here, Jung is presented with two options—either write the occurrences off as coincidence, or posit a relationship between them that is not dependent on causality. He opts for the latter course. He creates synchronicity.

"On the Significance of Number Dreams" provides one last example of Jung creating a frame through which to view apparently incomprehensible events. This paper, one of Jung's earlier works, tells of an adulterous patient who repeatedly had dreams revolving around numbers. For example, one night the patient had a dream that, while at his mistress's residence, he "played" on a high number—152 ("On the Significance of Number Dreams," 193). Through the associative method, Jung discovers that the patient's mistress has, in the past few years, lived at Number 17 X Street, Number 129 Y Street, Number 48 Z Street, and now she lives at Number 6 A Street. Taking into account the fact that the patient told his mistress to move from her Z Street address and thus ignoring it in his considerations, Jung adds together 17, 129, and 6 to come up with a sum of 152. The patient comes up with many such dreams; the one we have chosen merely represents the most easily encapsulated example. But of perhaps more interest is Jung's discovery that the phenomenon of number dreams was not exclusive to the patient. In a mirror of her husband's problems, the patient's wife also had number dreams, which Jung analyzes here as well. For example, her dream where the words "Luke 137" flashed in front of her eyes is analyzed in terms of her children and Jung's children, as well as in the biblical context ("On the Significance of Number Dreams," 197–98). This biblical context is more interesting for our purposes because of the verses it evokes. Jung does make a point of the fact that the wife had so little knowledge of the Bible that she did not know that "Luke" had to refer to one of the gospels ("On the Significance of Number Dreams," 197), so she referred to Acts 1.37 instead. This does not exist, so she looked to Acts 1.7, in which Jesus, when asked if he will now restore the Kingdom of Israel, replies, "It is not for you to know the times or periods that the Father has set by his own authority." Jung, however, looks to Luke 1.37, in which the angel Gabriel tells Mary that she will be the mother of Jesus in spite of her virginity: "For nothing will be impossible with God." Jung takes this to indicate that the patient's wife sees herself as actually fertile; in spite of having had several miscarriages, she is still able to produce children and to be a good mother. But since the patient's dream "Luke 137" does not necessarily imply splitting the number down to 1.37, Jung turns to Luke 13.7, where he finds this verse: "So he said to the gardener, 'See here! For three years I have come looking for fruit on this fig tree, and still I find none. Cut it down! Why should it be wasting the soil?' " This verse deals with the parable of the barren fig tree, the meaning of which is not explained in the biblical context.

Of course, this sort of circumstance is perfect for Jung. He takes the symbol of the fig tree, claims that antiquity gave it the symbolic meaning of male genitals, and attributes it to the wife's sadistic fantasies of cutting or biting off her husband's penis. Leaving aside the obvious Freudian implications of the interpretation, it is significant to note that Jung ascribes a definite meaning to the fig tree, that of the penis, and does so from a biblical source.

In that light, let us look at another, more well known reference to the fig tree:

> From the fig tree learn its lesson: as soon as its branch becomes tender and puts forth its leaves, you know that summer is near. So also, when you see all these things, you know that he is near, at the very gates. Truly I tell you, this generation will not pass away until all these things have taken place. Heaven and earth will pass away, but my words will not pass away. (Matt. 24.32–35)

Traditionally, this section has been interpreted to have an eschatological meaning because of its context, where the destruction of the temple, the persecutions of the believers, and the Second Coming are predicted. In *The Late Great Planet Earth,* an Evangelical Christian eschatological text, the passage from Matthew is said to refer to the nation of Israel, and the fig tree is called "a historic symbol of national Israel" (Lindsey, 43). According to *The New Strong's Exhaustive Concordance of the Bible,* the actual word "fig" in both the Matthew and Luke contexts is a translation of συκῆ, which in turn derives from σύκον, the word for "fig" in koine Greek. Neither usage of the word in the biblical context gives any reason to suspect a phallic reference, unless we assume Jung's interpretation of the fig tree symbol is the correct one. But the quotation from Lindsey gives us an alternate interpretation, which is far more in keeping both with the context from which it is derived and with the parable of the barren fig tree.

In that light, let us look at some other interpretive techniques to which Jung could have subjected the "Luke 137" reference. In the New Revised Standard Version of the Bible, the 137th word of the Gospel of Luke is "Elizabeth." Certainly, the allegation could be made that translations of the Bible differ, and word location is nothing to go by. Although this objection could be extended—after all, the woman's Bible knowledge is described as very poor, so comparing by word may well be as merited as by verse—we will let this criticism stand. In any case, the 137th verse of any translation of Luke in any Bible is Luke 3.5, which is a portion of John the Baptist's quotation from the book of Isaiah: "Every valley shall be filled, and every mountain and hill shall be made low, and the crooked shall be made straight, and the rough ways made smooth." If anything, this fits in better with the eschatological context in which we found the fig symbol than a phallic idea. And we could go on, turning to the book of Acts, which is held also to be written by Luke, and explore its various possibilities, but there is no need. All this would do is provide even more verses to which we could apply even more interpretive theories, obscuring even further the empirical fact of the woman's dream.

That brings us back to a very interesting point. Conspicuous by their absence throughout "On the Significance of Number Dreams" are any references to whether or not Jung's interpretations of the dream contents actually helped the patient in any way. That is, we have a whole host of dreams involving numbers, and a whole host of interpretations of them, but nowhere do we have any indication that Jung's interpretations ever helped the patient. This criticism can be leveled at Jung in countless places. In *Unconscious,* Jung undertakes a very in-depth analysis of the dreams of a woman he has never met. The material was provided by Théodore Flournoy, one of Jung's contemporaries, in the *Archives de Psychologie,* and was a synopsis of one of Flournoy's cases. To make a long story short, Miss Miller was able to work through her neurosis completely without Jung's help. The interpretations provided throughout *Unconscious* are entirely Jung's own—Miss Miller neither provided them nor benefited from them. She was treated entirely by someone whose interpretations were different from Jung's.

In this last consideration, perhaps we have returned to the crux of what we have meant to put forth in this chapter. That is, in spite of Jung's repeated insistence that he does not twist the facts to fit his theories, he really works only through those interpretive theories. He does not deal with the facts at all—instead, he takes a fact such as a dream and uses it as a springboard for association, and then takes associations as facts. Note that such a criticism of Jung's method should not be extended to say that all forms of investigation must be abandoned. However, when investigating ambiguous phenomena, we must maintain a clear distinction between where the empirical fact ends and the interpretation begins. It is one thing for critics to say that they believe *Moby Dick* to be an allegory, but quite another for them to say that it actually is an allegory. The difference is epistemological; equating the book with the allegory does not say that we know what we believe Melville meant, but that we know what he actually meant. We can analyze phenomena such as books or dreams from a purely empirical standpoint—the fact that the whale is so prevalent in *Moby Dick* certainly implies that it may well be a symbol for something, but we cannot say what without first asking Melville. In that case, we must be ready to accept Melville's statement that, for him, the whale symbolized nothing. For us, it may well symbolize an event. But it is one thing to say that it symbolizes something for us and quite another to say that it does so, or should do so, for everyone, and especially for the author.

In *Unconscious,* Jung commits that fallacy. He treats neither Miss Miller nor her dreams. He treats his interpretations of her dreams and both creates and solves the problem she allegedly faces. That Flournoy himself agreed with Jung's analysis of the situation ("On Psychological Understanding," *CW* 3:415) does not change the fact that we have no idea whether or not Miss Miller did. As far as Jung is concerned, this concern would be irrelevant. Psychoanalysis depends on the psychoanalyst providing guesses and suspicions, and if this is suggestion, Jung says, then so be it; people are only susceptible to "those suggestions with which [they] are already secretly in accord" ("The Aims of Psychotherapy," 74). If Miss Miller did not agree with Jung's interpretation, and did not see herself as possessed with the complexes Jung sees in her, she would be proving just how right Jung was. "Anyone who insists on denying it [i.e., projection] becomes identical with it" ("The Self," *CW* 9[ii]:44). But Jung repeatedly makes the point that, even if his interpretations are only accepted by the patient because of suggestion, the fact that the interpretations are accepted shows that the patient believes them. That is, if Miss Miller had agreed with Jung, she would be agreeing because his interpretation was right, but if she had disagreed, she would do so because she could not admit that he was right. With this, Jung's interpretations become unfalsifiable.

> There is an extremely serious problem in symbolic interpretation, whether it is behavior or anything else that is being interpreted: such interpretations are inherently nonfalsifiable. This is especially true in psychoanalytic theory . . . no matter whether [the patient] agrees with the interpretation or argues against it, her behavior will be seen by the psychoanalyst as supporting the interpretation. (Hines, 111)

In the field of cultural examination, Jung is presented with one fewer check, in that there is no patient to agree or disagree. A book can speak to us, but it cannot answer our questions. We can interpret the book in light of our questions to provide answers, but then we come dangerously close to performing suggestion upon ourselves. That is, when people ask questions of a text (such as the Bible) and then read it to determine answers, the critical observer should ask whether such people are not merely using the text to support a view that they already hold. Depending upon whom we ask, *Moby Dick* is either about a whale or a cosmic struggle. Jung would say the latter, and he could find support throughout the field of literary criticism. However, this support may not always be forthcoming. It is now for us to decide whether or not Jungian theory is in any way equipped to analyze cultural artifacts.

9

Jung and Popular Culture—
Archetypes or Archietypes?

Jung considered his archetypes part of the psychic makeup of every society and saw their expression in every aspect of life. In every culture, Jung saw symbols such as the dying hero or the terrifying mother, and while some cultures may have developed the symbols more fully than others, that did not mean the symbols themselves differed from culture to culture. For example, throughout *Unconscious,* Jung takes Miss Miller's dream and fantasy images and relates them to such diverse mythologies as the Christian, Hindu, Polynesian, and North American. We have already examined the philosophical problems with this approach, so there is no need to restate them here. However, as we have said, writing off the archetypes by both logical and logistic approaches is not sufficient to provide a complete rebuttal to Jung; natural phenomena are not subject to such rules of logic as Occam's Razor. Often physical phenomena do not take on the characteristics we would demand of them if they were to be a tight formulation; in a succinct system, light would be either a wave or a particle, but in nature it acts as both and it is as both that we must explain it. Jung could and did assert the same thing for archetypes—not that they fit the minimum possible requirements, but that their existence is unquestionable and irreducible.

It therefore becomes imperative that, to truly disprove the theory of archetypes, they must be shown wanting on terms even Jung would have to acknowledge. Perhaps we can do this through a typological approach. Keeping in mind Bergson's idea that every comic character is a type (Bergson: 1911b, 148), it may be worthwhile to consider various examples of popular culture from past and present, first in an attempt to find archetypes, then to see if the types might give some more coherent descriptions.

This approach follows one of Jung's own lines of proof—time and time again he appeals to works such as *Faust* to support his points. Jung could not and would not deny that he cites the presence of an archetype in myths and legends as supporting evidence for his arguments. These myths and legends being the dominant (if not only) forms of literature in preliterate societies and very important to the literate ones, they would form an inexorable part of popular culture throughout the ages. Even in today's most secular societies, the urban legend plays an important role in the cultural milieu. Whether or not the universality of the archetypes is adequate to prove their existence, showing them not to be universal would force even Jung to pause and reflect. As well, if any relation between popular culture and typology is borne out by our investigation, we will have some strong support for presenting it as an alternative to Jung's ideas.

One of Jung's more commonly cited archetypes is that of the hero. Throughout *Unconscious* Jung interprets Miss Miller's visions as dominated by an infantile hero, attempting to break free from the mother. In particular, the Chiwantopel dream teems with images that Jung interprets as epitomizing an entire society's quest for individuation. In "The Stages of Life," Jung asserts that the childhood stage (birth to fifteen years) is dominated by the unconscious (*CW* 8:795). This explains why he insists upon an "infantile" hero; the hero, while still bound by the mother, is infantile and cannot be brought into consciousness, cannot be assimilated into the "mature" personality by individuation. Since children are by definition immature, they cannot be expected to have assimilated the hero. As such, Jung's idea would require that media targeted toward the under-fifteen age group depict heroes of a superlative, almost surreal dimension. And a brief look through any average little boy's bedroom would reveal exactly that—their posters revere superlative athletes, their comic books describe the adventures of incredibly powerful heroes, and their toys allow them to vicariously save the world over and over by helping character figurines defeat the forces of evil in the safety of their own living rooms.

But to stop with characters such as those ignores another whole facet of this child's existence. Heroes and villains are not always presented in such black-and-white terms in real life, and the child's experience reflects this as well. On the bookshelf, alongside the chronicles of Superman or Spiderman, sit the adventures of Archie Andrews. Usually referred to as just "Archie," he is one of the most widely drawn comic book heroes in North America. Yet as far as a hero goes, the "Archietype" hardly fits the archetype. For this reason, it makes sense to look into Archie in some depth as we analyze the typical hero figure, to set him as a counterpoint to Jung's ideas. If we can show in this case that Jung's hero idea, as well as being logically unnecessary, is simply inapplicable, then we have gone a long way toward showing that it is irrelevant. That is, if Archie does not meet the strict criteria for an archetype, then the entire concept of the specific archetype may come under question. And since we have already shown that the idea of a general pool of archetypal energy is more ludicrous than the specific archetypes, being able to dismiss the specific archetype knocks out a substantial cornerstone to Jungian theory.

Very few of Archie's character traits are consistent from episode to episode—for example, while sometimes he is a champion surfer, other times he has never surfed before—but those traits that do remain constant do not represent someone trying to break free from an oppressive mother. While he will occasionally argue with his parents, Archie is nothing if not a model child. He washes dishes, he mows the lawn, he paints the house, and while sometimes he may be a bit lax in those responsibilities, he would never shirk them completely. It would not be too much to say that keeping his parents happy is a fundamental goal in Archie's life.

Two other phenomena of Archie's life make him an even more interesting hero to compare to Jung's archetypal version. First of all, it is significant to note that, while Archie never seems to age in the books, he is often presented as one of two temporally distinct characters (a third has begun to appear, where Archie can be approximately dated as fourteen years old, but this will not detract from our hypothesis). The youngest Archie, or "Little Archie," would be about six years old. The younger Archies are not depicted so often as the elder incarnation, perhaps because of his youth—the range of events that Archie experiences is more credible when presented in the guise of an older person.* The

---

*This is not to say that children do not believe that other cartoon characters have other experiences. But characters such as Mighty Mouse or Bugs Bunny are patently fantastic, and their experiences are patently fantastic as well. Archie is portrayed as living a believable, possible life with real-world problems (no matter how glibly presented).

oldest and most common Archie is a high school senior, approximately seventeen years old. If we take the fifteen-year period of childhood literally, this puts Archie and his friends outside Jung's first stage of life; a culturally adapted interpretation of the fifteen-year period puts Archie right at the transition between the stages of childhood and youth, at a time when Jung would see him as undergoing a rite of passage. Either way, Jungian theory would have to posit Archie as a role model who children should admire or try to emulate.

If Archie is a role model, the traits he personifies are interesting to note. Certainly, most adults would want to see duty and honor to parents as characteristics in their children, but Archie does far more than housework. Other constants in his life include pursuing dates, difficulties with authority figures, and below-average academic achievement. Jung might take Archie's service to his parents and attribute that to an infantile personality, relate the pursuing of dates to an attempt to find someone upon whom he could project his anima, ascribe the problems with authority to infantile strivings to individuate, and explain the poor academic performance by analogy with the substandard intellect of the child compared to the adult. The other characteristics could vary widely, Jung would say, because they are irrelevant to the process of individuation. Jung may want to attribute the variability in Archie's other characteristics to his being a young person, at a stage of life "without any conscious problems" ("The Stages of Life," *CW* 8:795). As we saw at the beginning of this chapter, Jung has said that the rules of logic do not govern the psychic life. If we accept that assertion unquestioningly, we effectively defuse any utility the Archie example would provide.

We have already discussed the philosophical grounds on which we cannot accept any statement exempting the archetypes from logical discourse, but here we have a concrete example and thus can demand that its logic be at least internally consistent. If Jung defines problems such as dealing with his girlfriend's parents and getting good grades in school—human interaction and material success—as unconscious, then neither Archie nor any other individual in the world has any conscious problems. However, this logic is horribly circular—since he defines the problem as unconscious, when he finds it Jung is able to describe the

---

This brings us back to the modality of belief mentioned in chapter two—both Mighty Mouse's and Archie's experiences are equally plausible for their respective characters. But it would be implausible for Mighty Mouse to have Archie's problems or vice versa.

person who displays it as submersed in the unconscious. However, if the problem were defined as conscious, Jung would have to call Archie conscious and therefore an adult. The difficulty actually arises when we call the problem anything beyond a problem *simpliciter*. For Jung to call something either conscious or unconscious is for him to apply his interpretive hypothesis to it, and if the hypothesis is applied to the assumptions, we cannot be surprised to find it also utilized in the conclusion.

In *Unconscious,* Jung unequivocally states that the fantasy hero must not fear death, for through death comes liberation from the devouring mother, and individuation. But when Archie is presented with danger, he acts in a manner radically different from Jung's archetypal hero. While he will often attempt to avoid a difficult personal situation and can be rather fickle when dealing with life's little problems, when Archie feels himself truly needed he is never slow to offer assistance. However, unlike Chiwantopel, Archie does seek out physical danger. Miss Miller's Indian may have bared his breast to the threatening arrow and proclaimed his magnificence, invoking this bravery as supporting evidence. When the serpent did finally rob him of his existence, Jung claims ("The Battle for Deliverance from the Mother," 176) it fulfilled Miss Miller's desire that he die and she become individuated. On the other hand, when Archie is confronted with physical danger, he acts to minimize it. Death is not a noble goal for the Archie-hero. While he is not afraid to put himself into perilous situations, he does so with the explicit intent of solving the crisis and coming out alive. Rather than baring his breast to the arrow, Archie invariably holds up a shield, blocks the attack, and turns over his attacker to the local authorities. And when the danger is past, Archie always insists on anonymity and refuses all pomp and circumstance, an even more interesting contrast to Chiwantopel and his boasts.

Enough of Archie; he is but one character in one comic series which, while without question is very popular, is nonetheless a fraction of the popular culture available in Western society. In any case, Archie's capacity as counterexample to Jung, while very telling, is limited. He and his friends entertain only a particular segment of the youth of Western society; for whatever reason, probably the social conditioning that "grownups do not watch or read cartoons," most people have abandoned Archie by the time they enter college. At this point, Jung would interject that the stage of childhood, and its corresponding period of unconsciousness, has ended. And although the popularity of comic books and animation with adults (e.g., "The Simpsons") serves to further our point, pursuing this tangent will not serve any further purpose here. After all, Jung would say, the child has grown up, and will become involved in "mature" problems such as self-doubt and the desire to return to that "childhood level of consciousness" ("The Stages of Life," *CW* 8:764). In calling self-doubt a "mature" problem, Jung again applies his interpretive filter to a basic fact and produces a loaded statement. He has made a point that must be hotly contested. Freud saw the idea that children are innocent and happy as arising from "the universal wish of all men, facing the inevitable disappointments of adulthood, to find something in their past that was supremely satisfactory" (Rieff, 7). Besides what this statement tells us about Freud and his theories, it should tell us something about Jung. One of Freud's major incentives in his speculation was to produce theories that degraded the previously held myth of the happy childhood, because he saw it as a lie. That is, he walked into his psychoanalytic sessions with an interpretive hypothesis, found it, and therefore saw it as justified. Jung has walked in with the idea that self-doubt is a problem of not being adapted to deal with the unconscious, and that children live immersed in unconscious contents. Therefore, when he finds self-doubt in children, he must explain it away. He, too, has a hypothesis about children which, when assumed, is easily "proved" by the evidence presented. And, like Freud's, the universality of Jung's ideas about children is very easily refuted when confronted with simple evidence.

> Oh mother, I can feel the soil falling over my head. And as I climb into an empty bed oh well, enough said.
> Oh mother, I can feel the soil falling over my head. See the sea wants to take me, the knife wants to slit me, do you think you can help me?
> I know it's over, and it never really began, but in my heart it was so real. . . .
> And you even spoke to me and said:
> *"If you're so funny, then why are you on your own tonight? And if you're so clever, then why are you on your own tonight? If you're so very entertaining, then why are you on your own tonight? If you're so very good looking, why do you sleep alone tonight?*
> "I know.
> *"Because tonight is just like any other night. That's why you're on your own tonight.* With your triumphs and your charms, while they're in each other's arms."

It's so easy to laugh, it's so easy to hate. It takes strength to be gentle and kind. . . .

Love is natural and real, but not for you my love, not tonight my love. . . . *Love is natural and real, but not for such as you and I, my love* . . .

Oh mother, I can feel the soil falling over my head . . .

(Morrissey, abridged)

The above quotation consists of the lyrics to a song by The Smiths, a 1980s musical group that targeted an audience of disaffected teenagers and were quite successful. The quoted lyrics hardly reflect the thoughts of someone totally unconcerned with self-doubt—rather, it bemoans the fact that the singer is not currently involved in a relationship, in spite of the fact that he thinks he should be. Especially in the italicized lines, we see the singer as plagued with what appears to be chronic self-doubt. If he is not with someone tonight "because tonight is just like every other night," this says something about how he perceives himself, and the fact that he feels like "the sea wants to take [him], the knife wants to slit [him]" could hardly be more explicit.

Just as he did when Chiwantopel bared himself to the serpent, Jung would attribute the suicidal urge of the above song to the infantile desire of the listener (and, perhaps, the writer as well) to die and be reborn. Unfortunately for Jung, more modern theories of suicide than his posit that actually, the last thing the suicidal person wants is to come back into the world in any form. The thoughts of a person about to commit suicide take on three specific forms: they show heightened inimicality, exacerbation of perturbation, and intellectual tunnel vision (Shneidman, 51). That is, suicidal people perceive elements of their psychological makeup as being unfriendly to their selves, they show a level of mental upset substantially greater than normal, and they entertain an unbearable feeling that the proverbial light will never appear at the end of the tunnel. Shneidman compares these three states to an explosive; by themselves they are dangerous but they only explode when presented with a match. In this case, the match is the idea that life, and the problems it presents, can be ended forever by suicide (ibid., 54). In short, the idea of getting a fresh start on life is the furthest thing from the thoughts of the suicidal person. Life has become too full of pain; the suffering must be stopped, and the idea of an eternal sleep carries with it the idea of freedom from the horrible state of being through which the suicidal person must suffer day after day. Certainly, the same contemporary musical groups that present the suicidal view often attempt to impel young people not to kill themselves (e.g., The Smiths and The Cure). But one look at the suicide statistics among teenagers today will attest to the seductive nature of this solution among those same young people who listen to songs like "I Know It's Over" (above), and whom Jung has called free from conscious problems and self-doubt.

Calling the right to suicide a fundamental human right, Thomas Szasz refuses to see killing oneself as universally the result of a mental illness. "It is precisely the elastic and strategic character of the concept that makes mental illness so attractive to the modern mind" (Szasz, 806). That is, suicide is the act of a moral agent, for which action that agent is ultimately responsible. For Jung to call self-doubt of the sort that drives people to suicide the sole province of the adult either denies the existence of teenage suicide or ascribes to teenagers the domain of moral agents on the same level as adults. Jung could not choose the latter course, because his views are meant to be universal, and any age group whose members can enjoy and identify with such a simple character as Archie cannot also be given the right to become the fully individuated personalities that his views demand.

Something has to give; reality, or Jung's views about it.

The case of popular culture serves as a perfect example of a view that we espoused back when we discussed the inadequacies of Jung's proofs, that his universal statements about humanity were in fact universal among the humanity consisting of traditionally educated, wealthy, middle-aged white people. There is more than a grain of truth in the statement that "being psychoanalyzed has become as much a bourgeois institution as going to college" (Sontag: 1961b, 259). For the most part, the debate over whether or not medical insurance should cover the cost of psychoanalysis has been a waste of time; psychoanalysts such as Jung or Freud would have little to say to an inner-city African-American woman. In Jung's eyes, Miss Miller has had a typical education. In fact, she has read and can discuss Leibniz and Anaxagoras ("The Hymn of Creation," 30), and knows enough to be able to describe the characteristic features of an Egyptian statue ("The Miller Phantasies," 24). We have already seen that another of Jung's "inexperienced" patients knew enough to make the connections between silver, quicksilver, and the god Mercury ("A Study in the Process of Individuation," 37), and had read some Swedenborg (ibid., 47). No matter what Jung may say, these are not typical people. Perhaps they are typical of a certain social class at a certain time; we will not question that. However, to say that the thoughts and ideas of someone with this kind of education would be identical to those of someone whose literary scope stops with Danielle Steel is to engage in sheer nonsense. Certainly, both the educated and the uneducated may well accept Jung's theories, but they would do so for different reasons. The educated person, having encountered roughly the same information in reading as did Jung, would agree with Jung because his ideas sound very familiar. The average person would simply not know how to respond and would acquiesce to the testimony of an expert. If people will willingly give up their own opinions in such a simple task as judging the lengths of two line segments when presented with conflicting testimony from an expert or a group (Asch, 33–34), it takes no great leap of faith to assume that, in more complex matters, they would only do the same, but more quickly.

However, that leap of faith may well land us in some very hot water. We are not going to try to contradict Asch's findings about people acquiescing to a group decision in the realm of line judgment, but the realm of popular culture can often be another matter. While we have no data to support this statement, and thus must phrase it in experiential terms, it seems often to be the case that culture can break down into two disparate strands with two disparate audiences. This dichotomy is best represented in the cinema. Looking at two films such as *Eraserhead,* by David Lynch and *Saturday Night Fever* by John Badham, most people would be hard-pressed to discover any points of similarity between the two beyond the simple fact that both were originally meant to be seen on a screen. Although the two films were nearly contemporary, the crossover of audiences would be very close to zero; it is entirely possible that, in any showing of one film, no one in the audience would have seen the other. Anyone who had seen both at the time of their release might well provide one of two responses: the person would think either that *Eraserhead* was a dull and boring "art film" with no plot whatsoever, or that *Saturday Night Fever* was an inane and poorly written story about disco music.

Jung would have to find some way to explain away this difference in light of the archetypes. Undoubtedly, he would be able to do exactly that, construing *Saturday Night Fever* as a reenactment of primitive dance scenes, and seeing *Eraserhead* as the product of one man trying to accept the fact that the warped creations he has produced are actually his own unconscious contents. We could not falsify interpretations such as these; film criticism is as hotly contested as that of literature, if not more so, and an idea such as that which we attribute to Jung would be only one of many. However, this is exactly where we can apply Sontag's idea of the interpretation in opposition to the primary fact to show us another possibility. Without becoming too embroiled in producing interpretations ourselves, we can say with reasonable certitude that, while *Saturday Night Fever* has a definite plot, *Eraserhead* does not. That is, the first film tells a story with a definite beginning, middle, and end; the second, if it tells any story at all, does so in a very disjointed and fragmented way. Therefore, *Eraserhead* requires the application of an interpretation in order to be comprehensible. It leaves the viewer asking, "What were those deformed creatures? Why was the protagonist both raising them as children and eating them for dinner?" As an independent entity, the film makes no sense. It cries out for an interpretive hypothesis to structure the elements into some sort of coherent whole. "Interpretation makes art manageable, comfortable" (Sontag 1961a, 17). *Saturday Night Fever,* on the other hand, needs no help for its audience to be comfortable. Demanding to be accepted on its own terms, it serves in this respect as a perfect example of American mass-market cinema. Certainly, we are free to apply as many interpretations to this film as to Lynch's. Nonetheless, it makes internal sense and can be enjoyed without such a practice.

We have said that Jung would try to find examples of the archetypes in both of these films, and while we belittled him for doing so, we did not provide an alternative. We will do that now. Application of Sontag's anti-interpretation to both of the films shows them to be of two categorically different types, which we shall call "comprehensible" and "incomprehensible" on the basis of their needing an interpretive hypothesis in order to make sense to the viewer. Now, let us combine this statement with the two general attitude types. When we removed the concept of the collective unconscious from introversion in the last chapter, we were left with a world view that perceives things through a subjective filter. The interpretive hypothesis provides such a filter. On the other hand, the extravert sees the world as a collection of objects and does not need to apply such a hypothesis to explain away the world. In this respect, when introverts are presented with an object whose interpretation is so blatant as to be ludicrous (*Saturday Night Fever*), they may well see it as banal. On the other hand, when extraverts are presented with an object so incomprehensible as to demand some sort of interpretation (*Eraserhead*), they may well balk.

Certainly, we have not proved anything here. The statements we made above are merely descriptions without the benefit of testing and data to back them up. As such, they are not to be seen as truths; we should make it clear that they are only hypotheses, subject to support or falsification from future examination. Nonetheless, positing a connection between cultural preference and general attitude type makes far more sense than invoking archetypes. It requires less of a departure from the areas covered by empirical science—while archetypes are untestable, personality types are. As well, making this connection may provide some order to what is currently a very chaotic field. Jung himself did deal with typology and culture together in one paper, but he looked at them from the end that produces the art object, rather than that which receives it ("The Problem of Typical Attitudes in Aesthetics"). We must not be too optimistic about how our new idea will be received; accepting it requires giving up far more specific "knowledge" about what the director or author "really meant" in the art object. Nonetheless, it does explain one very interesting phenomenon that few if any current theories can touch. No matter which school of interpretation is applied, one universal assumption made in interpreting is that the object of the study is exactly that—universal. That is, the film critic would say that everyone in the world could and should be able to appreciate *Eraserhead,* and they would, if only they would look at it in light of what it "really" is. On the other hand, our theory seems far more in line with reality. Throughout *Psychological Types,* Jung implies that extraverts are the norm in any society, while introverts are the exception (e.g., his comments about the introverted intuitive type in "General Description of the Types," 505–510). If this is true, then *Saturday Night Fever* would be a far more popular film than *Eraserhead,* because it is targeted toward the attitude type of the general public. That was in fact the case; while Lynch's film has become a cult favorite, Badham's achieved incredible commercial success at the time of its release. It might also explain the "unfathomable" popularity of some incredibly "awful" films. This successs is actually unfathomable only to the introverted minority of the population, but since the introverts comprise the majority of the intellectual community, the published opinion comes down against these films. The extraverted public supports the film with a different type of printed material—money.

It is somewhat ironic that, in an attempt to show the fallacies in Jungian theory, we have just given one aspect of it some empirical support. Granted, personality theory was one of Jung's more empirical concepts, and he did keep both feet at least near the ground throughout his investigations of it. Fortunately, we can see Jung's own response to our idea in his own writings:

> It would surely be a great folly if, for the sake of personal tendencies, we were to reduce values of universal reality down to mere personal undercurrents. That would be pseudo-psychology. Such, however, exists. ("The Problem of Types in the History of Classical and Medieval Thought," 52).

That is, no matter how correct any assumption based on the personality types may be, Jung was far more concerned with maintaining his universals, the archetypes. He would be more content to explain cultural artifacts in the way we posited he would look at Archie than to take a concept that he saw as personal and ascribe to it the power to interpret the art object. So, in fact, we have used Jung's own words against him, taking one part of his theory and using it to combat another. In truth, we did the same thing in citing Bergson at the end of the last chapter; when he said that every comic character is a "type" (Bergson 1911b, 148), he actually intended what Jung meant by the word "archetype"—the trickster, the buffoon, and so on. Nonetheless, through their statements both Bergson and Jung have helped us derive a new hypothesis, one that is both empirically testable and falsifiable. In that regard, they have become contributors to empirical science. In addition, Jung has contributed to the knocking down of his own house of cards, the archetypes, by providing us tools in the one reasonably sound portion of the *Collected Works*. The irony is striking.

10

Conclusions

It is desirable to have examined all of [the sciences], even to the most superstitious and false, in order to recognise their real worth and avoid being deceived thereby.

(Descartes: 1637, 6)

Whoever knows he is deep, strives for clarity; whoever would like to appear deep to the crowd, strives for obscurity. For the crowd considers anything deep if only it cannot see to the bottom . . .

(Nietzsche: 1882, 173)

Throughout this investigation, when we have looked at the constructs of analytical psychology, such as the self and the archetypes, we have seen them not to be actual objects. That is, although the archetype of the hero is well documented in literature, it cannot be called a universal phenomenon. However, this does not make examination of it a useless endeavor. If we were to psychoanalyze Jung, or someone of his educational background, looking at works of classical literature to find how such people perceive the world would be fruitful. The same procedure applied to an inner-city African-American or a Vietnamese peasant would be pointless. Having discarded the universal, archetypal hypothesis, we can state with some firmness that people can think and express themselves only in terms of the metaphors they know. According to Samuels, one school of post-Jungian thought has changed its views on the archetypes and looks at them as metaphors (Samuels, 242). Jung did not take this approach, so we have not discussed it in this work, but it would seem more logical and more empirically justified than the route

Jung himself followed in exploring the archetypes.

In fact, it seems that Jungian theory in general makes the mistake of taking itself too literally. Everywhere he looked, Jung found metaphors; he tried to make them literal structures—and failed. Some alchemists described the lapis in terms that Jung found similar to the self, others in terms of the shadow. Rather than say that some alchemists had a different conception of the lapis than others and structured their symbolism accordingly, Jung claims that the lapis symbolizes both the self and the shadow, and he goes to elaborate lengths to support this. It would have been better if he had limited himself. However, Jung was trying to formulate a body of theory universal to the entire human species, and as such could not limit his claims by any factor. Taking his claims not as literal structures but as metaphors does give them more power, in that it destroys the inductive criticisms that we have leveled throughout this investigation. If Jung claims that water is a symbol of the unconscious, not for everyone but for a select group of people, we cannot disprove this claim by saying that it does not symbolize the unconscious for someone not a part of this select group. By not limiting himself in this manner, Jung has simplified our job of proving his life's work to be not only unscientific but invalid.

But does this lack of universality mean that Jungian theory must be discarded totally? Just because psychoanalysis is not scientific does not mean it is without merit—people can appreciate Freud's genius without agreeing with his theories (as Eysenck did), and people can benefit from psychoanalysis without it being a science (Hook, 212), although whether or not they do is another question entirely. Many people experience great personal gain from reading a particularly moving book, or from going to church, or from traveling to foreign lands and experiencing other cultures; none of these are scientific, yet no one would call for their removal.

If we were to consider psychoanalysis an art, we would allow for the simultaneous and reasonably amicable expression of more than one school of thought. After reading a book or seeing a film, people often comment, "That didn't work for me." In the same vein, a person seeking analysis could consider the different schools of psychoanalysis and make a reasoned choice rather than working from the fallacy we touched on in a previous chapter, namely that just as all Protestant denominations are the same, so are all psychoanalysts. Those of a reductionist leaning could choose a Freudian analyst, while those of a mystical bent would know to consult a Jungian. Freud admitted that his theories could not work for everyone; that while neurotics could benefit from them, psychotics could not (Freud: 1949, 51). As well, Jung's theories seem more suited for people with a tenuous grip on reality than those who just feel insecure (Storr, 15).

Nonetheless, "when it comes to public health . . . vigilance, not tolerance, is the watchword" (Bunge and Ardila, 18). If, as Eysenck has documented, a patient's chances of being diagnosed as schizophrenic are five times greater if the diagnosing individual is American as opposed to British (Eysenck 1972, 358), this says something about the imprecision of diagnosis. Eysenck does not make clear whether the diagnosing individual is meant to be a psychologist or a psychoanalyst, but that is unimportant—if the discrepancy is so great among psychologists, with the successive Diagnostic and Statistical Manuals to help them diagnose, we cannot expect it to be smaller among those who use as tools various concepts that some psychoanalysts have admitted to be metaphors (Glass, 275), though others disagree (Waelder 1962, 635). In any case, theories need not be therapeutic in order to be psychoanalytic. In light of this, it is not surprising to see that most psychoanalysts are loath to provide data of their success rate. However, in a rare bit of numerical revelation, Jung is willing to provide just such a number, though granted in very rounded figures. At the end of his career, Jung estimated that of all his patients, one third were "really cured," one third were "considerably improved," and one third were "not essentially influenced" ("Psychiatric Activities," 143). However, he does make sure to emphasize that his final third was not necessarily left empty by the experience; they might not realize its true benefits even ten years later, but by the end of their lives that realization may come (ibid., 143).

Again, we see a classic case of unfalsifiability creeping into Jung's diagnoses. Freudians are notorious for saying that, if we have a dream that does not fulfill a wish, that dream fulfills the wish of having a dream that does not fulfill a wish (Salmon, 264). That is, it is not that the theory is inapplicable in this case, but that we have not figured out how to apply it. The same explanation comes out in Jung's case. It is not that undergoing the process of psychoanalysis did not help the "not essentially influenced" patients, but that they have not yet seen how it has helped them. Jung really hedges his bets on this one, even covering the contingency that the realization might never come.

We could propose countless hypotheses for the patient who is not essentially influenced by psychoanalysis. In the end, the one that best fits the approach that we have taken here is to say that this person has never learned to think in terms of Jungian metaphors. If we never learn to associate water with the unconscious, we will not "benefit" from that aspect of the Jungian method. Conspicuously, we have avoided talking in Jungian metaphors throughout our inquiry. However, as we approach the end, we can now come out of the closet, so to speak, and admit that Jungian discourse, when taken metaphorically, forms a very useful language that we can use to discuss cultural artifacts. Defining "anima" as "a feminine principle carrying certain characteristics and occurring in a certain setting" creates a term that could come in very handy when discussing novels, plays, and films. When the concept is no longer universal and no longer psychological, we can discuss whether or not a character such as *Faust's* Gretchen is an "anima." Basically, Jungian discourse makes quite good conversational shorthand, so long as we adequately define its terms. We should have no problem with people advancing interpretive hypotheses about popular culture, so long as they admit that the hypotheses are based on interpretations rather than the actual fact. In the beginning, the various schools of biblical criticism did exactly that—they admitted that they were describing a sequence of events in a purely hypothetical manner and then derived statements from this series. Certainly, the logic is circular, but admittedly so, and while this is still a questionable practice, at least it is not a hypocritical one. Later applications of the critical schools omitted the admission and based their statements on the idea that their hypotheses about ancient society, which could be neither supported nor falsified, were actually correct. This is the fallacy of which we have accused Jung, and as such, we can apply the criticism here as well.

After such a long investigation, the point could well be raised that Jung and his theories are hardly normative in the academic world, and that if I do not personally like Jungian theory, I can choose from numerous other schools. This would be a fair enough comment if Jungian theory were confined purely to the academic world. However, this is not the case. It is worth keeping in mind that Jung considered himself first and foremost a psychologist, not a metaphysician (see for example "Christ, a Symbol of the Self," *CW* 9[ii]:122). That is, he was not furthering scholarly theories but clinical tools. He saw his research into world religion as giving light to the fundamental archetypes around which human behavior is structured. Both his diagnoses and his treatments are predicated upon his having correctly ascertained the true nature of humanity, and that this true nature is expressed through such symbolic outlets as religion.

In short, Jung is not just building castles out of air, as we all too often do in the world of academia. He is out in the world, passing off himself and his method as the most suited to help people through personal difficulties. For example, for him to have been incorrect in his inquiries into religion, but to use these inquiries as the basis for clinical tools, is for him to base his theories on incorrect research. This is malpractice at its finest.

But our work here draws to a close, and as we finish, we have to leave the ideal world where, when something is disproved, it is therefore discarded as well. As such, we have to realize that, no matter how unscientific and useless and everything else we have found Jungian theory to be, we also have to agree with John Smith: people, when given the choice, would rather ascribe their origin to a myth than to random activity (J. Smith, 206). Analytic psychology will always find a ready audience, no matter how much we try to disprove it. Given the choice between banning all pseudosciences or allowing for individual decisions, we really have no choice at all. If the Jungians had their way, our investigation would never see the light of day; who is to say that our opinion is "right" and theirs "wrong?" Even if our system of thought is more rational than theirs, we should not delude ourselves that we are therefore "right." In the end, it is better to allow the expression of irrational systems of thought than to ban them. If we do not, someday the tables may be turned, and it could be our thoughts that become banned. Witch-hunts are horrible things, and we should not want to institute one.

Of course, this does not mean we have to advocate analytic psychology or any other type of psychoanalysis, nor does it mean our taxes and our efforts should go toward paying for them. When asked, we are more than within our own rights to put forth any and all objections that we may entertain in its regard. In this exposition, we have only dealt with what is wrong with Jung in a very general sense. It would take too long to enumerate point by point all of the various contradictions and inconsistencies in Jung's thought, and anyone whom we have not persuaded to abandon Jung by now we will never be able to persuade. However, we must never lose sight of the distinction between "persuade" and "coerce." It is more than verbal.

Bibliography of Works by C. G. Jung*

Section 1: General

Jung, Carl Gustav. *Psychology of the Unconscious.* Ed. and trans. Beatrice M. Hinkle. 1916. Reprint. New York: Moffat Yard, 1951.

———. *Collected Papers on Analytical Psychology.* Ed. Dr. Constance E. Long, trans. M.D. Eder except "The Psychology of Dreams"—trans. Dora Hecht. London: Balliere, Tindall, and Cox, 1917.

———. *Psychological Types.* Trans. H. Godwin Baynes. 1923. Reprint. London: Routledge & Kegan Paul, 1953.

———. *Contributions to Analytic Psychology.* Trans. H. G. Baynes, Cary F. Baynes. London: Routledge & Kegan Paul, 1928.

———. *Modern Man in Search of a Soul.* Trans. W. S. Dell, Cary F. Baynes. New York: Harcourt Brace, 1933.

———. *The Integration of the Personality.* Trans. Stanley Dell. New York: Farrar & Rinehart, 1939.

———. *Memories, Dreams, Reflections.* Ed. Anelia Jaffé. Trans. Richard Winston and Clara Winston. 1963. Revised 1973. Reprint. New York: Vintage, 1989.

———. "Approaching the Unconscious." In *Man and His Symbols.* Ed. Carl G. Jung. 1964. Reprint. New York: Doubleday, 1983.

———. *The Collected Works of C. G. Jung: Bollingen Series XX.* Executive Ed. William McGuire. Eds. Sir Herbert Read, Michael Fordham, Gerhard

---

*I have attempted to use selections both from the Bollingen *Collected Works* (1953–71) and from other sources in order to eliminate any allegations that I have been subject to the bias of one translator or revision. In addition, I have read some papers in both the *Collected Works* and other sources and have determined that there being different translators has not significantly affected the papers.

Adler. 20 vols. Trans. R. F. C. Hull, Leopold Stein, Diana Riviere. Princeton: Princeton University Press, 1953–71.

Section 2: *Collected Works* (1953–71) by Volume and Paper Title

Papers taken from the *Collected Works* when cited in the text are referenced by *paragraph* number in this format: *CW* XX:yy (XX is the volume number; yy is the *paragraph* number).

CW 1: Psychiatric Studies
　　"A Third and Final Opinion on Two Contradictory Psychiatric Diagnoses." 430–77.
　　"On the Psychological Diagnosis of Facts." 478–84.

CW 2: Experimental Researches
　　"The Associations of Normal Subjects." 1–498.
　　"Experimental Observations on the Faculty of Memory." 639–59.
　　"Psychoanalysis and Association Experiments." 660–727.
　　"Association, Dream, and Hysterical Symptom." 793–862.

CW 3: The Psychogenesis of Mental Disease
　　"The Psychology of Dementia Praecox." 1–316.
　　"On Psychological Understanding." 388–424.
　　"Mental Disease and the Psyche." 496–503.
　　"Recent Thoughts on Schizophrenia." 542–52.
　　"Schizophrenia." 553–84.

CW 4: Psychiatric Studies
　　"The Psychology of Number Dreams." 95–128.

CW 5: Symbols of Transformation
　　A second edition of *Unconscious*

CW 7: Two Essays on Analytical Psychology
　　"On the Psychology of the Unconscious." 1–201.
　　"The Relations Between the Ego and the Unconscious." 202–406.
　　"New Paths in Psychology." 407–41.
　　"The Structure of the Unconscious." 442–521.

CW 8: The Structure and Dynamics of the Psyche
　　"The Transcendent Function." 131–93.

"A Review of the Complex Theory." 194–219.
"The Significance of Constitution and Heredity in Psychology." 220–31.
"Psychological Factors Determining Human Behavior." 232–62.
"Instinct and the Unconscious." 263–82.
"The Structure of the Psyche." 283–342.
"On the Nature of the Psyche." 343–442.
"On the Nature of Dreams." 530–69.
"The Real and the Surreal." 712–48.
"The Stages of Life." 749–95.
"The Soul and Death." 796–815.
"Synchronicity: An acausal connecting principle." 816–968.
"On Synchronicity." 969–97.

CW 9 (i): The Archetypes and the Collective Unconscious
"Archetypes of the Collective Unconscious." 1–86.
"The Concept of the Collective Unconscious." 87–110.
"Concerning the Archetypes with Special Reference to the Anima Concept."
    111–47.
"Concerning Rebirth." 199–258.
"Psychology of the Child Archetype." 259–305.
"The Psychological Aspects of the Kore." 306–383.
"On the Psychology of the Trickster–Figure." 456–88.
"Concerning Mandala Symbolism." 627–712.

CW 9 (ii): Aion: Researches into the Phenomenology of the Self
"The Ego." 1–12.
"The Shadow." 13–19.
"The Syzygy: Anima and Animus." 20–42.
"The Self." 43–67.
"Christ, a Symbol of the Self." 68–126.
"The Sign of the Fishes." 127–49.
"The Prophecies of Nostradamus." 150–61.
"The Historical Significance of the Fish." 162–80.
"The Ambivalence of the Fish Symbol." 181–92.
"The Fish in Alchemy." 193–238.
"The Alchemical Interpretation of the Fish." 239–66.
"Background to the Psychology of Christian Alchemical Symbolism." 267–
    86.
"Gnostic Symbols of the Self." 287–346.
"The Structure and Dynamics of the Self." 347–421.
"Conclusion." 422–29.

CW 10: Civilisation in Transformation
"The Role of the Unconscious." 1–48.
"Mind and Earth." 49–103.
"Wotan." 371–399.
"After the Catastrophe." 400–443.
"The Fight with the Shadow." 444–57.
"Epilogue" to "Essays on Contemporary Events." 458–87.
"The Rise of a New World." 425–34.
"Flying Saucers: A Modern Myth of Things Seen in the Skies." 589–824.
"The Complications of American Psychology." 946–80.
"The Dreamlike World of India." 981–1001.
"What India Can Teach Us." 1002–1013.

CW 11: Psychology and Religion
"Psychology and Religion." 1–168.
"A Psychological Approach to the Dogma of the Trinity." 169–295.
"Transformation Symbolism in the Mass." 296–448.
"Answer to Job." 553–758.
"Psychological Commentary on *The Tibetan Book of the Great Liberation.*"
    759–830.
"Foreword to Suzuki's *Introduction to Zen Buddhism.*" 877–907.

CW 12: Psychology and Alchemy
"Introduction to the Religious and Psychological Problems of Alchemy."
    1–43.
"Individual Dream Symbolism in Relation to Alchemy." 44–331.
"Religious Ideas in Alchemy." 332–554.
"Epilogue." 555–65.

CW 13: Alchemical Studies
"The Visions of Zosimos." 85–144.
"Paracelsus as a Spiritual Phenomenon." 145–238.
"The Spirit Mercurius." 239–303.
"The Philosophical Tree." 304–482.

CW 14: Mysterium Coniunctionis
"The Components of the Coniunctio." 1–35.
"The Paradoxa." 36–103.
"The Personification of the Opposites." 104–348.
"Rex and Regina." 349–543.
"Adam and Eve." 544–653.
"The Conjunction." 654–789.
"Epilogue." 790–92.

CW 15: The Spirit in Man, Art, and Literature
  "Paracelsus." 1–17.
  "Paracelsus the Physician." 18–43.
  "In Memory of Sigmund Freud." 60–73.

CW 16: Specific Problems of Psychotherapy
  "Psychology of the Transference." 353–539

Section 3: Papers or Collections Not Part of the *Collected Works*

Papers or collections not part of the *Collected Works* are referenced in this
  format: "Paper Title" (Author and Year), pages. This should allow for
  easy location of any papers cited only by name in the body of this inquiry.

"The Aims of Psychotherapy" (Jung 1933), 63–84.
"The Apollonian and the Dionysian" (Jung 1923), 170–83.
"Approaching the Unconscious" (Jung 1964), 24–106.
"Archaic Man" (Jung 1933), 143–74.
"Archetypes of the Collective Unconscious" (Jung 1939), 52–95.
"Aspects of the Libido" (Jung 1916), 70–76.
"The Basic Postulates of Analytical Psychology" (Jung 1933), 200–225.
"The Battle for Deliverance from the Mother" (Jung 1916), 169–87.
"Commentary" on *The Secret of the Golden Flower* (Wilhelm, 1931), 81–137.
"The Conception and the Genetic Theory of the Libido" (Jung 1916), 77–86.
The Conception of the Unconscious" (Jung 1917), 445–74.
"'Concerning the Two Kinds of Thinking" (Jung 1916), 4–21.
"Confrontation with the Unconscious" (Jung 1963), 170–99.
"The Content of the Psychoses" (Jung 1917), 312–51.
"A Contribution to the Psychology of Rumor" (Jung 1917), 176–90.
"Definitions" (Jung 1923), 518–617.
"The Development of Personality" (Jung 1939), 281–305.
"Dream Analysis In Its Practical Application" (Jung 1933), 1–31.
"Dream Symbols of the Process of Individuation" (Jung 1939), 96–204.
"The Dual Mother Role" (Jung 1916), 188–236.
"First Years" (Jung 1963), 6–23.
"Freud, Sigmund" (Jung 1963), 146–169.
"General Description of the Types" (Jung 1923), 412–517.
"The Hymn of Creation" (Jung 1916), 26–46.
"The Idea of Redemption in Alchemy" (Jung 1939), 205–80.
"Instinct and the Unconscious" (Jung 1928), 270–81.
"Introduction" to *Psychological Types* (Jung 1923), 9–14.

"Introduction" to *MDR* (Jung 1963), v–xiv.

"Introduction" to *Secret of the Golden Flower* (Wilhelm, 1931), xiii–xv.

"Late Thoughts" (Jung 1963), 327–354.

"The Meaning of Individuation" (Jung 1939), 3–29.

"The Miller Phantasies" (Jung 1916), 22–25.

"On Life After Death" (Jung 1963), 299–326.

"On Psychical Energy" (Jung 1928), 1–76.

"On the Importance of the Unconscious in Psychopathology" (Jung 1917), pp. 278–86.

"On the Psychology and Pathology of So-Called Occult Phenomena" (Jung 1917), 1–93.

"On the Relation of Analytic Psychology to Poetic Art" (Jung 1928), 225–49.

"On the Significance of Number-Dreams" (Jung 1917), 191–99.

"Problems of Modern Psychotherapy" (Jung 1933), 32–62.

"The Problem of Types in Modern Philosophy" (Jung 1923), 372–400.

"The Problem of Types in the History of Classical and Medieval Thought" (Jung 1923), 15–86.

"The Problem of Typical Attitudes in Aesthetics" (Jung 1923), 358–71.

"Prologue" to *MDR* (Jung 1963), 3–6.

"Psychiatric Activities" (Jung 1963), 114–145.

"Psychological Commentary" (Evans-Wentz, 1927), pp. xxxv–lii.

"The Psychological Foundations of Belief in Spirits" (Jung 1928), 250–69.

"Psychological Types" (Jung 1928), 295–312.

"Psychology and Literature" (Jung 1933), 175–99.

"The Psychology of Dreams" (Jung 1917), 299–311.

"Psychotherapists or the Clergy" (Jung 1933), 255–82.

"The Question of the Therapeutic Value of Abreaction'" (Jung 1928), 282–94.

"Retrospect" (Jung 1963), 355–9.

"The Sacrifice" (Jung 1916), 237–67.

"School Years" (Jung 1963), 25–83.

"Septem Sermones ad Mortuos: Appendix V" (Jung 1963), 378–90.

"Sigmund Freud," see "Freud, Sigmund."

"The Song of the Moth" (Jung 1916), 47–69.

"Spirit and Life" (Jung 1928), 77–98.

"The Spiritual Problem of Modern Man" (Jung 1933), 226–54.

"Student Years" (Jung 1963), 84–113.

"A Study in the Process of Individuation" (Jung 1939), 30–51.

"Symbolism of the Mother and of Rebirth" (Jung 1916), 129–68.

"The Transformation of the Libido: A possible source of primitive human discoveries" (Jung 1916), 87–105.

"Travels" (Jung 1963), 238–88.

"The Type Problem in the Discernment of Human Character" (Jung 1923), 184–206.

"The Type Problem in Psychiatry" (Jung 1923), 337–57.

"The Unconscious Origin of the Hero" (Jung 1916), 106–28.

"Visions" (Jung 1963), 289–98.

"Woman in Europe" (Jung 1928), 164–88.

"The Work" (Jung 1963), 200–222.

General Bibliography

Abercrombie, M., C. J. Hickman, and M. L. Johnson. *The Penguin Dictionary of Biology*. 6th ed. London: Penguin, 1973.

Abraham, Karl. *Dreams and Myths—A Study in Race Psychology*. Trans. William A. White. 1913. Reprint. New York: The Journal of Nervous and Mental Disease, 1970.

Ahmad, Hazrat Mirza Tahir, ed. *The Holy Qur'an, with English Translation and Commentary*, vol. 3. 1949. Reprint, 1969. Rev. ed. London: Islam International, 1988.

Ali, Ahmed, trans. *Al-Quran: A Contemporary Translation*. 1984. Rev. ed. Princeton: Princeton University Press, 1988.

Andreason, Nancy C. "Brain Imaging: Applications in Psychiatry." *Science* 239 (1988): 1381–88.

Another Monty Python Record. Scarborough, Ont.: Quality Records, 1972.

Aristotle. "Physics." Books I–II. Trans. W. Charlton. In *A New Aristotle Reader*. Ed. J. L. Ackrill. Princeton: Princeton University Press, 1987.

———. *De Generatione et Corruptione*. Trans. Harold H. Joachim. Oxford: Oxford University Press, 1922.

Arlow, Jacob. "Psychoanalysis as Scientific Method." In *Psychoanalysis, Scientific Method, and Philosophy*. Ed. Sidney Hook, 1959. Reprint. New York: New York University Press, 1964, pp. 201–211.

Artemidorus. *Oneirocritica (The Interpretation of Dreams)*. Commentary and trans. Robert J. White. Park Ridge, N.J.: Noyes Press, 1975.

"Art in a War Zone." Atlanta: Cable News Network, 4 January 1991.

Asch, Solomon E. "Opinions and Social Pressure." *Scientific American* 193 (1955): 31–35.

Badham, John, dir. *Saturday Night Fever*. With John Travolta and Karen Lynn Gorney. U.S.A., 1977.

Bainbridge, William Sims. *Satan's Power: A Deviant Psychotherapy Cult.* Berkeley: University of California Press, 1978.

Barches, Jack D., Huda Akil, Glen R. Elliott, R. Bruce Holman, and Stanley J. Watson. "Behavioral Neurochemistry: Neuroregulators and Behavioral States." *Science* 200 (1978): 964–73.

Barlow, David H. "Causes of Sexual Dysfunction: The Role of Anxiety and Cognitive Interference." *Journal of Consulting and Clinical Psychology* 54 (1986): 140–48.

Barnes, Barry, and David Bloor. "Relativism, Rationalism, and the Sociology of Knowledge." In *Rationality and Relativism.* Eds. Martin Hollis and Steven Lukes. Cambridge: MIT Press, 1989, pp. 21–47.

Bauer, Bruno. "The Trumpet of the Last Judgement over Hegel." Trans. Lawrence S. Stepelevich. In *The Young Hegelians: An Anthology.* Ed. Lawrence S. Stepelevich. 1983. Reprint. Cambridge: Cambridge University Press, 1987, pp. 177–86.

Belicki, Kathryn, and Denis Belicki. "Predisposition for Nightmares: A Study of Hypnotic Ability, Vividness of Imagery, and Absorption." *The Journal of Clinical Psychology* 42 (1986): 714–18.

Bergson, Henri (1911a). *Creative Evolution.* Trans. Arthur Mitchell. London: Macmillan, 1911.

———. (1911b). *Laughter: An Essay on the Meaning of the Comic.* Trans. Cloudesley Brereton and Fred Rothwell. New York: Macmillan, 1911.

———. (1912). *An Introduction to Metaphysics.* Trans. T. E. Hulme. New York: G. P. Putnam's Sons, 1912.

———. (1935). *The Two Sources of Morality and Religion.* Trans. R. Ashley Audra, Cloudesley Brereton, W. Horsfall Carter. New York: Henry Holt, 1935.

Berkeley, George. *A Treatise Concerning the Principles of Human Knowledge.* In *Classics of Western Philosophy,* 2nd. ed. Ed. Steven M. Cahn. Indianapolis: Hackett, 1977.

Betty and Veronih . No. 23, February 1991. Mamaroneck, N.Y.: Archie Comic, 1990.

Bishop, Dale. "When Gods Become Demons." In *Monsters and Demons in the Ancient and Medieval Worlds: Papers Presented in Honor of Edith Porada.* Ed. Ann E. Farkas. Mainz on Rhine: Verlag Philipp von Zabern, 1987, pp. 95–100.

Boardman, John. " 'Very Like a Whale'—Classical Sea Monsters." In *Monsters and Demons in the Ancient and Medieval Worlds: Papers Presented in Honor of Edith Porada.* Ed. Ann E. Farkas. Mainz on Rhine: Verlag Philipp von Zabern, 1987, pp. 73–84.

Boas, Franz. *Anthropology and Modern Life.* New York: W. W. Norton, 1962.

Bodkin, Maud. *Studies of Type-Images in Poetry, Religion, and Philosophy.* London: Oxford University Press, 1951.

Book of Common Prayer and Administration of the Sacraments and Other Rites and Ceremonies of the Church according to the Use of the Anglican Church of Canada. Toronto: Anglican Book Centre, 1959.

Boyle, Robert. *The Works of the Honorable Robert Boyle in Six Volumes.* London: private printing, 1772.

Brenner, Charles. "Psychoanalysis: Philosophy or Science?" In *Psychoanalysis and Philosophy.* Charles Hanly and Morris Lazerowitz, eds. New York: International University Press, 1970, pp. 35–45.

Brown, Clifford A. *Jung's Hermeneutic of Doctrine—Its Theological Significance.* Chico, Calif.: Scholars Press, 1981.

Brundvand, Jan. *The Vanishing Hitchhiker: American Urban Legends and Their Meanings.* New York: Norton, 1981.

al-Bukhari. *Sahih.* Vol. 2. nd.

Bunge, Mario. *Scientific Research.* New York: Springer-Verlag, 1967.

Bunge, Mario, and Ruben Ardila. *Philosophy of Psychology.* New York: Springer-Verlag, 1987.

Burton, Sir Richard F., trans. *The Kama Sutra of Vatsyayana: The Classic Hindu Treatise on Love and Social Conduct.* New York: E. P. Dutton, 1964.

Campbell, Joseph, ed. (1972a). *The Portable Jung.* 1972. Reprint. London: Penguin, 1986.

———. (1972b). *Myths to Live By.* 1972. Reprint. New York: Bantam, 1973.

Cavallero, Corrado, and Piercarla Cicogna. "Comparing Reports of the Same Dream: Proposals for a Structural Analysis." *Perceptual and Motor Skills* 57 (1983): 339–56.

Chamberlain, Houston Stewart. *Foundations of the Nineteenth Century.* Trans. John Lees. 2 vols. London: John Lane, 1913.

Chapman, J. Harley. *Jung's Three Theories of Religious Experience.* Lewiston, N.Y.: Edwin Mellon Press, 1988.

Chaucer, Geoffrey. *The Canterbury Tales.* Trans. Nevill Coghill. 1951. Reprint. New York: Penguin, 1986.

Chetwynd, Tom (1974). *Dictionary for Dreamers.* 1974. Reprint. London: Paladin, 1987.

———. (1982). *A Dictionary of Symbols.* 1982. Reprint. London: Paladin, 1987.

Christman, John. "Constructing the Inner Citadel: Recent Work on the Concept of Autonomy." *Ethics* 99 (1988): 109–124.

Cocks, Geoffrey. *Psychotherapy in the Third Reich: The Goring Institute.* Oxford: Oxford University Press, 1985.

Cohen, Edmund. *C. G. Jung and the Scientific Attitude.* New York: Philosophical Library, 1975.

Conrad, Joseph. *Heart of Darkness.* 1902. Reprint. New York: Bantam, 1981.

Creuzer, Friedrich. *Idee und Probe Alter Symbolik.* 1806. Reprint. Stuttgart-

Bad Cannstatt: Friedrich Frommann Verlag, 1966.

Crowley, Aleister. *Aleister Crowley's Thoth Tarot Deck*. 80 cards. 1942. Reprint. Stamford, Conn.: U.S. Games Systems, 1987.

———. *The Book of Thoth: A Short Essay on the Tarot of the Egyptians*. 1944. Reprint. Stamford, Conn.: U.S. Games Systems, 1988.

Cumont, Franz: *The Mysteries of Mithra*. Trans. Thomas McCormack. New York: Dover, 1956.

Dalrymple, David J. " 'Images of Immortality': Jung and the Archetype of Death and Rebirth." In *Jung's Challenge to Contemporary Religion*. Eds. Murray Stein, Robert L. Moore. Wilmette, Ill.: Chiron, 1987, pp. 175–88.

Dante. *Inferno*. Trans. Laurence Binyon. London: Macmillan and Co., 1952.

———. *Paradisio*. Trans. Laurence Binyon. London: Macmillan and Co., 1952.

———. *Purgatorio*. Trans. Laurence Binyon. London: Macmillan and Co., 1952.

Davies, Robertson. *The Manticore*. 1972. Reprint. Markham, Ont.: Penguin, 1976.

de Givry, Grillot. *The Illustrated Anthology of Sorcery, Magic and Alchemy*. Trans. J. Courtenay Locke. New York: Causeway, 1973.

DeMartino, Richard. "The Human Situation and Zen Buddhism." In *Zen Buddhism and Psychoanalysis*. New York: Grove Press, 1960, pp. 142–71.

Descartes, René (1637). *Discourse on the Method of Rightly Conducting the Reason and Seeking Truth in the Field of Science. In Discourse on Method and Meditations*. Trans. Laurence J. Lafleur. 1960. Reprint. New York: Macmillan, 1988, pp. 3–57.

———. (1641). *The Meditations Concerning First Philosophy. In Discourse on Method and Meditations*. Trans. Laurence J. Lafleur. 1960. Reprint. New York: Macmillan, 1988, pp. 61–143.

Descola, Philippe. "Head-Shrinkers vs. Shrinks: Jivaroan Dream Analysis." *Man* 24 (1989): 439–50

Dols, William L., Jr. "The Church as Crucible for Transformation." In *Jung's Challenge to Contemporary Religion*. Eds. Murray Stein, Robert L. Moore. Wilmette, Ill.: Chiron, 1987, pp. 127–45.

Dostoyevsky, Fyodor. *Crime and Punishment*. 1866. Reprint. New York: Bantam, 1982.

Dunkell, Samuel. *Sleep Positions—The Night Language of the Body*. New York: William Morrow, 1977.

Dunne, Carrin. "Between Two Thieves: A Response to Jung's Critique of the Christian Notions of Good and Evil." In *Jung's Challenge to Contemporary Religion*. Eds. Murray Stein, Robert L. Moore. Wilmette, Ill.: Chiron, 1987, pp. 15–26.

Edelson, Marshall (1984). *Hypothesis and Evidence in Psychoanalysis*. Chicago: University of Chicago Press, 1984.

———. (1988). *Psychoanalysis: A Theory in Crisis*. Chicago: University of

Chicago Press, 1988.

Eliade, Mircea (1955). *The Myth of the Eternal Return.* Trans. Willard R. Trask. London: Routledge & Kegan Paul, 1955.

———. (1959). *The Sacred and the Profane: The Nature of Religion.* Trans. Willard R. Trask. San Diego: Harcourt Brace Jovanovich, 1959.

———. (1976). *Occultism, Witchcraft, and Other Cultural Fashions.* Chicago: University of Chicago Press, 1976.

Ellenberger, Henri F. *The Discovery of the Unconscious: The History and Evolution of Dynamic Psychiatry.* New York: Basic Books, 1970.

Ellis, Albert. "The Impossibility of Achieving Consistently Good Mental Health." *American Psychologist* 42 (1987): 364–75.

Engelsman, Joan Chamberlain. "Beyond the Anima: The Female Self in the Image of God." In *Jung's Challenge to Contemporary Religion.* Eds. Murray Stein, Robert L. Moore. Wilmette, Ill.: Chiron, 1987, pp. 93–105.

Evans-Wentz, W. Y., ed. *The Tibetan Book of the Dead.* Trans. Lama Anagarika Govinda. Foreword by C. G. Jung, trans. by R. F. C. Hull. 1927; first paperback ed. Oxford: Oxford University Press, 1960.

Eysenck, Hans (1953). *The Structure of Human Personality.* 1953. Reprint. London: Methuen, 1970.

———. (1957). *Sense and Nonsense in Psychology.* 1957. Rev. ed. 1958. Reprint. London: Penguin, 1968.

———. (1972). *Psychology is About People.* New York: Library Press, 1972.

Eysenck, Hans, and Michael W. Eysenck. *Personality and Individual Differences: A Natural Science Approach.* New York: Plenum, 1985.

Fernandez, James W. *Persuasions and Performances: The Play of Tropes in Culture.* Bloomington: Indiana University Press, 1986.

Festinger, Leon. *A Theory of Cognitive Dissonance.* 1957. Reprint. Stanford: Stanford University Press, 1962.

Fichte, Johann. *The Vocation of Man.* Trans. Peter Preuss. 1987. Reprint. Indianapolis: Hackett, 1991.

Fischer, Henry G. "Ancient Egyptian Attitude Toward the Monstrous." In *Monsters and Demons in the Ancient and Medieval Worlds: Papers Presented in Honor of Edith Porada.* Ed. Ann E. Farkas. Mainz on Rhine: Verlag Philipp von Zabern, 1987: 13–26.

Fix, William R. *Pyramid Odyssey.* Toronto: John Wiley & Sons, 1978.

Fordham, Michael. *Jungian Psychotherapy: A Study in Analytic Psychology.* Chichester, U.K: John Wiley & Sons, 1978.

Fox, Susan. *Not Part of the Bargain.* Toronto: Harlequin, 1989.

Freud, Sigmund (1907). "The Sexual Enlightenment of Children." In *The Sexual Enlightenment of Children.* 1963. Reprint. New York: Collier, 1974, pp. 17–24.

———. (1908a): " 'Civilised' Sexual Morality and Modern Nervous Illness." In *Civilisation, Society and Religion.* London: Penguin, 1985, pp. 33–55.

Freud, Sigmund. (1908b). "On the Sexual Theories of Children." In *The Sexual Enlightenment of Children*. 1963. Reprint. New York: Collier, 1974, pp. 25–40.

———. (1908c). "Family Romances." In *The Sexual Enlightenment of Children*. 1963. Reprint. New York: Collier, 1974, pp. 47–184.

———. (1913). "Infantile Mental Life: Two Lies Told by Children." In *The Sexual Enlightenment of Children*. 1963. Reprint. New York: Collier, 1974, pp. 185–89.

———. (1949). *An Outline of Psycho-Analysis*. Trans. James Strachey. 1949. Reprint. New York: W. W. Norton, 1989.

Friedlander, Shems. *When You Hear Hoofbeats, Think of a Zebra*. New York: Harper & Row, 1987.

Fromm, Erich (1957). *The Forgotten Language: An Introduction to the Understanding of Dreams, Fairy Tales, and Myths*. New York: Grove Press, 1957.

———. (1960). "Psychoanalysis and Zen Buddhism." In *Zen Buddhism and Psychoanalysis*. New York: Grove Press, 1960, pp. 77–141.

Gangestad, Steve, and Mark Snyder. "To Carve Nature at its Joints: On the Existence of Discrete Classes in Personality." *Psychological Review* 92 (1985): 317–49.

Glass, Arnold Lewis, and Keith James Holyoak. *Cognition*. 2nd ed. New York: Random House, 1986.

Glass, Leonard. "Man's Man/Ladies' Man: Motifs of Hypermasculinity." *Psychiatry* 47 (1984): 260–78.

Goethe, Johann Wolfgang von. *The Autobiography of Johann Wolfgang von Goethe*. Trans. Jim Oxenford. 2 vols; Chicago: University of Chicago Press, 1974.

———. *Faust, Part One*. Trans. Philip Wayne. London: Penguin, 1949.

———. *Faust, Part Two*. Trans. Philip Wayne. London: Penguin, 1959.

Goldsmith, Oliver. *She Stoops to Conquer*. 1958. Reprint. New York: Bantam, 1966.

Goldstein, E. Bruce. *Sensation and Perception*. 2nd ed., Belmont, Calif.: Wadsworth, 1984.

Graves, Robert. *The White Goddess: A Historical Grammar of Poetic Myth*. New York: Octagon, 1972.

Guntrip, Harry. "Psychoanalysis and some Scientific and Philosophic Critics." *The British Journal of Medical Psychology* 30 (1978): 207–224.

Gwatkin, Henry Melvill. *Selections from Early Writers, Illustrative of Church History to the Time of Constantine*. London: Macmillan, 1929.

Hacking, Ian. "Language, Truth and Reason." In *Rationality and Relativism*. Eds. Martin Hollis and Steven Lukes. Cambridge: MIT Press, 1989, pp. 48–66.

Halderman, Brent L., Thomas T. Jackson, and Paul F. Zelhart. "A Study of Fantasy: Determinants of Fantasy Function and Content." *Journal of Clinical Psychology* 41 (1985): 325–30.

Hall, Calvin S., and Vernon J. Nordby. *A Primer of Jungian Psychology*. New York: New American Library, 1973.

Hansen, Donald P. "The Fantastic World of Sumerian Art; Seal impressions from Ancient Lagash." In *Monsters and Demons in the Ancient and Medieval Worlds: Papers Presented in Honor of Edith Porada*. Ed. Ann E. Farkas. Mainz on Rhine: Verlag Philipp von Zabern, 1987, pp. 53–63.

Hartmann, Heinz. "Psychoanalysis as a Scientific Theory." In *Psychoanalysis, Scientific Method, and Philosophy*. Ed. Sidney Hook, 1959. Reprint. New York: New York University Press, 1964, pp. 3–37.

Hebb, D. O. (1951). "Role of Neurological Ideas in Psychology." In *The Conceptual Nervous System*. Ed. Henry A. Buchtel. Oxford: Pergamon, 1982, pp. 1–10.

——— (1958). "Intelligence, Brain Function, and the Theory of Mind." In *The Conceptual Nervous System*. Ed. Henry A. Buchtel. Oxford: Pergamon, 1982, pp. 53–63.

——— (1967). "Cerebral Organisation and Consciousness." In *The Conceptual Nervous System*. Ed. Henry A. Buchtel. Oxford: Pergamon, 1982, pp. 117–20.

——— (1968). "Concerning Imagery." In *The Conceptual Nervous System*. Ed. Henry A. Buchtel. Oxford: Pergamon, 1982, pp. 121–30.

——— (1969). "The Mechanism of Perception." In *The Conceptual Nervous System*. Ed. Henry A. Buchtel. Oxford: Pergamon, 1982, pp. 131–39.

Heinze, Thomas F. *Creation vs. Evolution Handbook: An Evaluation of the Theory of Evolution in the Light of Scientific Research*. 1973. Reprint. Grand Rapids, Mich.: Baker Book House, 1983.

Hess, Moses. "The Recent Philosophers." Trans Lawrence S. Stepelevich. In *The Young Hegelians: An Anthology*. Ed. Lawrence S. Stepelevich. 1983. Reprint. Cambridge: Cambridge University Press, 1987, pp. 359–75.

Hillman, James (1971). "The Inferior Function." In *Jung's Typology*. 1971. Reprint. Irving, Tex.: Spring, 1979, pp. 75–150.

———. (1975). *Re-Visioning Psychology*. New York: Harper & Row, 1975.

Hines, Terence. *Pseudoscience and the Paranormal: A Critical Examination of the Evidence*. Buffalo, N.Y.: Prometheus Books, 1988.

Hollis, Martin. "The Social Destruction of Reality." In *Rationality and Relativism*. Eds. Martin Hollis and Steven Lukes. Cambridge: MIT Press, 1989, pp. 67–86.

Holy Bible, The New Revised Standard Version. Nashville: Thomas Nelson, 1990.

Homans, Peter. *Jung in Context: Modernity and the Making of a Psychology*. Chicago: University of Chicago Press, 1979.

Homer. *The Odyssey*. Trans E. V. Rieu. Advisory Ed. Betty Ravice. London:

Penguin, 1946.

Homer. *The Iliad.* Trans. E. V. Rieu. Advisory Ed. Betty Ravice. 1950. Reprint. London: Penguin, 1988.

Hook, Sidney. "Science and Mythology in Psychoanalysis." In *Psychoanalysis, Scientific Method, and Philosophy.* Ed. Sidney Hook, 1959. Reprint. New York: New York University Press, 1964, pp. 212–24.

Horowitz, Mardi J., and Nathan Zilberg. "Regressive Alterations of the Self Concept." *American Journal of Psychiatry* 140 (1983): 284–89.

Hughes, Thomas Patrick. *Dictionary of Islam.* 1885. Rev. ed. London: W. H. Allen, 1964.

Hume, David. *An Enquiry Concerning Human Understanding.* Ed. Eric Steinberg. 1977. Reprint. Indianapolis: Hackett, 1988.

Hunter, Fumiyo, and Nissim Levy. "Relation of Problem-Solving Behaviors and Jungian Personality Types." *Psychological Reports* 51 (1982): 379–84.

Huston, John, dir. *Moby Dick.* With Gregory Peck. Screenplay John Huston, Ray Bradbury. Hollywood, 1956.

Huot, B., K. Makarec, and M. A. Persinger. "Temporal Lobes Signs and Jungian Dimensions of Personality." *Perceptual and Motor Skills* 69 (1989): 841–42.

Ireland, Mardy S., and Lucy Kernan-Schloss. "Pattern Analysis of Recorded Daydreams, Memories, and Personality Type." *Perceptual and Motor Skills* 56 (1983): 119–25.

Irvine, William C, ed. *Heresies Exposed: A Brief Critical Examination in the Light of the Holy Scriptures of Some of the Prevailing Heresies and False Teachings of Today.* 1917. Reprint. Neptune, N.J.: Loizeaux Brothers, 1983.

Jacobi, Jolande. *The Psychology of C. G. Jung.* Trans. Ralph Manheim. 1942. Reprint. New Haven: Yale University Press, 1964.

James, William. *The Varieties of Religious Experience.* 1902. Reprint. New York: Viking Penguin, 1985.

Jastrow, Joseph. *Error and Eccentricity in Human Belief.* 1935. Rev. ed. London: Dover, 1962.

Joke Book Comics Digest Annual: 1977 Edition. New York: Archie Comic, 1977.

Jones, Judy, and William Wilson. *An Incomplete Education.* New York: Ballantine, 1987.

Kierkegaard, Søren (1834a). *Philosophical Fragments.* Trans. Howard V. Hong, Edna H. Hong. Princeton: Princeton University Press, 1985.

———. (1843b). *Fear and Trembling: A Dialectical Lyric.* Trans. Walter Lowrie. Princeton: Princeton University Press, 1941.

———. (1849). *The Sickness Unto Death.* Trans. Walter Lowrie. Princeton: Princeton University Press, 1944.

Kipnis, David. "Psychology and Behavioral Technology." *American Psychologist*

42 (1987): 30–36.

Kirschenmann, Peter P. (1973). "Concepts of Randomness." In *Exact Philosophy*. Ed. Mario Bunge. Dordrecht, Netherlands: D. Reidel, 1973, pp. 129–48.

———. (1982). "Some Thoughts on the Ideal of Exactness in Science and Philosophy." In *Scientific Philosophy Today: Essays in Honor of Mario Bunge*. Eds. Joseph Agassi and Robert S. Cohen. Dordrecht, Netherlands: D. Reidel, 1982, pp. 85–98.

Koestler, Arthur. "The Urge to Self-Destruction." *The Nobel Foundation* (1970): 1–8.

Kogut, Dennis, and Denis J. Lynch. "Therapists and Quasi-Therapists in a Therapy Analogue Situation." *Journal of Clinical Psychology* 40 (1984): 72–77.

Kovel, Joel. *A Complete Guide to Therapy: From Psychoanalysis to Behavior Modification.* New York: Pantheon, 1976.

Krajewski, Wladyslaw. "On Hypotheses and Hypotheticism." In *Scientific Philosophy Today: Essays in Honor of Mario Bunge*. Eds. Joseph Agassi and Robert S. Cohen. Dordrecht, Netherlands: D. Reidel, 1982, pp. 99–109.

Kubie, Lawrence. "Psychoanalysis and Scientific Method." In *Psychoanalysis, Scientific Method, and Philosophy.* Ed. Sidney Hook, 1959. Reprint. New York: New York University Press, 1964, pp. 57–77.

Lakoff, George, and Mark Johnson. *Metaphors We Live By.* Chicago: University of Chicago Press, 1979.

Lambert, Wilfred G. "Gilgamesh in Literature and Art: The Second and First Millennia." In *Monsters and Demons in the Ancient and Medieval Worlds: Papers Presented in Honor of Edith Porada.* Ed. Ann E. Farkas. Mainz on Rhine: Verlag Philipp von Zabern, 1987, pp. 37–52.

Lane, Harlan, and Daryl Bem. "Collateral Control of Discriminative Verbal Behavior: An Experiment in Social Influence." In *A Laboratory Manual for the Control and Analysis of Behavior.* Belmont, Calif.: Wadsworth, 1965.

Lang, Fritz, dir. *Metropolis.* With Brigitte Helm, Alfred Abel, Gustav Froelich. Germany, 1926.

Lao Tzu. *Tao Te Ching.* London: Allen & Unwin, 1959.

Laurence, Theodor. *The Sexual Key to the Tarot.* New York: New American Library, 1971.

Lazerowitz, Morris. "The Problem of Justifying Induction." In *Psychoanalysis and Philosophy.* Charles Hanly and Morris Lazerowitz, eds. New York: International University Press, 1970, pp. 210–57.

Leahey, Thomas Hardy, and Grace Evans Leahey. *Psychology's Occult Doubles: Psychology and the Problem of Pseudoscience.* 1983. Reprint. Chicago: Nelson-Hill, 1984.

Lester, David, Jeffrey S. Thinschmidt, and Lisa A. Trautman. "Paranormal Belief and Jungian Dimensions of Personality." *Psychological Reports* 61 (1987): 182.

Levy, Nissim, and Stanley E. Ridley. "Stability of Jungian Personality Types Within a College Population Over a Decade." *Psychological Reports* 60 (1987): 419–22.

Lieb, Michael. "Ezekiel's Inaugural Vision as Jungian Archetype." *Thought* 64 (1989): 116–29.

Lifton, Robert Jay. *Thought Reform and the Psychology of Totalism—A Study of "Brainwashing" in China.* New York: W. W. Norton, 1961.

Lindholm, Lynn M. "Is Realistic History of Science Possible? A Hidden Inadequacy in the New History of Science." In *Scientific Philosophy Today: Essays in Honor of Mario Bunge.* Eds. Joseph Agassi and Robert S. Cohen. Dordrecht, Netherlands: D. Reidel, 1982, pp. 159–88.

Lindsey, Hal, with C. C. Carlson. *The Late Great Planet Earth.* 1970. Reprint. New York: Bantam, 1983.

Lynch, David, dir. *Eraserhead.* With John Nance and Charlotte Stewart. USA, 1978.

Lynn, Steven J., and Judith W. Rhue. "Fantasy Proneness: Hypnosis, Developmental Antecedents, and Psychopathology." *American Psychologist* 43 (1988): 35–44.

Madden, Edward H. *Philosophical Problems of Psychology.* New York: Odyssey Press, 1962.

Maltin, Leonard, ed. *Leonard Maltin's TV Movies and Video Guide, 1990 Edition.* Assoc. Eds. Mike Clark, Rob Edelman, Alvin Marill, Luke Sader, Bill Warren. 1969. Rev. ed. New York: New American Library, 1989.

Mann, Michael, dir. *The Keep.* With Scott Glenn, Ian McKellan, Alberta Watson. USA, 1983.

Marriott, Alice, and Carol K. Rachlin. *American Indian Mythology.* New York: Mentor, 1968.

McCreary, Charles. *Psychical Phenomena and the Physical World.* London: Hamish Hamilton, 1973.

Melville, Herman. *Moby Dick, or, The Whale.* New York: Random House, 1930.

Miller, David L. " 'Attack Upon Christendom!'—The Anti-Christianism of Depth Psychology." In *Jung's Challenge to Contemporary Religion.* Eds. Murray Stein, Robert L. Moore. Wilmette, Ill.: Chiron, 1987, pp. 27–40.

Milton, John. *Paradise Lost.* Ed. Merritt Y. Hughes. 1962. Reprint. New York: Macmillan, 1986.

Modell, Arnold H. "The Nature of Psychoanalytic Knowledge." *The Journal of the American Psychoanalytic Association* 26 (1978): pp. 641–58.

Money, John. "Sin, Sickness, or Status?—Homosexual Gender Identity and Psychoneuroendocrinology." *American Psychologist* 43 (1987): 384–99.

Moore, Robert L. "Ritual Process, Initiation, and Contemporary Religion." In *Jung's Challenge to Contemporary Religion.* Eds. Murray Stein, Robert L. Moore. Wilmette, Ill.: Chiron, 1987, pp. 147–60.

Moreno, Antonio. *Jung, Gods, and Modern Man.* Notre Dame: University of Notre Dame Press, 1970.

Morris, Errol, dir. *The Thin Blue Line.* USA, 1988.

Morrissey, Steve. "I Know It's Over." From *The Queen is Dead.* London: Sire Records, 1986.

Murphy, Warren, and Richard Sapir. *The Destroyer.* 63 vols; last vol. New York: New American Library, 1986.

Myers-Briggs Type Indicator (Form G—Self-Scorable). Palo Alto: Consulting Psychologists Press, 1987.

Nagel, Ernest. "Methodological Issues in Psychoanalytic Theory." In *Psychoanalysis, Scientific Method, and Philosophy.* Ed. Sidney Hook, 1959. Reprint. New York: New York University Press, 1964, pp. 38–56.

Nichols, Sallie. *Jung and Tarot: An Archetypal Journey.* 1980. Reprint. York Beach, Maine: Samuel Weiser, 1982.

Nietzsche, Friedrich (1872). *The Birth of Tragedy.* Trans. Walter Kaufmann. In *Basic Writings of Nietzsche.* Ed. Walter Kaufmann. 1966. Reprint. New York: Modern Library, 1968, pp. 3–144.

———. (1880). Excerpts from *The Wanderer and His Shadow.* Trans. Walter Kaufmann. In *Basic Writings of Nietzsche.* Ed. Walter Kaufmann. 1966. Reprint. New York: Modern Library, 1968, pp. 159–66.

———. (1882): Excerpts from *The Gay Science.* Trans. Walter Kaufmann. In *Basic Writings of Nietzsche.* Ed. Walter Kaufmann. 1966. Reprint. New York: Modern Library, 1968, pp. 171–78.

———. (1885). *Thus Spoke Zarathustra.* Trans. R. J. Hollingdale. London: Penguin, 1961.

———. (1886). *Beyond Good and Evil.* Trans. Walter Kaufmann. In *Basic Writings of Nietzsche.* Ed. Walter Kaufmann. 1966. Reprint. New York: Modern Library, 1968, pp. 192–435.

———. (1887). *The Geneaology of Morals.* Trans. Walter Kaufmann. In *Basic Writings of Nietzsche.* Ed. Walter Kaufmann. 1966. Reprint. New York: Modern Library, 1968, pp. 439–602.

Nurbakhsh, Javad. *Sufi Symbolism: The Nurbakhsh Encyclopedia of Sufi Terminology,* volume 1. Trans. Javad Nurbakhsh, with Leonard Lewisohn and Terry Graham. London: Khaniqahi-Nimatullahi, 1984.

O'Flaherty, Wendy Doniger (1973). *Siva: The Erotic Ascetic.* 1973. Reprint. Oxford: Oxford University Press, 1981.

———. (1980). *Women, Androgynes, and Other Mythical Beasts.* 1980. Reprint. Chicago: University of Chicago Press, 1982.

Orwell, George. *Nineteen Eighty-Four.* London: Martin Secker & Warburg, 1949.

Paracelsus (1656). *The Archidoxes of Magic*. Trans. Robert Turner. 1656. Reprint. London: Askin, 1975.

———— (1894). *The Hermetic and Alchemical Writings of Paracelsus the Great*. Trans. Arthur Edward Waite. 2 vols. 1894. Reprint. New York: University Books, 1967.

Pargeter, Margaret. *Kiss of a Tyrant*. Toronto: Harlequin, 1980.

Pennebaker, James W., Janice K. Kiecolt-Glaser, and Ronald Glaser. "Disclosure of Traumas and Immune Function: Health Implications for Psychotherapy." *Journal of Consulting and Clinical Psychology* 56 (1988): 239–45.

Persinger, Michael A. *Neurological Bases of God Beliefs*. New York: Praeger, 1987.

Piaget, Jean. *Epistemologie et Psychologie de la Fonction*. Paris: PU de France, 1968.

Piaget, Jean, and Bärbel Inhelder. *L'Image Mentale Chez L'Enfant*. Paris: PU de France, 1966.

Plato. *Meno*. Trans. Benjamin Jowett. 1949. Reprint. New York: Macmillan, 1987.

————. *Phaedo*. Trans. G. M. A. Grube. Indianapolis: Hackett, 1977.

Popper, Karl. *The Logic of Scientific Discovery*. 1934. Reprint. New York: Science Editions, 1961.

Porada, Edith. "Introduction." In *Monsters and Demons in the Ancient and Medieval Worlds: Papers Presented in Honor of Edith Porada*. Ed. Ann E. Farkas. Mainz on Rhine: Verlag Philipp von Zabern, 1987: 1–13.

Pumpian-Midlin, E., ed. *Psychoanalysis as Science*. 1952. Reprint. New York: New York Basic Books, 1956.

Qur'an. *See* Ali and Ahmad above.

Ramachandran, T. M. "Film Censorship in India." In *70 Years of Indian Cinema (1913-1983)*. Ed. T. M. Ramachandran. Bombay: CINEMA India-International, 1985.

Rapp, Friedrich. "Distrust of Reason." In *Scientific Philosophy Today: Essays in Honor of Mario Bunge*. Eds. Joseph Agassi and Robert S. Cohen. Dordrecht, Netherlands: D. Reidel, 1982, pp. 287–98.

Reiner, Erica. "Magic Figurines, Amulets, and Talismans." In *Monsters and Demons in the Ancient and Medieval Worlds: Papers Presented in Honor of Edith Porada*. Ed. Ann E. Farkas. Mainz on Rhine: Verlag Philipp von Zabern, 1987: 27–36.

Rhine, J. B. *The Reach of the Mind*. London: Faber and Faber, 1946.

Richardson, James T. "Introduction." In *The Brainwashing/Deprogramming Controversy*. Toronto: Edwin Mellen Press, 1983, pp. 1–11.

Ricoeur, Paul. "The Question of Proof in Freud's Psychoanalytic Writings." *The Journal of the American Psychoanalytic Association* 25 (1977): 835–71.

Rieff, Philip. "Introduction" to *The Sexual Enlightenment of Children*. 1963. Reprint. New York: Collier, 1974, pp. 7–16.

Rollins, Wayne G. "Jung's Challenge to Biblical Hermeneutics." In *Jung's Challenge to Contemporary Religion*. Eds. Murray Stein, Robert L. Moore. Wilmette, Ill.: Chiron Publications, 1987, pp. 107–125.

Rosenberg, Alfred. *Race and Race History and Other Essays by Alfred Rosenberg*. Ed. Robert Pois. New York: Harper & Row, 1970.

Rudolph, Kurt. *Gnosis: The Nature and History of Gnosticism*. Trans. Robert McLachlan Wilson. 1977. First U.S. edition. New York: Harper & Row, 1983.

Ruse, Michael. "Teleology Redux." In *Scientific Philosophy Today: Essays in Honor of Mario Bunge*. Eds. Joseph Agassi and Robert S. Cohen. Dordrecht, Netherlands: D. Reidel, 1982, pp. 299–309.

Russell, Bertrand (1912). *The Problems of Philosophy*. 1912; 13th imp. Oxford: Oxford University Press, 1986.

———. (1959). *Wisdom of the West*. London: Crescent Books, 1959.

Salmon, Wesley. "Psychoanalytic Theory and Evidence." In *Psychoanalysis, Scientific Method, and Philosophy*. Ed. Sidney Hook, 1959. Reprint. New York: New York University Press, 1964, pp. 252–67.

Samuels, Andrew. *Jung and the Post-Jungians*. London: Routledge & Kegan Paul, 1985.

Sapir, J. David. "The Anatomy of Metaphor." In *Social Use of Metaphor: Essays on the Anthropology of Rhetoric*. Eds. David Sapir, Christopher Crocker. Philadelphia: University of Pennsylvania Press, 1977.

Sargant, William Walters. *Battle for the Mind: A Physiology of Conversion and Brain-Washing*. Garden City, N.Y.: Doubleday, 1957.

Schwartz, Robert M. "Cognitive-Behavior Modification: A Conceptual Review." *Clinical Psychology Review* 2 (1982): 267–93.

Schwartz-Salant, Nathan. "Patriarchy in Transformation: Judaic, Christian, and Clinical Perspectives." In *Jung's Challenge to Contemporary Religion*. Eds. Murray Stein, Robert L. Moore. Wilmette, Ill.: Chiron, 1987, pp. 41–71.

Scott, Ridley, dir. *Blade Runner*. With Harison Ford, Rutger Hauer, Sean Young. U.S.A., 1982.

Scriven, Michael. "The Experimental Investigation of Psychoanalysis." In *Psycho-analysis, Scientific Method, and Philosophy*. Ed. Sidney Hook, 1959. Reprint. New York: New York University Press, 1964, pp. 226–51.

Segal, Robert A. "A Jungian View of Evil." *Zygon* 20 (1985): 83–89.

Sheridan, Richard Brinsley. *The School for Scandal*. 1958. Reprint. New York: Bantam, 1966.

Shneidman, Edward S. "A Psychological Theory of Suicide." *Psychiatric Annals* 6 (1976): 51–60.

Sieber, Joan E., and Barbara Stanley. "Ethical and Professional Dimensions of Socially Sensitive Research." *American Psychologist* 43 (1988): 49–55.

Singer, June. "Jung's Gnosticism and Contemporary Gnosis." In *Jung's Challenge to Contemporary Religion*. Eds. Murray Stein, Robert L. Moore. Wilmette, Ill.: Chiron, 1987, pp. 73–91.

Skinner, B. F (1959a). "A Critique of Psychoanalytic Concepts and Theories." In *Cumulative Record*. 1959. Reprint. New York: Appleton-Century Crofts, 1961, pp. 185–94.

———. (1959b). "Psychology in the Understanding of Mental Disease." In *Cumulative Record*. 1959. Reprint. New York: Appleton-Century Crofts, 1961, pp. 194–202.

———. (1959c). "Superstition in the Pigeon." In *Cumulative Record*. 1959. Reprint. New York: Appleton-Century Crofts, 1961, pp. 404–409.

———. (1959d). "What is Psychotic Behavior?" In *Cumulative Record*. 1959. Reprint. New York: Appleton-Century Crofts, 1961, pp. 202–219.

Skinner, B. F., and W. H. Morse. "A Second Type of Superstition in the Pigeon." In *Cumulative Record*. 1959. Reprint. New York: Appleton-Century Crofts, 1961, pp. 409–412.

Small, Stephen A. R. Shepherd Zeldin, and Ritch C. Savin-Williams. "In Search of Personality Traits: A Multimethod Analysis of Naturally Occurring Prosocial and Dominance Behaviors." *Journal of Personality* 51 (1983): 1–16.

Smith, Huston. *The Religions of Man*. 1958. Reprint. New York: Harper & Row, 1965.

Smith, John Maynard. "Symbolism and Chance." In *Scientific Philosophy Today: Essays in Honor of Mario Bunge*. Eds. Joseph Agassi and Robert S. Cohen. Dordrecht, Netherlands: D. Reidel, 1982, pp. 207–216.

Smith, Robert. "Fight." From *Kiss Me Kiss Me Kiss Me*. London: APB Music, 1987.

———. "If Only Tonight We Could Sleep." From *Kiss Me Kiss Me Kiss Me*. London: APB Music, 1987.

Solzhenitsyn, Alexander. *One Day in the Life of Ivan Denisovich*. Trans. Ralph Parker. 1962. Reprint. London: Penguin, 1985.

Sontag, Susan (1961a). "Against Interpretation." In *Against Interpretation and Other Essays*. 1961. Reprint. New York: Dell, 1969, pp. 13–23.

———. (1961b). "Psychoanalysis and Norman O. Brown's Life Against Death." In *Against Interpretation and Other Essays*. 1961. Reprint. New York: Dell, 1969, pp. 258–64.

———. (1969a). "The Aesthetics of Silence." In *Styles of Radical Will*. New York: Farrar, Straus & Giroux, 1969, pp. 3–34.

———. (1969b). "The Pornographic Imagination." In *Styles of Radical Will*. New York: Farrar, Straus & Giroux, 1969, pp. 35–73.

———. (1969c). "What's Happening in America (1966)." In *Styles of Radical Will*. New York: Farrar, Straus & Giroux, 1969, pp. 193–204.

Sperber, Dan. "Apparently Irrational Beliefs." In *Rationality and Relativism*.

Eds. Martin Hollis and Steven Lukes. Cambridge: MIT Press, 1989, pp. 149–80.

Stafford, Judith. *The Lemon Cake.* Toronto: Harlequin, 1990.

Steel, Danielle. *Fine Things.* New York: Dell, 1987.

Stein, Murray. "Jung's Green Christ—A Healing Symbol for Christianity." In *Jung's Challenge to Contemporary Religion.* Eds. Murray Stein, Robert L. Moore. Wilmette, Ill.: Chiron, 1987, pp. 1–13.

Stern, Paul. *C. G. Jung—The Haunted Prophet.* New York: George Braziller, 1976.

Storr, Anthony. *Jung.* 1973. Reprint. London: Fontana, 1974.

Strauss, David Friedrich. "The Life of Jesus." Trans. George Eliot, Marilyn Chapin Massey. In *The Young Hegelians: An Anthology.* Ed. Lawrence S. Stepelevich. 1983. Reprint. Cambridge: Cambridge University Press, 1987, pp. 21–51.

Strong, James. *The New Strong's Exhaustive Concordance of the Bible.* Nashville: Thomas Nelson, 1984.

Suzuki, D. T. "Lectures on Zen Buddhism." In *Zen Buddhism and Psychoanalysis.* New York: Grove Press, 1960, pp. 1–76.

Swartz, Paul. "Personal Myth: A Preliminary Statement." *Perceptual and Motor Skills* 58 (1984): 363–78.

Sykes, J. B., ed. *The Concise Oxford Dictionary of Current English.* 7th ed. Oxford: Oxford University Press, 1982.

Szasz, Thomas. "The Case Against Suicide Prevention." *American Psychologist* 41 (1986): 806–812.

Taylor, Charles. "Rationality." In *Rationality and Relativism.* Eds. Martin Hollis and Steven Lukes. Cambridge: MIT Press, 1989, pp. 87–105.

Taylor, Richard. *Metaphysics.* 1963. Reprint. Englewood Cliffs, N.J.: Prentice-Hall, 1983.

Tellegen, Anke. "The Analysis of Consistency in Personality Assessment." *Journal of Personality* 56 (1988): 621–63.

Tobayck, Jerome, and James E. Wilson II. "Paranormal Beliefs and Beliefs About Lunar Effects." *Psychological Reports* 63 (1988): 993–94.

Tobayck, Jerome, James E. Wilson II, Mark Miller, Patsy Murphy, and Thomas Mitchell. "Comparisons of Paranormal Beliefs of Black and White University Students from the Southern United States." *Psychological Reports* 63 (1988): 492–94.

Tolkien, J. R. R. *The Lord of the Rings.* Toronto: Methuen, 1971.

Traweek, Sharon. *Beamtimes and Lifetimes: The World of High Energy Physicists.* Cambridge: Harvard University Press, 1988.

Trope, Yaacov, Miriam Bassok, and Eve Alon. "The Questions Lay Interviewers Ask." *Journal of Personality* 52 (1984): 90–106.

Ulansey, David. *The Origins of the Mithraic Mysteries: Cosmology and Salvation in the Ancient World.* Oxford: Oxford University Press, 1989.

Veyne, Paul. *Did the Greeks Believe in Their Myths? An Essay on the Constitutive Imagination.* Trans. Paula Wissing. Chicago: University of Chicago Press, 1988.

von Blanckenhagen, Peter H. "Easy Monsters." In *Monsters and Demons in the Ancient and Medieval Worlds: Papers Presented in Honor of Edith Porada.* Ed. Ann E. Farkas. Mainz on Rhine: Verlag Philipp von Zabern, 1987, pp. 85–94.

von Franz, Marie-Louise. "The Inferior Function." In *Jung's Typology.* 1971. Reprint. Irving, Tex.: Spring, 1979, pp. 1–74.

Waelder, Robert H (1962). "Psychoanalysis, Scientific Method, and Philosophy." *The Journal of the American Psychoanalytic Association* 10 (1962): 617–37.

———— (1970). "Observation, Historical Reconstruction, and Experiment: An Epistemological Study." In *Psychoanalysis and Philosophy.* Eds. Charles Hanly and Morris Lazerowitz. New York: International University Press, 1970, pp. 280–326.

Wasserman, James. "Aleister Crowley's Thoth Tarot Deck." In *Instructions for Aleister Crowley's Thoth Tarot Deck,* 1944. Reprint. Stamford, Conn.: U.S. Games Systems, 1988, pp. 3–22.

Waterman, Alan S. "On the Uses of Psychological Theory and Research in the Process of Ethical Inquiry." *Psychological Bulletin* 103 (1988): 283–98.

Wilde, Oscar. "The Critic as Artist." In *The Portable Oscar Wilde.* Eds. Richard Aldington, Stanley Weintraub. 1946. Rev. ed. 1981. Reprint. London: Penguin, 1987.

Wilhelm, Richard, trans. *The Secret of the Golden Flower: A Chinese Book of Life, with a Portion of The Book of Consciousness and Life.* Trans. to English Cary F. Baynes. 1931. Rev. ed. New York: Harcourt, Brace & World, 1962.

Wirtz, Philip, and Adele V. Harrell. "Effects of Post-Assault Exposure to Attack-Similar Stimuli on Long-Term Recovery of Victims." *Journal of Consulting and Clinical Psychology* 55 (1987): 10–16.

Woolfolk, Robert L., and Frank C. Richardson. "Behavior Therapy and the Ideology of Modernity." *American Psychologist* 39 (1984): 777–86.

Zimbardo, Philip G., Ebbe B. Ebbesen, and Christina Maslach. *Influencing Attitudes and Changing Behavior.* 1969. Reprint. Reading, Mass.: Addison-Wesley, 1977.

Zusne, Leonard, and Warren Jones. *Anomalistic Psychology: A Study of Magical Thinking.* 2nd ed. Hillsdale, N.J.: Lawrence Erlbaum, 1989.

Index

213

DATE DUE

FEB 2 5 2005			
GAYLORD			PRINTED IN U.S.A